NARROW BUT ENDLESSLY DEEP

THE STRUGGLE FOR MEMORIALISATION IN CHILE SINCE THE TRANSITION TO DEMOCRACY

NARROW BUT ENDLESSLY DEEP

THE STRUGGLE FOR MEMORIALISATION IN CHILE SINCE THE TRANSITION TO DEMOCRACY

PETER READ & MARIVIC WYNDHAM

Published by ANU Press
The Australian National University
Acton ACT 2601, Australia
Email: anupress@anu.edu.au
This title is also available online at press.anu.edu.au

National Library of Australia Cataloguing-in-Publication entry

Creator: Read, Peter, 1945- author.

Title: Narrow but endlessly deep : the struggle for memorialisation in Chile since the transition to democracy / Peter Read ; Marivic Wyndham.

ISBN: 9781760460211 (paperback) 9781760460228 (ebook)

Subjects: Memorialization--Chile.
Collective memory--Chile.
Chile--Politics and government--1973-1988.
Chile--Politics and government--1988-
Chile--History--1988-

Other Creators/Contributors:
Wyndham, Marivic, author.

Dewey Number: 983.066

All rights reserved. No part of this publication may be reproduced, stored in a retrieval system or transmitted in any form or by any means, electronic, mechanical, photocopying or otherwise, without the prior permission of the publisher.

Cover design and layout by ANU Press.

Cover photograph: The alarm clock, smashed at 14 minutes to 11, symbolises the anguish felt by Michele Drouilly Yurich over the unresolved disappearance of her sister Jacqueline in 1974.

This edition © 2016 ANU Press

I don't care for adulation
or so that strangers may weep.
I sing for a far strip of country
narrow but endlessly deep.

No las lisonjas fugaces
ni las famas extranjeras
sino el canto de una lonja
hasta el fondo de la tierra.[1]

---

[1] Victor Jara, 'Manifiesto', tr. Bruce Springsteen, *The Nation*, 2013.

Contents

Illustrations ix
Glossary xi
Acknowledgements xiii
1. Introduction: Narrow but endlessly deep 1

Part I

2. Victor Jara, the State University of Technology
   and the Victor Jara Stadium 23
3. From state terror to state error: Patio 29, General
   Cemetery, Santiago 39
4. Carved cherubs frolicking in a sunny stream:
   The National Stadium 59
5. Last stand of the MIR: Londres 38 81
6. The chosen one: 1367 José Domingo Cañas 105
7. A garden of horror or a park of peace: Villa Grimaldi 127
8. A memorial destroyed: Loyola, Quinta Normal 155

Part II

9. The memorials today and the advance of the state 177
References 215

Illustrations

Interior, the Victor Jara Stadium. Students and staff from the State University of Technology were forced to sit on the left, workers on the right. Several detainees in terror and despair jumped from the balconies to the right of the picture. 37

The seat painted white, in the 'dangerous prisoners' section, is that believed to have been occupied by Jara for a period after being recognised. 38

Nena González, caretaker of Patio 29, General Cemetery. 40

In 1973 the caretaker hut of Nena González stood on this site in Patio 29. From here, unobserved, she witnessed the disposal of hundreds of those killed in the first weeks after the coup. 47

Roberto Sanchez. 60

The principal memorial, main entrance, National Stadium of Chile. 77

The smaller structure at the left is the swimming pool changing room, National Stadium of Chile, occupied by the women detainees. The larger, more modern structure attached to it is the display area opened in 2014. 78

The front façade, Londres 38, showing the marks of burning candles resting against it during the vigils held for the detained-disappeared. 88

Londres 38 with its message of November 2015, 'Break the pact of silence'. On the darker flagstones are inscribed the names of the detained-disappeared believed held here, and their political affiliation. 103

Poster, 1367 José Domingo Cañas, featuring Laura Moya Diaz and Lumi Videla Moya. 106

Lumi Videla Moya's name is the only one to appear on this side of the memorial stone at José Domingo Cañas. The names of others believed held here but who may have been killed elsewhere are on the other side, facing the pavement. 123

Bureaucratically destroyed signage, José Domingo Cañas. Originally the message read, 'Here were committed the/Most ferocious violations/Of human dignity/For this reason we demand/JUSTICE AND PUNISHMENT'. 125

Michele Drouilly Yurich. 129

Fragment of electrified barbed wire, one of the few remaining artefacts surviving from Cuartel Villanova (Villa Grimaldi). 147

The Ombú tree, Villa Grimaldi. No signage attaches to it. Only Michele Drouilly's 'Memory room' gives an account of what happened here. 151

Josefina Rodriguez in her home at Renacer, Loyola. 157

Little is left of the once-guarded exterior wall of the Loyola CNI Depot. 173

Glossary

CNI Central Nacional de Informaciones (National Information Centre) the Chilean state security service, 1977–90

Compañero/a Comrade

Concertación Concertación de Partidos por la Democracia A coalition of centre-left parties in Chile founded in 1988. Presidential candidates under its banner won every election from when military rule ended in 1990 until the conservative candidate Sebastián Piñera won the Chilean presidential election in 2010

Detainee The name universally applied in Latin America to individuals secretly held by the state

Detained-disappeared The name universally applied in Latin America by the human rights movement to political detainees in the context of state terrorism, and presumed murdered by the state

DINA Dirección de Inteligencia Nacional, the Directorate of National Intelligence, Pinochet's first state security and secret police service, established 1 November 1973

Extermination used by Latin American and other state authorities to describe the violent disposal of political enemies

Frentistas Followers of 'El Frente', an extreme left group dedicated to armed opposition during the Pinochet years

MIRista Member of the political party el MIR (Movimiento de Izquierda Revolucionaria, Movement of the Revolutionary Left), particularly marked for destruction by Pinochet in the first years after the coup

Pinochetistas Followers of General Augusto Pinochet, head of Chile's military government, 1973–90

Politically executed Commonly used Latin American phrase to distinguish between the detained-disappeared and those whose bodies have been found

Rodriguistas Members of 'El Frente Rodriguista', an extreme left group dedicated to armed opposition during the Pinochet years

Site of conscience Term used by the human rights movement to describe centres of torture or execution, usually carried out by the state

Acknowledgements

We thank the Australian Research Council for the award of a Discovery Grant that made this book possible. We also thank our colleagues Judith Keene, Elizabeth Rechniewski and Adrian Vickers, with whom we held many discussions on 'Judging the past in a post–Cold War world'. We thank the members of the Social Sciences Editorial Board of The Australian National University for their meticulous care in seeing the manuscript through its initial stages, particularly Professor Marian Sawer and Dr Frank Bongiorno. ANU Press handled production with its usual friendly efficiency. Thanks to Con Boekel for his technical assistance with the photographs using Lightbox. Thanks also to Geoff Hunt for his bright thoughts.

We thank, in particular, our friends who have for many years contributed so much to our understanding of Chile's recent past: Mario Artigas, the late Mauricio Barrientos, Bernardo de Castro, Luigi Cecchetto, Isolda Cid, Crifé Diaz Cid, Katie Hite, Mario Cortes Muñoz, Viviana Diaz, Michele Drouilly Yurich, Diana Duhalde, Francisco Castro, Mireya Garcia, Paula Gonzáles-Dolan, Nena González, the late Laura Moya, Elias Padilla, Victor Peña, Josefina Rodriguez, Roberto Sanchez and Denni Traubmann.

The following people conducted formal or spontaneous guided tours of the sites we discuss in this book, often more than once. We are particularly grateful because to them, of course, these were no ordinary tours, but entries into sites of enormous traumatic significance to both themselves and their families: Michele Drouilly Yurich, Juan Espina Espina, Nena González, Josefina Rodriguez, Juan Medina, Leopoldo Montenegro, Rogelio Rodriguez, Roberto Merino Jorquera, Roberto Muñoz, Laura Moya, Victor Peña, José Uribe.

Lyrics of Victor Jara songs, courtesy Fundación Victor Jara.

1

Introduction: Narrow but endlessly deep

On 11 September 1973, the Chilean Chief of the Armed Forces Augusto Pinochet overthrew the Popular Unity government of Salvador Allende and installed a military dictatorship. He believed he had two justifications that were shared by almost all of his senior officers and many civilians. The first was that under the rule of President Allende the country had become ungovernable. The second was that Allende's Chile might swing even further to the left to become a Cuban-style dictatorship of the proletariat. By 1990, when Pinochet stood down after an unsuccessful referendum to legitimate himself, the danger to conservative Chile had passed. The country was uneasy but stable, and the possibility of a second Cuba remote.

The victory of the right had come at a heavy cost to the small nation. By 1990, beginning what is known in Chile as the Transition to Democracy, Chilean society was severely traumatised. More than 30,000 people had been tortured either to extract information or simply to terrorise them. Issues of truth and justice remained unresolved; more than half the bodies of the 3,000 detained-disappeared remained disappeared. There seemed little prospect of prosecuting even the well-known perpetrators of Pinochet's bidding. The 1980 Constitution, enacted to preserve the significant features of the 'conservative revolution',[1] was still largely intact. Pinochet remained head of the armed forces and was created Senator for Life. This book traces the attempts of survivors, their families, descendants and supporters to memorialise the experiences of torture, terror and state murder at seven infamous Sites of Conscience, all within Santiago. For everyone it has been a hard and bitter journey, and one by no means complete.

Why hard and bitter? The first obstacle to memorialisation has been the Chilean state. This may surprise, since all of the governments since 1990 save one have been of the centre-left. A principal reason for their lack of enthusiasm is that, while what some Chileans call the transition to democracy began in 1990, for a time no government could be sure that the military would not again intervene, if provoked. A second reason is that an agenda of national reconciliation did not necessarily include state support for memorialising the persecution of every left-wing political party, particularly those once dedicated to its own overthrow! Hence the Chilean state's stance has been tentative, supporting a museum here, opposing another there, privileging one memorial, obstructing another, vacillating, unpredictably encouraging or denying. We will follow closely its support, or absence of support, at each of the seven sites, from the beginning of the transition to democracy to the present day.

The second obstacle is the relationship, then and now, between the vast array of leftist opinion and parties. At the time of the coup the spectrum was wide indeed. On the far left stood the highly educated, articulate, idealistic and often well-born members of the MIR, the Movement of the Revolutionary Left. Its members saw themselves as the Che Guevarist vanguard that would lead the masses to a communist utopia – without the need for elections. They never joined Allende's coalition. Next came Allende's own party, the Socialists, favouring force where necessary to achieve a democratic state: it was they who formed the most stable element in Allende's fluid government. More moderate again were the less doctrinaire Communists and the MAPU (Popular Unitary Action Movement),

---

1   For example, Art. 43 of the 1980 Constitution held that 'by the declaration of a state of emergency, the President of the Republic is enabled to suspend or restrict personal liberty, the right of assembly and the freedom to work. He can, also, restrict the exercise of the right of association, intercept, open, or record documents and all classes of communications, order requisition of assets and establish limitations on the exercise of the right of ownership'; 'Chile's Constitution of 1980 with Amendments through 2012'.

ready to work when necessary with other groups towards a pragmatic program of wages and conditions. They formed the second stable element of Allende's government. Towards the political centre, moderates like the Christian Democrats filled out the conservative end of left-wing opinion, and served for a time with Allende. Such were the political parties whose conflicting diversity was to unsettle Allende and, 30 years later, was to divide those bent on establishing memorials at the sites at which they or their comrades had suffered so hideously. The role of the Chilean state and the political factions, then, are the two elements that we will follow most closely in the bitter and painful struggles that are to follow. Of the 45,000 people arrested during the initial three-month reign of terror and of the more than 1,000 people killed, the majority were trade unionists and/or former members of the radical leftist parties, particularly those advocating armed revolution against the right.

In the analysis of each site we follow a chronological journey that is also a physical one: it is possible that a single person might have been held consecutively in five of these torture and extermination sites where the struggle for memorialisation has been so intense and bitter. But we will never know, and neither would that detainee – he or she was moved generally at night and always blindfolded. Only after the transition to democracy in 1990 did it become a little clearer who had been moved, where to, and why. Much even now remains unknown, especially the identities of the some of the perpetrators, though obviously the unreleased state archives and former military and security personnel together could reveal almost everything.

Yet there remains the issue: would releasing the documents aid or hinder the process of national reconciliation?

The psychologist Elizabeth Lira and the political scientist Brian Loveman examined a number of formal and informal strategies, known as the Via Chilena de Reconciliación Política, developed in Chile over two centuries to restabilise the nation after a period of state violence, a set of procedures for reconciliation after political cataclysm. The measures were partly constitutional, partly informal, but each was designed to help the government and nation function again with the approval of a majority of its citizens. Such measures have included commutation of prison sentences for crimes committed by police and military, the return of exiles sometimes with restitution of property or pension, one-off payments to sufferers on both sides of the recent conflict, special laws for named individuals for purposes of reparation, and symbolic measures like public memorials. They also looked to the creation of new political coalitions involving some of the losers in the conflict; redefinition of key actors, parties and worker organisations to carry on under new names; reincorporation of some of the politically defeated into cabinet, universities or bureaucracy; and constitutional and legal reforms to ratify the re-establishment of the 'Chilean family'. Though few Chileans surviving a coup d'etat or revolution believed that political forgetting was possible, Chileans held it to be necessary periodically to 'start again'. Such attempted reconciliation did not necessarily signify forgiveness, more that certain violent measures taken by the state in a period of crisis were not later to be openly discussed. Measures of reconciliation demanded that officials of a new political regime avert their gaze from certain events; citizens who refused to do so were held to be in bad taste, or worse. Lira and Loveman argue that such measures have been to a point enacted even by post-Pinochet centre-left governments.[2]

No post-Pinochet government has as yet been prepared to release the secret information that would identify lists of perpetrators, arguably because it is consistent with the Via Chilena. That is to say, each government since 1990 has calculated that the *majority* of Chileans agree that the mass prosecution of malefactors by the state itself, whatever the moral imperative, was undesirable in the interests of national workability. Even President Bachelet, her father dead after torture, her mother and she herself tortured and exiled, has presumably thought better of pursuing the morally justified path. All the national leaders, in fact, have steered a careful course. The first elected president after the dictatorship, Patricio Aylwin, made it clear that his government would take no part in prosecuting the perpetrators: that was a matter for the courts.[3] He declared that his presidency signified not the 'return' to democracy but the 'transition' towards

---

2   Elizabeth Lira and Brian Loveman, 'Truth, Justice reconciliation and impunity as historical themes: Chile 1814–2006', *Radical History Review*, no. 97, 2007, 42–76; see also Peter Read, 'Reconciliation without history: State crime and state punishment in Chile and Australia', in Frances Peters-Little, Ann Curthoys, John Docker, eds, *Passionate Histories*, Aboriginal History Monograph 21, ANU E Press, Canberra, 2010, pp. 281–82.
3   Chile has jailed more perpetrators of violence committed in the name of the state than any other nation in South America; but it is the victims who have proceeded against them, not the state itself.

it, conceding even-handedly that if Allende carried no mandate to convert Chile into a Socialist state, then the intervention of Pinochet had divided the country still further. But it was not only the political right, he asserted, whom Allende had alienated.[4] The inference that some of the left had become disillusioned with Allende, or might even carry some of the blame for the coup, was left hanging. It needed the centre-right President Sebastián Piñera (2010–13) to shift the blame further to the left in carefully suggesting that, in his opinion, the first to bear responsibility should be those who promoted hatred and armed violence and who despised democracy as the simple tool of the bourgeoisie, while themselves attracting no more than a third of the popular vote.[5]

A national reconciliation by which left and right embrace rather than tolerate each other is clearly impossible while the protagonists of those decades remain alive. Yet it is possible to achieve it in later generations if the evidence is preserved to make it possible. At Myall Creek, Australia, in 1838, white men massacred 28 Aborigines. Unusually, the government took the crime seriously, gathered evidence, conducted a trial and executed seven of the perpetrators. In June 2000, descendants of the perpetrators and descendants of the victims gathered at the site for the unveiling of a monument. Side by side, some even holding hands, they walked through the sacred smoke towards a giant boulder whose signage included the words:

> Erected on 10 June 2000 by a group of Aboriginal and non-Aboriginal Australians in an act of reconciliation and in acknowledgement of the truth of our shared history.

The extraordinary ceremony, so rare in Australia, was only possible because the police had minutely gathered evidence from witnesses, survivors and perpetrators – 142 years earlier. Such a symbolic

---

4   Azócar Patricio Aylwin, 'El desafío de mirar al futuro' [The challenge to foresee the future], in Hernán Larraín and Richard Nuñez, eds, *Las Voces de la Reconciliation*, Instituto de la Sociedad, Santiago, 2013, pp. 35–36.
5   Sebastián E. Piñera, 'Por un Chile reconciliado y en paz' [For a reconciled and peaceful Chile], in Larraín and Nuñez, *Las Voces de la Reconciliation*, pp. 27–29. Probably Piñera referred to the more radical Socialists and the MIRistas, even though the latter had been banned as a political organisation since 1969.

reconciliation may in time be possible in Chile too; provided that the unreleased evidence and oral history programs still under way are preserved for the great-grandchildren of the future.[6]

Many times in the following chapters we will find evidence of successive governments stopping short of releasing documents, but still following a moderate Via Chilena to assuage the left while not antagonising the right. We will follow a (failed) attempt, unaccompanied by prosecutions, to identify the bodies uncovered in the General Cemetery. At a Site of Conscience in José Domingo Cañas we investigate the establishment of an (underfunded) museum to placate a prominent leftist critic. We will see how the state paid for a Wall of Names of victims at the best known of all such centres, Villa Grimaldi, and how it commissioned a team of architects and urban planners to memorialise the National Stadium. All governments have tolerated community-based denunciations of identified perpetrators by the ceremony known as the '*funa*'; we follow a particularly spectacular example of the *funa* that denounced 'el Príncipe' (the Prince), the military officer most closely associated with the murder of the Chilean musician Victor Jara. We test Aylwin's assertion that it was not only the conservatives who were alienated by Allende, by following the clash of two working-class ideologies over if and where to site a memorial to urban guerillas. At the better-known Site of Conscience Londres 38, we will note the reluctance of any administration to allow a state-owned building to be a platform of the MIR, which party, in Piñera's opinion, once portrayed democracy as the simple tool of the bourgeoisie. Perhaps each of these measures, sponsored by one or other of all post-Pinochet governments, are the clearest expression of a contemporary Via Chilena and a perceived desire to 'start again'.

The same might be said about the Museum for Memory and Human Rights, initiated and opened by Bachelet in 2010 in the last few months of her first term. The name itself suggested the tensions among the members of the planning committee. Memory is not the same as Memories, and neither, as we shall see, is necessarily to be equated with human rights. The same tensions are evident on every

---

6   Further discussion, see Peter Read, 'The truth that will set us all free: An uncertain history of memorials to Indigenous Australians', in Louise Purbrick, Jim Aulick and Graham Dawson, eds, *Contested Spaces: Sites, Representations and Histories of Conflict*, Palgrave Macmillan, Basingstoke, 2007, pp. 150–52.

floor of the exhibition. Victor Jara's song, written as a detainee in the last days of his life and displayed movingly over 10 metres of the entry passageway, sits a little awkwardly beside a rather less prominent catalogue of atrocities committed in Rwanda, Thailand and a dozen other countries. Clearly this museum will focus not on international but Chilean memory and human rights. Upstairs, noisily jostling schoolchildren watching footage of running troops may find themselves close to a woman shaking in grief as she listens to an audio recording.

Whose human rights? The display begins on 11 September 1973, without information on what might have precipitated the coup. Online comments on the display often criticise the emphasis on violations of human rights rather than explaining the cause of the military intervention. The same concerns are manifest in many academic conferences. In 2013, the historian Andrés Estefane concluded a discussion of the implication of the displays with the acerbic observation:

> Pain, suffering, disorientation, mutilation, solitude, disappearance, torture, murder, darkness, all these tropes are here introduced as the result of the 'unnatural' coincidence between violence and politics. Thus, there is no reflection on the political function of violence. There is pure violence represented in a fashion that directly appeals to the fragility of the body. Furthermore, by emphasizing the atrocities perpetrated in the past by a state that magically does not resemble and has no relationship with the actual state, by promoting an ideological and practical distance between the material and symbolic benefits of today and the brutality and precariousness of a dark past, by suggesting that outside the liberal state the individual citizen becomes vulnerable, Latin American governments are now recycling and subverting a classic socialist maxim: the precept of these times seems to be *liberal democracy or barbarism*.[7]

***

The origins of the museum's lack of historical analysis can perhaps be found in Bachelet's inaugural address in March 2006 – that violations of human rights can have many explanations but absolutely no

---

7   Andrés Estefane, 'Materiality and politics in Chile's Museum of Memory and Human Rights', *Thresholds* 41, Spring 2013, p. 169.

justification.[8] Here, surely, is the left's version of Aylwin's dictum that if Allende carried no mandate to convert Chile into a Socialist state, then the intervention of Pinochet had divided the country still further. The Via Chilena, like the museum itself, suggests that any historical display sponsored by the state should take care not to revive antagonisms that might hinder the nation 'moving on'.

***

The narrative of each study is carried by a single individual closely connected with it, as detainee, caretaker, curator or witness. It begins on the first day of the coup at the State University of Technology (UTE) where Victor Jara and hundreds of students and staff were trapped. From the UTE the detainees were marched to the Stadium of Chile, now known as the Victor Jara Stadium, to join thousands of others to be interrogated, tortured or killed. We follow Jara's life and death as it is remembered – or not remembered – at the university and the stadium that now bears his name. The university's confused signage today indicates the paralysing terror and uncertainty of the first few days of the coup. At the stadium, successive Ministers for Sport, by refusing funding and discouraging interest, have actively obstructed any kind of memorialisation.

Nena González leads the third chapter as we follow the bodies of those murdered at the Stadium of Chile and elsewhere, to an obscure precinct of the Santiago General Cemetery, Patio 29. The state security began to secretly and unceremoniously bury its victims shortly after the coup. The post-Pinochet state found a role for itself here too, in exhuming and identifying hundreds of victims; but in its haste to pacify the families and to deflect demands to identify and punish the perpetrators, it relied too heavily on the then crude science of DNA profiling. Most of the human remains were misidentified. Immediately after the coup, and from an unobtrusive corner as she worked, Nena saw the trucks carrying hundreds of naked bodies to be thrown into holes and, nine years later, Pinochet's hurried exhumations to conceal the makeshift burials; she spoke to officers who despised her and an endless array of terrified families asking what she knew. She carries the trauma to this day.

---

8   Cited, Peter Kornbluh and Katherine Hite, 'Chile's turning point', *The Nation*, 17 February 2010.

1. INTRODUCTION

Those who survived the first days of executions at sites like the Stadium of Chile were trucked within days to another, and much bigger holding area, the National Stadium. Our focus is on an accidental victim. Don Roberto Muñoz first was a worker at the stadium, then arrested, detained, tortured, released, and today is a worker at the site again. We follow the painful tensions between the state and memorialisers, heritage design professionals and those who experienced the terror, and between the survivors themselves as to what form the monuments should take.

The fourth chapter follows the journey of at least 42 detainees taken from the National Stadium to the 'House of Memory' at 1367 José Domingo Cañas (Street). Here we confront a formidable personality, Laura Moya Diaz, who almost single-handedly created the display. Her passing in 2013 signified a new direction to the memorial and museum that she had created and dominated for so long.

From José Domingo Cañas certain detainees were trucked to a larger and more specialised site of torture in the middle of the CBD, at 38 Londres (Street). In 2008, undecided as to the building's future, the state at first allowed a variety of left-wing interpretations of the recent past. By 2010 it had begun to grasp the potential of the site for the presentation of its own less confrontational interpretation of the Pinochet era right in the centre of the city, and installed itself as the principal voice of the building's remembrance. Such is the multiplicity of contending voices that no single personality can carry the narrative, but we follow in particular Roberto D'Orival Briceño, the brother of a detained-disappeared, whose collective pressed the government to install the MIRistas as inheritors of the building.

Should a site of terror evoke feelings of horror or serenity? At the best known of all the Chilean memorial parks, Parque por la Paz Villa Grimaldi (known colloquially as Villa Grimaldi), prolonged debate at length produced a park of peace in which the horrors of torture and disappearance were presented much less graphically than some of its corporation members demanded. Michele Drouilly, sister of the detained-disappeared Jacqueline, guides us through the intense debates over the priorities of detained-disappeared or survivor.

Lastly, we examine a site on which a spotlight fell in the last years of the dictatorship. Here in 2009 was unveiled a memorial stone dedicated principally to four urban guerillas of the armed revolutionary cell known as Rodriguistas. Josefina Rodriguez, founding member of a local chapter to construct new housing for Chile's needy, opposed the memorialisation from the beginning. Today that memorial stone is nowhere to be seen.

***

Haifa Zangana was imprisoned and tortured in the infamous prisons Qasr al-Nihaya and Abu Ghraib, near Baghdad, in 1971. She asks:

> What would you do with such sites of torture? What should happen to a building where thousands of civilians, including women and teenagers, many of whom have been picked up in random military sweeps and at highway checkpoints, have experienced or witnessed degrading and dehumanizing practices? A place where, in some cases, torture resulted in death? Where photographs and videos, kept as memorabilia, show breaking chemical lights and pouring the phosphoric liquid on detainees; pouring cold water on naked detainees, beating detainees with a broom handle and a chair; threatening male detainees with rape … sodomizing a detainee with a chemical light and perhaps a broomstick …[9]

President George W. Bush, after revelations of US atrocities enacted on prisoners in 2003, wanted Abu Ghraib demolished. Yet most prisoners, artists and human rights advocates, including Zangana, wanted it saved, conserved and a part set aside as a museum as a reminder of the 'scar that runs deep within our collective memory … No screams of the abused, no howling of the tortured, no whispers of women begging for mercy. Silence will be the language that howls out to condemn atrocities, violence, humiliation and degradation and protests our pain.'[10] Such a memorial might seem unobjectionable, but we shall see how creating a desolate silence in a former place of agony can be anathema to other survivors of identical experience.

---

9   Haifa Zangana, 'Foreword: Abu Ghraib: Prison as a Collective Memory', in Purbrick, Aulick and Dawson, *Contested Spaces*, p. xiv.
10 Ibid., pp. xiv–xv.

1. INTRODUCTION

Groups representing victims of the German Democratic Republic rejected the first designs of a memorial to the Berlin Wall because they believed it belittled its real horror.[11]

This is a book not of parties or ideologies but public history. It focuses on the memorials and memorialisers at each of the seven sites, engaging with worldwide debates about why and how should deeds of state violence to its own citizens be remembered, and by whom. Visits to such sites of violence have produced hundreds of reflections in academic journals or periodicals. Many are superficial, and how could they not be after an author's single visit? Our book traces the long period of memorialisation, from design proposals, commission, construction and unveiling; in whose name were they created, who remained disappointed? Who wrote the signage, whose words were excluded? How did rival groups change their positions over a decade or more? What moral, poetic, historical, political or ideological positions do the memorials present?

Some 250 memorials to the victims of the Pinochet repression, the majority only plaques, exist throughout Santiago. Many of these can be seen to parallel, or even substitute for, the prosecution and punishment of the perpetrators for crimes of disappearance, torture and detention, even of forced exile.[12] They can speak, through memory, of victimhood, heroism and martyrdom. They can demand recognition, reparation, reconciliation or justice. Memorials are one way – and the least likely to be condemned by apologists for the violence – for a state to appear to take responsibility for its past. But memorials to state violence are also, in the words of the politics of memory scholar Katherine Hite, 'battlegrounds, as artists, designers, states and societies negotiate how to convey, or evoke, or even shock, passers-by into contemplation and reaction'.[13] Hite distinguishes 'human rights' commemoration, sponsored by survivors and their advocates, from 'political' commemoration, led by states often in an attempt to heal

---

11   Gerd Knischewski and Ulla Spittler, 'Competing pasts: A comparison of National Socialist and German Democratic Remembrance in two Berlin memorial sites', in Purbrick, Aulich and Dawson, *Contested Spaces*, p. 175.
12   'Exiles File Civil Suits', Memoria y Justicia – Human Rights Today – Exiles.
13   Katherine Hite, 'Chile's National Stadium: As monument, as memorial', *ReVista*, Spring 2004, p. 61.

societal fractures.¹⁴ Typically, 'human rights'-driven memorials list the names of victims. The decision to erect a memorial, decide upon its form and content, secure funding and arrange a particular location will almost always be lengthy and divisive. The various protagonists – survivors, families of the disappeared and politically executed, and human rights activists – will not by any means share the same preferences or intentions. The memorial may register the emotions of loss and pain, but also of anger, or horror, or serenity and peace. There may be artefacts collected and displayed. Dedicated unpaid officials will need to care for the memorial, and as they age, or funds diminish, the memorial may show signs of neglect, even vandalism.

By contrast, state memorials are less likely to name victims; often they will be grand, impersonal, perhaps majestic. Debate as to the memorial's final form will remain internal. Very rarely will the public be granted a right of consultation. None of the features of design or wording, so important to human rights activists, will be open for debate for the state will follow its own priorities. There will be only one 'memory', one inscription, and that is the state's. At least one feature, however, will be common to the state and non-state memorial: the names of the perpetrators will not be listed.¹⁵

The struggles of Chilean memorialisers have many international parallels. The government's 'oblivion by passive hostility' of the Victor Jara Stadium is a milder version of the fate of the 'Gulag Museum', Perm-36, in Russia, whose private sponsors in 1996 created it in their euphoria at the Soviet collapse. But regional governments first showed little interest, later hostility towards its development. Bureaucratic passive resistance reduced, then cut, the museum's funding, and 2014 saw its closure.¹⁶ Nor was the forensic scientists' catastrophic misidentification of bodies exhumed from Patio 29 unknown elsewhere. In 2014 the South Korean government, in haste to satisfy the demands of distraught relatives, also misidentified many of the

---

14 Katherine Hite and Cath Collins, 'Memorial fragments, monumental silences and reawakenings in 21st century Chile', *Millenium* 38(2), 2009, p. 380.
15 The trend towards avoidance was set in the 'Rettig Report' and the 'Valech Report', the two major state-sponsored investigations into the Pinochet Regime. Both named victims, but neither identified perpetrators (the 'Report of the National Commission for Truth and Reconciliation', 1991, and the 'Report of the National Commission on Political Imprisonment and Torture', 2004).
16 'Perm-36', Wikipedia; 'Russian activists rally round embattled museum of Soviet repression', Radio Free Europe, 2 October 2014.

bodies recovered from a sunken ferry and returned them to the wrong families.[17] At the Vietnam Veterans Memorial in Washington DC, as at the Chilean National Stadium, opinions divided sharply not only between the professional design team and the veterans as to the form of the Washington Memorial, but just as sharply between the veterans themselves.[18] The dangers in a project leader failing to persuade the community-of-interest to follow, which we will see at José Domingo Cañas, had a more extreme counterpart at the Smithsonian Museum in Washington DC. It followed a decision of Martin Harwitt, director of the Smithsonian's National Air and Space Museum, to display 'Enola Gay', the plane that dropped the atomic bomb, without sufficient discussion of the context. Harwitt was forced to resign.[19] Many governments, as at Londres 38, use historic sites for their own interpretative purposes. In the interest of fostering national unity, the Singaporean government saw the advantage in stressing the role of Singaporean Malay soldiers in the World War Two Changi prison camp museum, and in the 1990s rewrote the signage to support this wider purpose.[20] The opposing polarities of horror or the serenity of contemplation to be invoked at a historic site are, first, at Auschwitz-Birkenau, which exhibits the crematoria, piles of clothing, shoes and human hair, and conversely at the Park of Peace at Hiroshima, intended 'not only to memorialize the victims, but also to establish the memory of nuclear horrors [by preserving the Genbaku Dome] and advocate world peace'.[21]

Memorials can invoke the strongest emotions. The destruction of one that we will meet in Quinta Normal, Santiago, is echoed in Germany, where it is universally considered too dangerous to name perpetrators on World War Two memorials for fear of reprisals to the memorial, or to the designers![22] In central Queensland, Australia, a memorial to the qualities of Kalkadoon Aboriginal warriors in fighting white invaders has been defaced or blown up several times.[23] At Knin Castle near

---

17 'South Korea admits ferry disaster dead bodies given to wrong families', *The Guardian*, 25 April 2014.
18 Denise Kirsten Wills, 'The Vietnam Memorial's history', *Washingtonian*, 1 November 2007.
19 Debbie Ann Doyle, 'Historians protest the new Enola Gay exhibit', *Perspectives of History*, December 2003.
20 Peter Read, 'Where are you Uncle John?' *Australian Cultural History* 27(9), 2009, 13–24.
21 Hiroshima Peace Memorial Museum website; 'Hiroshima Peace Memorial Park', Wikipedia.
22 Klaus Neumann, *Shifting Memories: The Nazi Past in the New Germany*, University of Michigan Press, Ann Arbor, 2000.
23 Lisanne Gibson, and Joanna Besley, *Monumental Queensland: Signposts on a Cultural Landscape*, University of Queensland Press, St Lucia, 2005, pp. 51–54.

Split, Croatia, just the top half of a memorial plaque dedicated to a Croatian patriot killed by Italian soldiers in the World War Two was preserved in the civil war (1991–95), but the bottom half – attesting to the plaque's erection by Serbo-Croatians – has been smashed. In Warsaw, patriots chose a random, neutral space in a cemetery to mourn their compatriots killed in Katyn Forest for fear that anything more tangible would be destroyed and the mourners punished.[24] Those who live through times of state violence, even those who participated in it, are likely to cast themselves as victims rather than victimisers. Descendants of perpetrators may deny responsibility for the actions of their forbears. Memorials protesting against state violence thus are ever in danger of defacement.

The sites that we will investigate are among the most iconic of more than 1,000 sites of torture and extermination throughout the country. Their multiple interpretations vary from oblivion to detailed and passionate expositions. The centre 'Simon Bolivar', a site chosen for the interrogation and execution of Communist Party leaders, was a complex of buildings completely unknown to investigators until a former guard confessed in 2007 to having worked there.[25] Terrible details emerged of fingerprints burnt off corpses with a blowtorch to prevent identification, of murders with Sarin gas or asphyxiation by plastic bag, of at least one communist being dropped into the sea by helicopter. Yet today the site is again a private house offering no acknowledgement to visitors, while the street numbering has been altered to confuse the ignorant. Only a crude, recently painted inscription on the fence indicates the true location of 'Simon Bolivar'. In 2013 a plaque marked the site. Next day it was gone and it has not been replaced. Oblivion.

A prototype of memorial-as-passionate-ideology is 'The House Museum of Human Rights Alberto Bachelet Martinez', known to the security forces as 'Nido #20', in the middle-class Santiago suburb of La Cisterna. Here a single dedicated individual, Juan Espina Espina, ex-militant and torture victim, maintains the small private house as a museum. Probably the dwelling was never much more than a

---

24   Lynn Olson and Stanley Cloud, *A Question of Honor: The Kościuszko Squadron: Forgotten Heroes of World War II*, Vintage Books, New York, 2007, p. 412.
25   Jorge Escalante and Javier Rebolledo, 'The "Dolphins" that exterminated the Communist Party', *La Nación*, 1 April 2007.

holding centre, but four people are known to have been tortured to death within its walls. Owned by the state since 2006, the house stands near the home where Bachelet, Chile's current president, grew up. Her father, General Alberto Bachelet, died after arrest and torture in the Air Force War Academy.[26] Precise information about Nido #20, as about nearly all such Chilean centres, is scarce. In reconstructing its history, little information could be gained from neighbours, for the guards, on the arrival of each detainee, would fire their guns in the air to scare everyone inside. In the bathroom is displayed an imitation *parrilla* (grill) on which detainees were tortured by electricity; in a bedroom, a tiny cupboard containing a life-sized two dimensional bound and gagged detainee almost bent double, is jammed into this tiny space. None of those known to have died here, however, are named. Rather, the overall message of the museum is less personal than unashamedly political. A sign in the entrance room reads:

> The opposition to the Popular Unity Party and to the movement began the political struggle that sought to declare government measures unconstitutional, and saturate the media with alarming information. Also, social and economic destabilisation by creating food shortages, strikes by employees and college professionals, commercial and transport stoppages that built upon the climate of commotion.

Finally, the use of violence, assassination and sabotage to promote the coup against the state:

> The US government opposed Salvador Allende and promoted the destabilization, violence and the military uprising.

The stress on the role of the United States, the wrongful loss of legitimate government and state-sanctioned murder of its own citizens, contrasts with the public presentations at the larger centres and indicates that split in historical interpretation noted by Hite. At the more notorious sites, we shall see that the dominant interpretation will be the violation of universal human rights, rather than evoking sympathy for the Chilean political left: the polarities of the Cold War are less fashionable today and draw fewer visitors. Juan Espina Espina

---

26 'Alberto Bachelet', Wikipedia.

himself concedes that by far the greatest number of visitors to his museum in 2013 came not for the 11 September anniversary of the coup, but to see an exhibition on Anne Frank.[27]

Yet even in these smaller centres, the tensions we will encounter throughout this study are never absent: between the universal and the particular, the survivor and the detained-disappeared, the state and the family of the victim, and not least, the abysses between the Rodriguista Patriotic Front, the MIR, Socialist, MAPU, Communist and Christian Democrat parties. Each suffered under the dictatorship, and each still seeks particular recognition of its sacrifice. It is between and within this aggressive diversity that the heritage professional must negotiate a path.

Sources on the dictatorship and its aftermath are surprisingly plentiful. Two vital bases of information are the two government reports, the so-called Rettig Report on the politically executed and detained-disappeared, and the Valech Report, on the victims of torture.[28] A multitude of autobiographies of dictatorship experience and analyses published by LOM Ediciones/Colección Septiembre supplement the substantial academic discussion, including the major trauma sites. It is hard to keep up with the constant web postings of supporters of leftist political parties, or interest groups associated with each site that we discuss. How, then, in a country saturated in memory can non-Chilean historians contribute something different?

In 2008 we published the article 'Putting site back into trauma studies: A study of five detention and torture centres in Santiago Chile'.[29] Here we argued that much recent scholarship had lost sight of that close connection between a generalised societal trauma and the actual sites where the trauma was inflicted. Within the field of public history, scholars of state terrorism and victims of Pinochet themselves

---

27 Juan Espina Espina, guided tour and interview, 9 November 2013.
28 Memoria Viva is the 'Digital archive of the Violations of Human Rights committed under the Military Dictatorship in Chile, 1973–1990', containing separate sections under criminals, the disappeared, executed and tortured (www.memoriaviva.com/); Archivo Chile (www.archivochile.com/) claims to be the 'Documentation of the political, social, and contemporary popular movements of Chile and Latin America'. While both sources should be used cautiously, much of their information is drawn from the two major government reports into the Pinochet dictatorship, see footnote 15, this chapter.
29 Peter Read and Marivic Wyndham, 'Putting site back into trauma studies: A study of five detention and torture centres in Santiago, Chile', *Life Writing* 5(1), 2008, 79–96.

insist that the loss of a site means a loss of a precise memory that is very often of benefit to the state that committed acts of terrorism. Hernán Valdéz wrote:

> If we, conscious of the terror which was established in the country, pass through here without suspecting the existence of this place, what remains for those who want, deliberately, to deny the terror over the others?[30]

We believe that the status of overseas historian, that is, unassociated with a particular interest group that any Chilean is likely to be, has given us considerable freedom. Outsiders can sometimes move more easily in a number of competing circles of class and party, win some trust and, in part, peer through the fabric of secrecy and mistrust that still exists so strongly within Chilean society. Partisans who have long exhausted their local audiences have a fresh opportunity to express their strongest passions to foreign academics, less biased in either direction. Our biggest contribution, though, may be longevity. Our researches are based on minute examination of specific sites through observation, a continuous photographic record, oral history, curatorial discussions and site visits over a decade and more to track the ascendancy of groups or individuals, changing signage, new memorial constructions or the removal of what was previously displayed. More generally we can track the incipient intrusion of the state into the process of memorialisation that will inevitably elude the casual visitor.

We may ask also: why, at this point, write a longitudinal study of memorialisation? Our answer is that, while moral outrage and street demonstrations will endure for many years, the journey towards physical memorialisation has almost run its course. People understand that the impulse to build new memorials to the victims of the dictatorship is not the force it was. Younger activists recall their own years of fighting for the return of democracy in the 1980s rather than the first murderous years of the coup. What the survivors of the first years of the dictatorship are currently inscribing on their own memorials may be their last chance to write their own history. Their demands for justice and for information still controlled by the state will continue, but it is improbable that following generations will

---

30 Hernán Valdéz, *Tejas Verdes*, LOM Ediciones, Santiago, 1996, p. 56.

engage with the Pinochet era with quite the same passionate intensity of those who endured the suffering. Never will they be able to claim 'I was here'.

***

Our intention in this book is not to dwell on the politics of the coup itself: it is as legitimate to celebrate the heroism of Allende's last radio address from his besieged office in the presidential palace, La Moneda, as it is to cite figures of the plunging economy and strike-ridden chaos of his regime. But in order to contextualise why the passions of the early 1970s continue to haunt the memorialisation of sites of state violence, we outline here some key events under Allende's rule up to September 1973. They grant a glimpse of the depth of feeling of the early 1970s, its idealism and hope, courage and frustration, hatred, excitement, resentment, sadness, fear, division and disillusion.

Truly the conservatives had much to resent and fear; truly the left could neither forget nor forgive what was visited upon them from 11 September 1973.

***

By January 1972, Allende's Popular Unity Party government was failing. The first Marxist ever to be become president of a Latin American country through open elections, his was an uneasy coalition of political allies from the moderate to the radical left. But after only a year in power, its divisions, always potential, were rapidly widening. Already he had nationalised the copper and textile industries and confiscated the largest estates; but reluctant to be seen to be dominated by Cuba or dictated to by the United States, Allende was steering a much more erratic course than he would have preferred. In January, one of his volatile and unpredictable political allies, the armed revolutionary political party MIR, was demanding more radical change. In February a more certain ally, the Socialists, was insisting that he spend less of his energies appeasing the MIR and more on dialogue with the Christian Democrats – who were not members of the Popular Unity Party at all. In May his generals warned him that galloping inflation and flagging productivity would weaken the defence forces. In July the National Congress, ever unsympathetic to the Popular Unity Party, tried to impeach the Interior Minister for authorising the importation of small arms from Cuba. In August 1972 the association of small businesses declared a national strike. Allende responded with a declaration of a State of Emergency. In October the truck drivers struck also; in an attempt to restore calm and guard against the much discussed possibility of a military coup, the president appointed several senior Defence Force officers to his Cabinet. By November the rate of expropriations of large land holdings and businesses in the name of the people had slowed, but another State of Emergency was declared. January 1973 brought the rationing of 30 basic items. In March the military officers withdrew from the Cabinet. In April the United States, pursuing a policy of economic sanctions against Chile for failure to compensate for nationalisation of US-dominated industries, broke off negotiations to refinance the ballooning national debt. In May the copper workers, whose relief from foreign exploitation had been such a key point of the Allende promise, called yet another national strike. June 1973 brought street fighting as leftist groups battled the police and right-wing gangs.[31] Late that month a coup attempt failed. Known as 'El Tanquetazo' because the rebel Army officers used tanks, it was successfully quashed by loyal Constitutionalist soldiers led by Army Commander-in-Chief Carlos Prats. In early September, just before the coup, and amidst much dissatisfaction, and with parts of the country in economic paralysis, Allende devalued the currency by 40 per cent.[32] Again and again Chile's Nobel prize winner Pablo Neruda warned of re-enacting the hideous Spanish Civil War that he had witnessed at first hand. But when it came, Chile's civil war was much more one-sided than anyone imagined.[33]

So deep had become the animosity not only between the government and its opponents but between the government and many of its so-called supporters, that Allende planned a national plebiscite. A popular vote, he hoped, would re-endorse majority support for his Popular Unity Party. The scheduled venue to announce the plebiscite

---

31 The most significant of the para-military right-wing groups was 'Patria y Libertad' (Fatherland and Liberty), disbanded the day after the coup; en.wikipedia.og/wiki/Fatherland_and_Liberty.
32 Drawn from various sources including Hutchison, Elizabeth Quay, Thomas Miller Klubock, Nara B. Milanich and Peter Winn, eds, *The Chile Reader*, Duke, Durham and London, 2014, ch. 4, pp. 343–432; Helen Osieja, *Economic Sanctions as an Instrument of US Foreign Policy: The Case of the US Embargo against Cuba*, Universal Publishers, 2006, pp. 97–100; 'Las raices de desabastecimiento y el "mercado negro"' [The roots of scarcity and the black market], 7 February 2002.
33 For example, Mario Amorós, *Neruda: El Príncipe de los Poetas*, Ediciones B, Santiago, 2015, p. 496.

was the most radical of Santiago's universities, the State University of Technology (the UTE), which during Allende's term had become first choice for engineering and technical training for young people of the rural poor. To its friends, the UTE was known as the launching pad of the new professionals. To its critics, it was said to be the Chilean equivalent of the Paris Polytechnic.

The scheduled date of Allende's plebiscite was 11 September 1973.

In this long, narrow country, the passions of remembrance, justice and punishment run endlessly deep: they could scarcely be deeper.

Part I

2
Victor Jara, the State University of Technology and the Victor Jara Stadium

The principal entertainer scheduled for the announcement of Allende's plebiscite at the State University of Technology (Universidad Técnica del Estado, UTE) was Victor Lidio Jara Martínez, known as Victor Jara, idolised and controversial folk-singer, hero of the poor and the left, scourge of the rich and conservative. Jara was from the oppressed copper mining and rural poor. His alcoholic, abusive father abandoned the family when Victor was a child; his mother gathered herbs from the hills, while her son collected firewood and grass for the pigs. In the 1950s the family moved to Santiago.[1] In the early 1960s, he visited the Soviet Union and Cuba and was impressed by both; returning he joined the Communist Party of Chile. He performed usually in his peasant's poncho, but a photograph in Joan Jara's biography of her husband, *Unfinished Song*, shows him equally at home at Stratford Upon Avon, Great Britain, strolling sedately in a suit with such artists as Dame Margot Fonteyn. Allende named him a Cultural Ambassador of his Popular Unity Party government, through which role he performed in most Latin American countries in 1971–73.

---

1   'Victor Jara biography', Encyclopaedia of World Biography; see also 'Víctor Jara', Biographías y Vidas.

Jara's nearest contemporary equivalents were, perhaps, Bob Dylan, John Lennon or Pete Seeger, but none is an apt comparison. Committed Communist, he was highly talented, passionate, brave, sarcastic, bitter, adored – and hated. Perhaps nothing better exemplifies the passion for social change, the depth of conservative hatred, and the manifestation of that hatred, than the life and death of Victor Jara.

Chile's upper classes believed that they had good reason to hate him. In 1969, following the massacre of eight landless peasants squatting on their absentee landlord's farm, he wrote the song 'Questions for Puerto Montt', aimed at the commander (whom he refers to as a 'Puerto Monkey'), about the would-be farmers who:

> Died not knowing because
> they blasted them in the chest
> fighting for the right
> to a plot of land to live,
> oh, to be unhappier
> the one who ordered fire
> knowing how to avoid
> a vile massacre[2]

Another number that did nothing to improve his relations with conservative Chileans was the re-release, in his first album (1966), of 'The pious woman' who fell in love with her confessor. Through various not very subtle references to shoes, sandals, cassocks and short candles, Jara was again satirising not only the country's establishment, but any Chilean who distrusted the direction of what might seem, under Allende, to be Chile's apparent and inevitable march towards Cuban dictatorship.

Worse followed. In 1971 he adapted the 1967 hit 'Little Boxes' by the US singer Malvina Reynolds, later popularised by Pete Seeger, to his own, much more biting version.[3] No longer a cover, it became more his own creation in making the rhythm more spiky, altering the melody and adding jarring discords. While Reynolds's little boxes were cheap postwar housing covering the hillside of Daly City, California, Jara's were in the 'barrio alto', the wealthy and much better constructed suburbs on the foothills of Santiago's cordillera. The first

---

2 Victor Jara, 'Questions for Puerto Montt', LyricsTranslate.
3 'Little Boxes', Wikipedia; 'Malvina Reynolds: Song Lyrics and Poems: "Little Boxes"'.

verse of 'Las Casitas del Barrio Alto' ('Little Houses of the Barrio Alto', or more colloquially, 'Little boxes of the flash district') did not mince matters:

> The Little Houses of the Barrio Alto
>
> The little houses of the barrio alto
> With railings and gardens in front
> A pretty entrance for the garage
> Waiting for a Peugeot.

Entertaining as this may have been for those who did not live in the 'barrio alto', Jara's critique now sharpened. Reynolds's 'doctors, lawyers and business executives' became:

> … dentists, businessmen
> Large scale landowners, drug traffickers,
> Lawyers and slum landlords
> All wearing polycron [polyester]
> and all triumphant on Prolen [equivalent of Prozac]
>
> They play bridge and drink dry Martinis
> And the kids are little blondies
> And with other little blondies
> They go all together to private schools.
>
> Daddy's little boy
> Later goes to university
> Starting off with his problems
> And his little social intrigues.
>
> Smokes joints in the Austin Mini
> Plays with bombs and politics
> Assassinates generals
> And is a seditious gangster.[4]

A Peugeot, even a TV set, were symbols of luxury in Chile of the early 1970s; even the profession of dentist smacked of privilege and conservative power. Yet it is possible that Jara, of dirt-poor rural origins, and with an irony that possibly escaped even his critics, was aiming his sarcasm at more than the extreme right with their exclusive education. He may also have been condemning the mostly high-born leadership of the MIR, that Movement of the Revolutionary

---

4   Translation and interpretation by Paula González Dolan.

Left which, through its ceaseless demands for armed revolution, was causing almost as much trouble to Allende as was the right. In this interpretation, the idle critics of the socialist revolution, both left and right, were content to fool around with explosives, political theorising, plots and criticism, instead of committing themselves to lending a hand without which the state experiment in workers' rights could not survive.

The following year brought another, even more famous, Jara number, 'Ni Chicha Ni Limona'. Now Jara made an appeal to everyone not already committed to the government to join the revolution 'where the potatoes are burning', that is, at the driving-point of social change. The title literally means 'Neither *chicha* nor lemonade', a Chilean expression hard to translate, but here contrasting *'chicha'*, a home-produced alcoholic drink, with home-produced lemonade; the peoples' simple drinks, aimed at those who accepted neither one nor the other, the uncommitted, the unwilling to decide, sniffing the air to see what the future held before joining in. Jara's wife Joan believes that Victor aimed his lyrics also at the Christian Democrats who still, in 1973, were undecided as to how far they should cooperate with the Allende experiment.[5] In 'Ni Chicha Ni Limona', the sharp sarcasm of 'Little Boxes of the Barrio Alto' was darkened by a threat, in the last verse, of what would happen to those who did not cooperate. In one of the still-current YouTube performances, clad in his poncho, Jara unequivocally presents the threat of expropriation. The song is even now an astonishing performance: catchy, invocatory, arrogant, clever, funny, menacing. It is the voice of the many thousands who had expected so much of their first democratically elected Marxist government, but who now, day by day, could see their hopes and their nation disintegrating. Jara begins:

> The party's already started
> Here where the sun shines
> If you're still used to twisting and turning
> No harm will come to you
> Where the potatoes are burning
>
> You're nothing
> Neither *chicha* nor lemonade
> you keep massaging – Caramba! – your dignity

---

5   Joan Jara, *Un Canto Truncado*, Punto de Lectura, Madrid, 1983, p. 267.

2. VICTOR JARA, THE STATE UNIVERSITY OF TECHNOLOGY AND THE VICTOR JARA STADIUM

> The party's already started
> It's burning bright
> You who were the quiet one
> (now) want to join in the dance
> finally for those still sniffing the wind
> There's no smell that will not escape them
>
> If we want a bigger party
> First we'll have to work
> And we'll have for everyone,
> Shelter, bread, friendship
> And if you're not with us
> It's up to you
> The party's [the social revolution] still advancing
> There's no question of retreating
>
> Leave your sideburns
> Come and make good your sins
> Even here, underneath my poncho,
> I don't have any dagger
> And if you continue pulling us down
> We're going to expropriate
> The pistols, the tongues
> And everything else as well

Following this last verse, in a televised performance Jara's smile fades as he turns to camera in close up to repeat the chorus:

> You're nothing
> Neither *chicha* nor lemonade
> Hey listen, you,
> you keep massaging – Caramba! – your dignity.[6]

Neither the President's attempted Cuban-style reforms nor the biting sarcasm of Jara would be forgotten by their enemies in the events that were now to follow.

---

6 Tr. Paula González Dolan.

NARROW BUT ENDLESSLY DEEP

11 September 1973, 5.30 am

Today is not only the day scheduled for the announcement of the plebiscite at the State University of Technology, but that also chosen secretly as the moment for the armed forces' coup against Allende. The trucks that will take the detained to prearranged holding centres throughout the city have been ordered days ago from distant locations. The principal interrogators heading for the UTE, led by their commanding officer Colonel Juan Manuel Guillermo Contreras Sepúlveda, have already departed the College of Military Engineers, two hours from Santiago. Thousands of young conscripts are being trucked from their bases in southern Chile towards the capital for a purpose still undisclosed. At first light detachments will start rounding up hundreds of proscribed workers in the industrial ports and mines. Some marked leaders will be dead by noon. The engineers' base at the port town of Tejas Verdes will shortly become the first headquarters of the new state security service later known as la DINA (National Intelligence Directorate) and commanded by Contreras. It will be here that the first strategic torture methods learned from the School of the Americas will be refined.[7] It will be here that the DINA agents will first enact what they have learned at the centres for training in torture, extermination and disappearance.[8] Simultaneously, tanks are moving into position to surround the seat of government, La Moneda, in the city centre. Planning seems complete, except that the military have failed to foresee the problem of how to dispose of the bodies of the many hundreds of leftists – whether Allende supporters or not – that they propose now to kill. Plans for the plebiscite are of course abandoned, as Allende, contrary to the advice of his bodyguards, rushes to La Moneda. At about the same time, a university official rings the home of Vice-Chancellor Enrique Kirberg of the State University of Technology, to inform him that soldiers have just destroyed the university's radio station. With a long history of communist sympathy and participation, Kirberg rushes to his own headquarters, the Chancellery, known as the Casa Central, in the main

---

7   The School of the Americas (now the Western Hemisphere for Security Co-operation) was founded in 1946 to teach 'anticommunist counterinsurgency training', especially in Central and Latin America.
8   Javier Rebolledo, *El Despertar de Los Cuervos*, CEIBA, Santiago, 2013, pp. 1–20.

2. VICTOR JARA, THE STATE UNIVERSITY OF TECHNOLOGY AND THE VICTOR JARA STADIUM

UTE campus. From the upper storey he can see bombers circling the city, especially threatening to La Moneda, the centre of government, where Allende shortly will make his last speech and his last stand.[9]

***

At home Victor Jara, like everyone else in Santiago, understood exactly the significance of the circling aircraft and the thunder of distant heavy weapons. Already a marked man, he knew that they would be coming for him. As a visiting Professor of Music at the UTE, his duty was to the campus, to his colleagues and to his friend Allende. He filled the car with the last of the petrol he kept for such an emergency. A neighbour, a pilot, came out on his balcony to shout an insult at him. Getting into the car he called out to Joan, 'I'll see you when I can, mamita. You know what you have to do ... Keep calm. Bye.' When she turned to look, Victor had gone.[10] At the campus he joined the hundreds of other students and staff still gathering to demonstrate no longer their support for the plebiscite but rather their solidarity against the coup despite the obvious danger to themselves. Few had any conception of what the Pinochetistas had in store for them.

Within the Chancellery Kirberg, having summoned his senior officials, announced through the public address that it was time to abandon the campus. Some students responded that their orders were to return to their urban zones to fight, and left. Some of the other leftist groups dispersed to their local headquarters or homes; several offered Kirberg sanctuary. By 9, troops had entered the campus itself. Staff and students who remained gathered to hold a nervous rally amidst bursts of machine guns in the close vicinity.

At noon Jara managed to put a call through to Joan. 'How are things, mamita? I couldn't call you before. I'm here, at the Technical University. You know what's happening, yeah?' Joan told him of the dive-bombers, Jara replied that everything was okay. 'When will you come back?' 'I'll call you later. Now they need the phone ... Bye.' Next door Joan's neighbours were all on the upstairs patio talking

---

9   Kirberg's narrative is taken from a transcribed interview by Luis Cifuentes S., 'Kirberg. Testigo y Actor del Siglo XX' [Kirberg: Witness and Actor of the Twentieth Century], 2nd edition, August 1999, especially chs 4 and 5.
10   Jara, *Un Canto Truncado*, pp. 389–90.

excitedly, standing on chairs the better to see the aerial attack on La Moneda, drinking toasts or waving a flag.[11] At about 4.30, Jara managed another phone call. In Joan Jara's account, he said '"I'll have to stay here ... It'll be difficult to return because of the curfew. At first light tomorrow morning, as soon as I wake up, I'll come home. Mamita, I love you." "Love you too." But I'm choking up while I'm saying it, and then he's cut the call.'[12]

Shortly before, a senior armed forces officer had imposed a curfew on the campus, followed by a summons to Kirberg to meet the military delegation. The vice-chancellor retorted that he would meet no one except off campus. There they told him that the university was cordoned off, that no one could enter or leave, and that tomorrow buses would come to take everybody to their homes. By mid-afternoon soldiers in army trucks had completely surrounded the university. The 800 students and staff were ordered not to attempt escape. They scattered to rooms and offices for warmth and mutual comfort on the bitter September night. All night, shooting resounded round the campus; several people died. Jara remained with his friends. He again phoned Joan to inform her that he would not be able to return at present. It was the last time she heard his voice. Survivors recalled that that night he and his friends wrapped themselves in newspapers, terrified of what the dawn would bring. In the darkness, the campus students and staff crept about to make contact with their friends and planned the morrow. Others crept into the metallurgical workshop to make Molotov cocktails out of whatever materials were to hand.

At 7 next morning Kirberg, after not much sleep in an office armchair, was awakened by a tremendous concussion of artillery. The phone rang:

'Ah, Rector, things have changed. Surrender.'
'Look, tell your commanding officer whoever he is, to cease fire, and everyone will leave.'
The officer replied, 'I'll see what I can do. Things aren't that simple.'
Presently a shout from outside,
'Come out with your hands up'.

---

11   Ibid., p. 391.
12   Ibid., p. 392.

2. VICTOR JARA, THE STATE UNIVERSITY OF TECHNOLOGY AND THE VICTOR JARA STADIUM

A soldier addressed him in what is, in Spanish, the very discourteous second person singular when addressing a figure of authority. 'Now you're going to learn what university autonomy means.' An army Captain came up rapidly to confront him. 'Ah, so you're the Vice-Chancellor, are you? Now you'll see, what we do with people like you, you shitty mother-fucker.' A soldier stood him facing the wall, warning him that he had 15 seconds to tell him where the arms were concealed. But apart from a few pistols, and whatever had been manufactured in the Metallurgical workshop in the past 12 hours, there were none. The heavy weapons opened up on the Chancellery to blast it to bits.[13]

Most of the UTE captives – for that was what they now were – spent the morning lying flat on their stomachs, ordered not to move. By mid-afternoon of 12 September, Jara was trucked or marched, like everyone else who had chosen not to escape the day before, six city blocks into the Stadium of Chile.

In most accounts, based on the memories of surviving eyewitnesses, several hours passed before Victor was recognised at the stadium by one of the military. 'You're that fucking singer, aren't you?' Set apart from the others, he was taken away to be interrogated and beaten up, at first in a broadcast booth. A particular swaggering guard, tall, blonde, Germanic, known as 'el Príncipe' (the Prince), mimed guitar playing, ran his fingers round his neck in mock execution. He is supposed to have said, 'What's this bastard doing here? Don't let him move from here. He's reserved for me.'[14]

Returned to the arena, smashed and broken, Jara found comfort with his friends. They washed his face, shared with him a small jar of marmalade and biscuits. He asked for pen and paper and began to scribble.

> In this small part of the city
> We are five thousand.
> I wonder how many we are in all
> in the cities and in the whole country?
> ...

---

13   Cifuentes, 'Kirberg', pp. 170ff; Carlos Orella, in Sergio Villegas, ed., *El Estadio*, LOM Colección Septiembre, Santiago, 1974/2013, p. 166.
14   See also Joan Jara's account, *Un Canto Truncado*, pp. 410–12.

> Six of us lost themselves in the space of the stars
> One dead, with a blow like I never believed
> Could be dealt to a human being.
> The other four wanted to end their terror
> One throwing himself into space, others beating their heads against the wall
> What fear is brought by the face of fascism
> They make their forward plans with such cunning precision…
> Without letting anything get in the way.
> Blood is medals for them
> Massacre the proof of heroism.
> Oh my God, is this the world you created
> Was it for this the astonishing seven days of labour?[15]

The meaning of 'six lost themselves in the space of the stars' emerged during a tour of the Stadium of Chile in 2014. What was already apparent then in these words was Jara's incomprehension of the depth of violent hatred that the military was visiting upon the detainees, and soon to be further visited upon him.

During the afternoon, as the military continued dividing up those who were to remain, those to be released, and those to be sent to the much larger National Stadium, Jara was dragged to a concrete downstairs changing room below the military corridor, reserved for 'important or special prisoners'. An unnamed eyewitness account continued:

> Up comes the chief of the 'prisoners section' and proposes 'Let's bust the hands of this mother's cunt'. He gives him blows with his stick. 'Sing now, you bastard. Get up' he orders. They bend his wrists over a bar and begin to beat his hands and wrists until they're a bloody mass. All this happens in the passage … Victor is on the floor … They show him up as a war trophy. Up come three officials from the Air Force. They arrange themselves in front of him, insulting and beating him by turns. 'Do you want a smoke, cunt?' they ask mockingly. Victor doesn't answer. They push a lighted cigarette into one of his hands.[16]

In the evening Jara was dragged back to the main stadium, bleeding, broken, barely alive.

---

15 Abbreviated version. The full song is reproduced in ibid., pp. 415–17.
16 Testimony of eyewitnesses, in Villegas, *El Estadio*, pp. 101–10.

Though he handed the words to his comrades, nobody knows if he finished the song. Perhaps he could endure no more. Oral history relates, though the story may have improved with the telling, that he managed to croak these broken words that night on the basketball court, along with 'Venceremos' (We shall Overcome) from his repertoire.[17] The last words he dictated, part of this last song, were an appeal to the mecca of the Chilean radical left:

> And Mexico, Cuba and the world?
> Scream this shame! ...

And the enduring incomprehension of violence as unforeseen as it was unimaginable:

> What I see I have never seen
> What I have felt and feel
> Will give birth to the moment.

***

It was probably in the pre-dawn of 16 September that he died. With many bones broken, including his spine, one account has him killed by a single bullet in an extended game of Russian roulette in the underground changing room, after which his guards were told to put as many bullets in him as they liked.[18]

The tour, 2009[19]

As we shall find at almost every site of torture and disappearance before 2009, no official tour exists either at the State University of Technology or the Stadium of Chile. At the UTE a campus official expresses surprise that anyone should be interested in exploring the UTE's part in the coup. He finds another employee, Don José Uribe, soon to retire, who not only holds the information, but is anxious to share it.

---

17   'Venceremos' was composed by Sergio Ortega for Allende's 1970 election campaign.
18   At great personal risk, Joan Jara and several Communist Party members buried Jara in an empty niche in the Santiago General Cemetery. It remained as a site of international veneration until he was reinterred, at the state's expense, in December 2009; 'Chile reburies coup victim and singer Jara', BBC News, 5 December 2009.
19   José Uribe, interview and guided tour, December 2009.

He begins with memorial plaques scattered about the campus. Near the main gate is a list of 18 students, officials and staff known to have been executed during the whole 17-year period of Pinochet's dictatorship, the figure known, that is, in 2003 when the plaque was erected by the 'politically exonerated'[20] staff of the university in September of that year. In the main campus student rallying point, stands a 4-metre mural, erected in 1991, removed in the later 1990s under orders of a conservative vice-chancellor, now reinstalled. Its dedication reads:

> With Victor with Kirberg the UTE lives.

Close by, erected in 2006, is a memorial to all students and staff associated with the university who died during the dictatorship, a three-dimensional sculpture of three figures, at least one a woman, bearing a body between them. Their heads are bent in grief in what seems a direct allusion to Michelangelo's *Pieta*.[21]

Uribe's next stop is the plaque dedicated to Gregorio Mimica Argote, in 1973 the president of the engineering student body, and well-known Communist Party member, detained on 12 September, but inadvertently released. On the 14th a patrol of 14 troops re-arrested him 'by order of the Ministry of Interior' in his parents' house. No one had realised how lucky he was to have been released at all. This time Argote's parents were ordered to say goodbye to him for they would not see him again. And they did not: their son remains one of the 'detained-disappeared', that is, one of the many thousands whose families join the cry *Donde está*? Where is he? Where is she? On 11 September 2003, 30 years after his disappearance, a memorial plaque to him as a detained-disappeared was fixed on a classroom corridor. A second student victim whose disappearance threw her family into agonising confusion and doubt is that of Michelle Peña, who was disappeared eight months into her pregnancy. The whereabouts of her baby, if it was born, remains unknown. The university crèche is named after her, and every year Michelle's mother, so relates the Alumni website, returns to the campus to remember her and others who disappeared. The plaque to her memory was dedicated 'thirty years

---

20 Those dismissed from the Pinochet regime and later vindicated and/or re-employed by the State University of Technology.
21 Reproduced in Alejandro Hoppe, photographer, *Memoriales en Chile: Homenajes a las Víctimas de Violaciones a Derechos Humanos*, Ocho Libros Editores, Santiago, 2007, p. 62.

2. VICTOR JARA, THE STATE UNIVERSITY OF TECHNOLOGY AND THE VICTOR JARA STADIUM

after the commemoration of her death', 11 September 1973; yet now it is understood that she actually was murdered by the security forces in 1975.[22] Even the date of Jara's death, inscribed on the sculpture to his memory in 1991, is wrong – 14 September. The plaque reads:

> Victor Jara Plaza
> Assassinated 14 September 1973
> For the right to live in peace

The inaccuracy and confusion evident in this and other campus signage equally reflects for how long relatives were kept from knowing what had happened to their siblings, parents, partners or children, an ignorance indicating either the security forces' bureaucratic carelessness, or its intention that nobody should find out.

Yet there is no mistaking the emotion of the sculptor of the Jara memorial. Above the plaque, at the edge of a grassy plaza stands his monument, 3 metres tall, a bronze guitar on a plinth. Above the body of the guitar, the neck transforms into an arm and hand, fingers outstretched and bent slightly backwards, outflung in the face of the horrors he is witnessing and suffering during his last terrible days.

Perhaps anxious not to confront his memories, the impromptu guide saves the most difficult moments till last. It's obvious that some of the events that occurred on the campus on 12 September are too painful to mark, even discuss. Entering the cafeteria, Uribe points to a small entrance in the wall. It is whispered, he says, that when the military discovered that some students had crept into this tunnel leading down from the cellar of the café (tipped off, perhaps, by the aggressive right wing 'Patria y Libertad' (Fatherland and Liberty) student movement) they bricked it up. If so, then their bodies must remain immured somewhere beneath the campus. No plaque marks the site. Meanwhile, in the metallurgical workshop, the bomb manufacture continued until soldiers, perhaps following a second tip-off, burst in, machine-gunned everyone, raped at least one woman on the workshop table and, it is said, threw at least one of the bodies into the workshop furnace. Again, the story is only whispered and known to very few. On the wall of the workshop, some of the marks of bullets are still plainly visible. Any explanatory signage is absent.

---

22 'Michelle Marguerite Peña Herreros', Memoria Viva.

> Should there not be some kind of marker?
> Maybe. I've never shown anyone this place before.
> Doesn't anyone else know about it?
> Yes, maybe. But we never talk about it.

Today the Stadium of Chile, renamed the Victor Jara Stadium, is owned directly by the state and controlled by the Minister for Sport. In 1973 it hosted gatherings not much larger than table tennis and boxing matches, while today its uses are similarly limited. A roofed structure of 6,000 seats, it stands in a rundown area of Santiago city. One enters unceremoniously through a dingy side street. In 2009 a caretaker expresses his pleasure as well as surprise that anyone should visit the stadium on such a mission, though it is surely memory for some as well as uninterest for others that restrains Chileans themselves.[23] Indeed, more than at the UTE, memorialisation is not to be found on plaques but in the oral history of the stadium workers. Once, a bronze marker, says the caretaker, was fixed on the wall outside but that was destroyed by Pinochet supporters and has not been replaced. The one remaining is the bronze relief, there above the foyer, the only evidence of the terrible events of September 1973. Part of Jara's last song is inscribed there. Beneath the inscription are the words:

> In this place they took the life of Victor Jara, the popular artist. In his honour, 12 September 2003, during the governorship of Don Ricardo Lagos, this stadium was renamed Victor Jara Stadium. To the memory of Victor and others like him who lost their lives here. He lives in our memory always.

The caretaker continues. Detainees escorted from the UTE were forced through the main entrance, past the ticket office, down this right-hand passage into the main arena. The arena is surprisingly small, holding only a single basketball court. Totally enclosed and roofed, it booms and echoes oddly to the sounds of traffic outside. The prisoners must have heard the sound of daily life so clearly through the stadium walls.

---

23   Juan Medina, interview.

2. VICTOR JARA, THE STATE UNIVERSITY OF TECHNOLOGY AND THE VICTOR JARA STADIUM

Interior, the Victor Jara Stadium. Students and staff from the State University of Technology were forced to sit on the left, workers on the right. Several detainees in terror and despair jumped from the balconies to the right of the picture.
Source: Photograph by Peter Read, editing Con Boekel.

Downstairs now, to a 'vestuario' (changing room). This is the room where Jara was first taken, but after the 15th used as a morgue. Its entrance leads to a steep metal staircase where a slamming steel door reverberates for several seconds. Cement walls, roof and floor, 7 metres long, 5 wide. The exhaust fans make a deafening roar: perhaps this is what Jara meant by the phrase 'the pulse of the machines' in his last song. When switched off, the roar becomes the silence of the grave, for this chamber is 3 metres below ground level. The night watchman, says the caretaker, has only recently stopped feeling the spirits of the murdered, although a 'spiritual cleanser' has been here twice. It is here that Jara was killed.[24]

---

24 'Ex soldier confessed to shooting Victor Jara', Freemuse, 8 June 2009.

The seat painted white, in the 'dangerous prisoners' section, is that believed to have been occupied by Jara for a period after being recognised.

Source: Photograph by Peter Read, editing Con Boekel.

3

From state terror to state error: Patio 29, General Cemetery, Santiago

This chapter traces the journey of the many hundreds of bodies of victims killed in the first few months of the coup, from sites like the Stadium of Chile, to an obscure and humble precinct of the city's principal cemetery. Doña Nena González, caretaker of Patio (Precinct) 29 carries the story. She holds all its memories. Nena has seen its every phase: evidence of secret, nocturnal burials, brazen disposals in broad daylight, of coffinless naked bodies slung two at a time into any open grave, brutal repression of demonstrators, clandestine meetings, official exhumations, investigations, mass rallies at the Patio 29 endpoint of city marches, reburials, state ceremonies of recognition, mourners' families seeking information, and today, a flowing caterpillar of journalists and film crews who want to know everything and pay nothing. Once one of the most dangerous places in the country to ask questions, Patio 29 is today a national monument, still cared for, as it has been for 45 years, by Nena González. You'll still see her seven days a week, raking, tidying, sweeping, boiling a kettle outside her tiny shelter, lined, weary, rising with difficulty. The sadness in her eyes comes not from personal tragedy: it is the sadness of what she has seen, and not seen, what she was told, and not told; and, as a true secondary victim of Pinochet's coup, of what she has endured.

Nena González, caretaker of Patio 29, General Cemetery.
Source: Photograph by Peter Read, editing Con Boekel.

3. FROM STATE TERROR TO STATE ERROR

***

It is 2001. From the principal Santiago thoroughfare Providencia, a 66-year-old wife of a missing factory worker crosses the Mapocho River confined in its concrete channel. Left and right turns take her past the tourist area of Bellavista: down the Avenida de la Paz until on the right she comes to the grand entrance of the General Cemetery of Santiago. She does not go straight ahead into the space reserved for the heroes of the Republic; rather, she turns right, past the imposing mausolea of the nation's dominant families. Fifty metres from the main entrance, the orderly blocks of graves in their precincts or 'patios' begin to look less imposing but by no means neglected. At the very end of the cemetery, she turns left to walk beside the rear wall pierced with hundreds of regular niches into which a coffin will just fit. This woman has not seen her husband since 14 September 1973 when the military burst in their home, seized him and threw him into a truck. Today is their 44th wedding anniversary. And so she comes to Patio 29 with its characteristic white-on-green signage that the Chilean state uses for its national monuments:

> Patio 29. Emblematic place of the human rights violations that took place between 1973 and 1990 as it was used to cover up the bodies and identities of the detained disappeared and politically executed during the military regime.

She greets the elderly caretaker in a blue dustcoat sweeping the paths between the empty holes and iron crosses with a worn-out broom. 'Buenos dias, Señora.'

Patios 28 and 30 on either side of Patio 29 blaze with colours, artificial blooms, little windmills and shade houses to shelter the dead and to reassure them that that they are not forgotten. Fresh flowers are constantly replaced. Birds hop about in the shrubs planted at the time of each interment. Everywhere there are people, on weekends the patios 28 and 30 are packed.[1] Yet Patio 29, which this widow is visiting, is bare and ugly, has few visitors. Iron crosses, many with 'NN' (No Name) painted crudely on them, intersperse with unsightly holes where bodies have been exhumed. At times the patio is green and verdant but more often dry and blasted. The widow has for

---

[1] Recently, the cemetery patios have been renumbered, but for convenience here we refer to the old numeration.

company only photographs of the detained-disappeared blowing about or stuck crudely on the crosses. *Donde está?* they ask. Where is he? Where is she? Like many thousands of other Chileans she has no idea; but it is here at Patio 29 that she can contemplate where the body of her missing husband *may* have been surreptitiously dumped all those years ago. It is here that his body *may* have been surreptitiously exhumed in 1983 and disposed of elsewhere when the Pinochetistas began to realise that a reckoning of the disappeared would have to be made; but it is also from here that the human remains that she was assured were really *his* body were exhumed. The legitimate authorities examined and in 1995 identified the remains; but 18 months later told her that it wasn't her husband after all, and that whoever's body she had buried alongside her mother-in-law's, would have to come out again. It is here, in the end, that she can ponder on no more than this desolate, unprepossessing space *may* have been the last site on earth where sunlight or starlight touched the body of her missing husband for the last time.

Or his body may never have been here at all.

Sola Sierra, whose husband had been missing for more than 20 years at the time she was interviewed in 1994, stood at the same ugly space of Patio 29 to reflect:

> All that makes one think rationally that he is dead. But emotionally, until one confronts that situation, 100%, no, I just can't assume it. Sometimes when one hears of cases where remains have been recently discovered somewhere, one immediately begins to assume the possibility, that the person one was searching for over so many years might be in that gravesite. But when the remains are identified and they don't correspond, one feels a kind of release. Ah, it wasn't him.[2]

Maria Eugenia Horvitz is almost certain she is the widow, not the wife, of her husband Enriquez Paris, one of Allende's close advisers, who was with the President on the morning of the coup. By noon he had disappeared; yet she can never be completely certain that his body was one of those thrown into Patio 29:

---

2   Sola Sierra, interview, June 1994, in Mark Ensalaco, *Chile Bajo Pinochet, La Recuperación de la Verdad*, Alianza Editorial, Madrid, 2002, p. 160.

You have the same sensation described by Kafka. You fight against state terrorism, against giant machinery which has fallen over all your loved ones. And that all you're morally compelled to do is absolutely worthless. Except as the rescue of a truth that has to remain for others. It produces great anguish.[3]

***

The disposal of the bodies of those murdered at the Stadium of Chile and round the city presented a problem that the armed forces, for all their secret planning, evidently had not foreseen. In that first week after the deaths of Allende and Jara, hundreds of bodies lay rotting in the streets of the capital. Over 80 bodies were counted floating down the Mapocho. The carnage of the first four months after the coup amounted to half the total of those murdered or disappeared during the 17-year period of the dictatorship.[4]

The first military thoughts of how to dispose of the bodies were of mass cremations, turning quickly to secret burials in a handy location. But where? According to the then cemetery director Rogelio Rodriguez, Patio 29 by chance had 320 vacant lots ready for immediate use.[5] Out of sight at the very back of the cemetery, it seemed ideal; so far, in the life of the cemetery, it had been used only for the graves of paupers who had died in the public street or the State Psychiatric Hospital.[6] Thus from mid-September 1973, truckloads of makeshift coffins began to arrive from the morgue or the freezers of the Medical-Legal Institute. When the supply of coffins ran out, bodies were piled two or three at a time in wooden boxes, even on planks of wood. Under close military watch the bodies went into the front four rows of 80 waiting graves, each unmarked except for a tin

---

3 Horvitz in Estéban Larraín, *Patio 29: Historias de Silencio*, Fondo de Desarrollo de los Artes y la Cultura, Ministerio de Educación, Chile, Fundación Ford, documentary, 1998.
4 Larraín, *Patio 29*; Padilla Ballesteros Elías, *La Memoria y el Olvido – Detenidos Desaparecidos en Chile*; Marivic Wyndham and Peter Read, '"From state terrorism to state errorism": Post Pinochet Chile's long search for truth and justice', in J. Keene, ed., *Where Are the Bodies? A Transnational Examination of State Violence and Its Consequences. The Public Historian* 32(1), February 2010, 32–33.
5 Rogelio Rodriguez, interview, 7 and 8 November 2008.
6 Javier Bustamante and Stephen Ruderer, *Patio 29. Tras La Cruz de Fierro*, Ocholibros, Santiago, 2008, p. 40.

cross bearing NN.[7] Three months later Patio 29 was bursting; excess bodies went into Patio 7. Workers were warned to keep strict silence, while any unauthorised approach to the area was strictly forbidden.

***

Every patio or precinct of the cemetery has a *cuidadora,* or caretaker. Each is charged with keeping her patio neat and welcoming: to rearrange flowers disordered in the wind, keep the weeds down, water the fresh flowers, keep the paths raked, keep track of who is buried where. She is expected to be able to answer questions and know most visiting family members by name. It is in her interest to be well informed: *cuidadoras* work mostly seven days a week during the opening hours of the cemetery, but receive no income from the state; they rely entirely on tips and donations. Each caretaker has a tiny shed where she can keep out of the rain, prepare a meal, lock up her tools.

The caretaker of Patio 29 was, and is, Nena González. Her grandmother and mother had served in the cemetery all their lives. Nena herself was born, she says, to the work. The site of the home where she was born is now inside the cemetery itself.

The news of Allende's death came to her as personal tragedy: as her family doctor he had fought to save her brother, suffering from polio, before he died. On the morning of the coup, like most Santiagans, she stayed at home, while the 'shoot on sight' curfew prevented her return for the rest of the week.

The first role of Rogelio Rodriguez, the cemetery director-general, was to find and dispose of the dozens of bodies arriving daily:

> I saw how the dead bodies came all dismembered. Because if they were shot in front then their backs were all destroyed, it was atrocious. Later I had to go inside the trucks, to go and collect bodies in the streets. We went with the staff, to take bodies from the streets. It was September, October, November, at this time, to take bodies from the River Mapocho, we took the dead from the Mapocho River. Sometimes the corpses were piled up outside the Medical-Legal Institute in the Avenida de la Paz, because there was a curfew between eight at night

---

7   Larraín, *Patio 29*; Rogelio Rodriguez, interview, 22 September 2007.

3. FROM STATE TERROR TO STATE ERROR

till seven, in the morning, nobody could walk in the streets. Yes, it was a time of tremendous terror. [Unknown people] would bring and leave the bodies for me and my staff to bring them in and register them.[8]

Nena returned to her post as caretaker of Patio 29 on 15 September and found herself ignored by the military almost as if she wasn't there, but watching, from her shelter, at a distance of no more than 10 metres. She recalled in horror:

> I saw the boxes when they came in twos, when they came naked, when they came stiff as if frozen, and that's not all I saw, I saw everything in the world. So I didn't resist. One day I fainted …

Every day two trucks, one red, one grey, came bringing corpses from the morgue.

Nena had no option but to get used to the daily arrivals:

> Later it became harder, later it didn't hurt me so much to see when the corpses came. It's like a scar that gets harder. Yes, it's a difficult thing to forget. It's a bad comparison, but it's like that you had realised that it was a slaughterhouse, animals hanging together with the difference that they came inside a box. All naked, men and women. And also children.

While burials continued until the end of 1973, Nena remained the only civilian allowed within 50 metres of her patio. By 1974 as the military patrols became intermittent, grieving relatives cautiously approached Nena – at great risk to everyone – to ask her if she had seen their loved one. Almost always she had to answer no, for all she had seen was the frozen disfigured corpses tipped two at a time into the holes. 'But are you sure? Are you sure?' Nobody, not even the military itself, could be sure.

Any information was precious, and for one family at least, Nena's luckily precise memory of a victim's location in her patio led to a late-night clandestine exhumation and reburial in the family plot in the nearby Catholic cemetery. When news of the relatives' bold operation eventually reached – and outraged and embarrassed – the military authorities, the blame and the punishment fell on the cemetery

---

8   Rogelio Rodriguez, interview.

workers. Some were dismissed. Some were detained and tortured. Nena somehow managed to escape suspicion. It was the only known case of a family exhumation from Patio 29 during the dictatorship.[9]

For the rest of 1973 Rogelio Rodriguez remained at the Medical-Legal Institute where bodies dragged from the river, university campuses and shanty towns must first be brought to be identified and registered:

> And the people, so many people came to the Medical-Legal Institute to ask for news but I couldn't give them any reports. Yes, the family members came to me. There were tons of them, it seems like the soldiers were giving them orders to ask me.[10]

Eventually, suspected of concealing information, Rogelio Rodriguez was detained and tortured:

> They threw me onto the ground and were going to cover me up, they were going to bury me alive. They threw a bucket of earth on top of me. Then they shoved my head into a bucket of water. Torture. And I, and everyone who came there, we were to be tortured there. I was with other comrades, workers and other sections who were taken because they accused them of being MIRistas or Communists. There was about thirty of us in this period, they threw each one of us into solitary confinement, without a bed, without anything, on the ground.

The tour, 2009

Seemingly harmless, unobtrusive, never staring the wrong way, Nena remained at her post. From her vantage point a little away from her patio, close to the tomb of Victor Jara and generally unnoticed by the cemetery workers and soldiers looking in the opposite direction, Nena was in the best position to surreptitiously follow all the daily events. Her tiny livelihood relied entirely on speaking with those grasping for every tiny detail.

---

9   Nena González, interview.
10 Ibid.

3. FROM STATE TERROR TO STATE ERROR

In 1973 the caretaker hut of Nena González stood on this site in Patio 29. From here, unobserved, she witnessed the disposal of hundreds of those killed in the first weeks after the coup.
Source: Photograph by Peter Read, editing Con Boekel.

Almost every hole in the ground for her now tells a story. Once she hid two surreptitious visitors in an empty tomb nearby, and on another occasion concealed Neruda's widow Urrutia in her own tiny shelter when the military approached. Walking and reminiscing through her patio, she recalled perhaps the most disturbing incident revealing, incidentally, the extreme danger awaiting everyone trying to discover information:

> The other thing I wanted to tell you, which I've never told anyone before – I knew one person here. He was in that section just there, so I got everything that happened here. One day a priest arrived, he came to the tomb. He always was very furtive. To the same tomb also came a mother and father. He was a young priest, but separately. And I had never worked out that they left a bit of paper under a stone. I'm frightened to tell you, but I'll tell you anyway. They hid the paper beneath the stone and the Señora, the mother, came and took out the paper and put another one [in the same place]. Up came the priest and he left another one. They interchanged in this way. And one day I stuck my nose in, which I regret all the days of my life, because I said to myself that they must have put something in it. I stuck my nose in

> and read the paper ... The paper said 'My son, I love you profoundly, your mother and father love you, please take care of yourself, wherever you are or if you're away'. And the one by the little priest said, 'Mami I love you very much, I told Papi that I love him very much, look after yourselves, I am well, don't worry, that's all, I'm well, don't worry'.

From weeks of observation, and more note reading, she realised that the young priest, always dressed as a Carmelite, and supposedly executed by the military, was actually the son of the old people! An official must have bungled the identification; the priest had gone into hiding and somehow managed to let his parents know that he was alive, and that they could communicate by messages left beside what was supposed to be his grave. Nena's patio had become a family's clandestine post office. Once or twice the priest came to Nena to ask her wistfully what the old people looked like. 'Always sad', Nena replied. Though she had twigged to what was afoot, she kept the secret quite to herself. An overheard chance remark, to priest, parent, or anyone, might mean death for the son, tragedy for the parents, detention and torture, probable disappearance for herself. Did the young priest survive years in hiding in a Carmelite monastery? Did he escape overseas? She concluded her walk through the second pathway of her patio with a message to the priest himself: 'If you are still alive, and read these words, come and see me, because you know who I am, but you don't know that I know your story.'

Stopping by another empty grave beside the third pathway, Nena explains the deadly danger to anyone associated with Patio 29 of sudden and arbitrary arrest.

> I'd be lying if I told you if I'd ever been harassed at any time here, no, never, never. The [military] sometimes made rude remarks but I always felt bad. I felt bad because they told me not to get involved here, or talk, not to talk to anyone. (I'd reply) 'How could I not speak to anybody if the public asked me questions about it?' Yes, I told them, it's the public who pays me and also talks with me in the gardens about the caretaking and everything else. 'You tell me not to talk about anything I have seen, but I haven't seen anything.'

Often she protected herself by feigning ignorance. But even a gentle or pious action on behalf of the dead invited retribution. She recalls that when she and a fellow caretaker made up a wreath of red carnations to place outside the niche containing the body of Victor Jara – she points to a niche 30 metres away – two soldiers ripped them up. (Red was the colour always used to honour the dead of the political left.) She points to a rusty iron cross still bearing the initials NN. She recalls that she, two of her children and a friend were gathering a few flowers from the wreaths lying in other patios to place on the unnamed graves in 29:

> One first of November, just the first of November of that year [the day of the Dead] 1973, I was here with two kids, now they're grown men. We were taking flowers right here, there were so many flowers and put them on the NN [No Name] graves. There were so many wreaths, I tell you, so we put them so they weren't NN any more. And one day up comes a Lieutenant and this Lieutenant tells us, me and the kids, here, and he says to us 'What are you doing here?' 'No, we're putting flowers on the deadies who don't have flowers, they're without little flowers.' And the Lieutenant says to me – I'm never going to forget – he says that 'these dogs aren't worth flowers' and it was a kick in the guts ... He obviously knew that I was working here. 'These dogs don't deserve a single flower.'

Observation and intuition could only take her so far. One afternoon a team of DINA troops arrived to hurriedly excavate and depart with a body she knew to be that of a 'gringo' (she meant an American). Was that the body of Charles Horman, subject of the film *Missing*?[11] To this day Nena González still does not know.

Yet traces of common humanity remained here and there among the military. A 'guardian angel' appeared, who when not doing cemetery duties, revealed himself to be a guard at Pinochet's house. He whispered information to her when seeming to converse officially; once he smuggled a carton of cigarettes for her. All thanks to Saint Lucy, says Nena, the patron saint of female martyrs. The risk to the soldier was much worse than for Nena: disgrace, torture, a terrible death.[12] She wonders what happened to him. Like so much else, that information too is lost in night and fog.[13]

---

11 Costa-Gavras, *Missing*, 1982, starring Jack Lemmon and Sissy Spacek. Seven months after the American businessman Ed Horman visited Chile to demand information on his son's whereabouts, he received the body of his son. An autopsy was, however, impossible.
12 For the punishment of a guard found to be aiding prisoners at Villa Grimaldi, see Chapter 7.
13 'Night and fog' was the policy of intimidating the population through causing individuals to disappear through arrest, then to deny all knowledge about them. Pinochet modelled the policy on Wehrmacht Chief of Staff Wilhelm Keitel (Ensalaco, *Chile Bajo Pinochet, La Recuperación de la Verdad*, p. 84).

In 1976, at great risk to herself, Nena passed the first of many messages to the Chilean Vicariate of Solidarity.

The Vicariate was a human rights organisation sponsored by the Catholic Church in a building next door to the Santiago Cathedral. It was even possible to enter its offices clandestinely through an underground passage from the cathedral itself. Officially set up by Pope Paul VI in 1976 at the request of the redoubtable Chilean primate Cardinal Raúl Silva Henriquez, it established first a public advocacy service for bereaved families; equally important, it began secretly to gather any information, from any source, about human rights violations, especially disappearances, clandestine burials and exhumations.[14] Information gathering was highly dangerous for anyone caught communicating or receiving such information. Nena, thought to be a key informant, was invited on a clandestine visit to recount what she knew. Circuitously she made her way to the cathedral to appear as a worshipper. Trembling in fright she entered the Vicariate itself through the tunnel well used by anyone engaged in secret information seeking or gathering. There her nerve failed her. She returned to Patio 29. The second time in 1974 the Vicariate, promising to look after her, brought her in a taxi. This time Nena revealed all she had learned through her observations and her prohibited discussions with other workers. The director of the Vicariate, his information to no small extent based on Nena's, made public his belief that Patio 29 contained many hundreds of unidentified victims of the dictatorship.[15] Continuing to appeal to international human rights bodies, in 1981 the Vicariate director demanded that the identities of those buried in Patio 29 should be revealed. A half-hearted Commission of Enquiry by a Judge Espejo required the Vicariate to provide him with all its information, including a map (provided by Nena), and Pinochet's newly established security agency known as the DINA, to hand over any of the inadequate and muddled autopsy information held by its

---

14 Technically it took over the work of the Chilean Committee for Cooperation for Peace until Pinochet closed it in May 1974. For 14 years it provided legal services, collated information, and recorded the human rights abuses of many thousands of Chileans; 'Historia', Arzobispado de Santiago, Fundación Documentación y Archivo de la Vicaría de la Solidaridad.
15 Rogelio Rodriguez holds the online registrations of several hundred people buried in Patio 29.

predecessors.[16] Espejo's preliminary finding was that six of the bodies bore some characteristics of workers disappeared from the little town of Paine not far from Santiago; but after ordering the state not to cremate, disturb or transfer any further bodies buried in Patio 29, he unexpectedly declared himself to be incompetent and abruptly abandoned the commission. A year later, in 1982, the military government showed its scorn of this order by removing, as part of its contemptuously named 'Operation Removal of TV Sets', at least 200 of the 320 bodies conjectured to have been buried there. Probably they were then cremated. The identities of these bodies, and their final resting place, have never been discovered.

Meanwhile an anonymous tip-off from a cemetery worker to the Vicariate caused it to lay a formal complaint to the Military Prosecutor.[17] Following the tip, Nena was again asked to come to the Vicariate to reveal what she had seen of the 'TV sets'.

> Here when they took out (bodies) nobody knew what was going to happen. No, nothing, suddenly I saw that they were opening the patio that's all, and later I said to them [the Vicariate officials] that they're going to raze it, and later that's what happened, they took most of them out. They took them out and I don't know what they did with them, if they took them away or they burned them. To me, they [must have] burned them. So what happened was that I warned them [the Vicariate] that on another day they would take out quite a few more. So the Vicariate came around, and the journalists as well and everyone. But they couldn't do anything about it and it stayed that way. Of course, I warned them, I told them ...
>
> Of course, I didn't want to go because I was terrified. And told them how it was, I told them everything.

Little was achieved beside gathering a bit more evidence. No one was able to stop the rumoured second mass exhumation.

***

---

16   The DINA was established in November 1973, with powers including the ability to aggregate all the existing intelligence services, and to enter homes and arrest and hold persons. The first director was Colonel Manuel Contreras Sepúlveda; Bruno Serrano, *Exhumación del Olvido*, CEIBO, Santiago, 2013, p. 33.

17   'Declaran Monumento Nacional al Patio 29' [Patio 29 declared a National Monument], CIREN, *Cronica Digital*, 13 July 2006, p. 1; Maxine Lowy, 'How Patio 29 was saved from (Total) Disappearance', *Human Rights Today*, 2006.

As we shall see so often in this discussion, it was not possible for the victims' families either to locate missing persons or to begin to memorialise a site of disappearance until after 1989, following the first free elections in 19 years. After the election, the new President and leader of an uneasy alliance of moderate Left and Centrist parties, Patricio Aylwin, declared that the transition to democracy had begun. Yet Aylwin was not encouraging to those whose relatives remained disappeared. The press reported that 'Each moment that passes makes the possibility more remote that the remains will reappear'.[18] Aylwin's Commission of Enquiry into the Disappeared stressed, significantly, the need for national reconciliation in its working brief. The so-called Rettig Commission named 979 detained-disappeared (including illegal executions and death from torture) and 1,319 politically executed.[19] The Vicariate issued criminal charges against those believed responsible either for the initial 'burials' or the 1982 illegal exhumations from Patio 29. Thus, in 1991, a government-appointed team of forensic anthropologists and doctors began the process of exhumation and identification. Patio 29 was the first priority, but which victims would be found and how would they be identified? Would the perpetrators be discovered, or named, or punished?

Aylwin remained adamant that his first priority was a national reconciliation that would include no punishment initiated by the state: 'there were to be no penal consequences in solving the issue of the identities of those responsible for the crimes'.[20] The lack of 'penal consequences' seemed the most secure way of preventing the military interrupting the process.

Patio 29, then, would be investigated – but no perpetrator would be prosecuted, nor even named. Indeed, the compromise suited the government and the immediate needs of most families. It also suited the military, which, thus protected from judicial procedures, could afford to appear conciliatory. In this way Patio 29 was becoming a site of unusual cooperation between all sides of politics. Everyone desired a successful and prompt resolution.

---

18 Gonzalo Vial, *El Mercurio*, Santiago, 30 April 2006.
19 Amnesty International's calculations in 1996 totalled 3,107 victims of all forms of disappearance and death.
20 Pamela Pereira, daughter of a Paine detained-disappeared and human rights lawyer, in Larraín, *Patio 29*.

Exhumations proceeded – with enormous difficulty. This memorable analogy was provided by Paco Etcheverria:

> Imagine that a plane carrying you don't know how many passengers crashes in some place in the mountains which no one finds nor is interested in. Then later, a planeload of passengers whose identity you don't know, disappears. Ten years pass in these mountains until explorers climbing the mountain discover an abandoned cemetery in an abandoned town. The plane has crash-landed on top of it and the dead from this catastrophe remain buried mixed with the other dead who are already in this cemetery, and then, additionally, it happens that this plane has burnt on impact so that the remains of the rest of the passengers have disappeared. Bearing in mind that in Patio 29, when the judicial intervention happened [in 1981] they had already exhumed some, no, just a few ... They have had to make disappear also other detained-disappeared. To reiterate, so when they [authorities] announce that they have found the place where the plane definitely came down, they removed the rest of the bones of people who had nothing to do with it. The situation about the passengers who came down isn't clear, and you've got in the laboratory I don't know how many bone fragments which now are mixed up.[21]

In 13 days the forensic team unearthed 126 bodies in 107 graves. Some of the skeletons, in Nena's recollection, were still bound in barbed wire, wrapped around them in a figure of eight.

Most of the exhumed were aged between 20 and 30. In the laboratory each was laid out anatomically to determine age, height, sex, condition of teeth and special characteristics.[22] Naturally, anxious relatives were active participants, recognising, or thinking they were recognising – their relative at first glance. 'This is my son. I would recognise him anywhere.' 'I knew him by his skull. My children inherited the same shape.'[23] Throughout the lengthy, well-intentioned and painful

---

21 Paco Etcheverria, interview in Bustamante and Ruderer, *Patio 29*, pp. 9–10.
22 'Memorias del Grupo de Antropología Forense y Suporte al Campo de los Derechos Humanos en Chile', V Congreso Chileno de Antropología, 8–12 November 2004.
23 Larraín, *Patio 29*.

process, staff and families worked closely together. 'Could you bring a photo of him, especially one in which he's smiling so we can compare tooth for tooth?' 'Do you have one of his shoes?'[24]

The act of returning the remains was solemn and traumatic both for the families and the staff of the Medical-Legal Institute. Close relatives followed the specialist, often enough, by now, a friend, to inspect the assembled skeleton. He or she explained in painstaking and excruciating detail every injury detected: a fractured rib, an arm broken in childhood, a punctured skull. 'This is the trajectory where the bullet entered and exited his brain.' 'The lack of any scar tissue suggests that he was still alive when they applied a soldering iron to his legs.' No one wished to be spared the narrative of horror. Devastating as it was, it was now *their* narrative, a central element of family history for decades to come. It was truth at its cruellest, but it was *their* truth. The son, daughter, husband or wife was no longer 'disappeared' but 'executed'. The relatives could now join the 'normal' community of mourners, decide on a burial place, place a name on the plaque with a date and loving message, bring flowers and offerings to the grave. Some were buried nearby, or in family mausolea. A few remains were flown overseas. The wives of the detained-disappeared became, overnight, widows with considerable legal and financial benefits. Theirs to claim were now a pension, subsidies for their children's health and education.[25] Rituals and visits to the grave on birth or wedding days became part of family life. Widows remarried. Parents died secure in the knowledge that their child's remains now lay safe at last.[26]

Between 1993, the year of identification, and 1998, 96 of the 126 remains had found their resting place. The rest remained unidentified. Though other remains from elsewhere in the country had been identified and reinterred, Patio 29 remained the centrepiece of successive Concertación (centre-left) governments' claims that they had done all they could.

---

24 Silvio Caiozzi Caiozzi, *Fernando Ha Vuelto*, Andrea Films Production, documentary, 1998; Enrique Ahumada, 'Dr Patricia Hernández: La ardua tarea de identificar los cuerpos de detenidos desaparecidos' [The difficult task of identifying the bodies of the detained-disappeared], *Caso Pinochet*.
25 The benefits available today for the victims and families are available through Instituto Nacional de Derechos Humanos, 'Beneficios establecidos por ley a las víctimas y familiares de violaciones ocurridas durante la dictadura', www.indh.cl.
26 Caiozzi, *Fernando Ha Vuelto*.

April 2006 brought an urgent request by the institute staff to all of the 96 family representatives to attend a meeting. Without warning of what to expect, they were subjected to a powerpoint presentation in which the names were listed of several categories of remains wrongly identified. Individual families had to search a list on the screen to find the names of their loved ones. The latest DNA techniques undermined all the findings. The terrible revelation was that eight of the 96 remains had been definitely wrongly identified, and all the rest were in doubt. Families who had waited 25 years to discover the fate and whereabouts of their missing family member now discovered that the remains they had laid to rest years before did not – or might not – belong to them after all. A parent exclaimed:

> Misidentified means reopening the wounds, restarting the search. It means our loved ones have disappeared once again: a pain that we never thought we would live through again.[27]

The revelations demanded re-exhuming the remains from the family tombs, relinquishing widows' pensions, returning the narratives of torture and murder that the families had come so agonisingly to possess. They now belonged to someone else's family. But whose? The Medical-Legal Institute issued a public apology, peremptorily rejected by a daughter of a newly redesignated detained-disappeared:

> Let him go to church and ask for forgiveness, This is not a matter of forgiveness ... We are not here to commiserate with anybody.[28]

A leading figure from the Group of Families of Detained-Disappeared conceded that while anything had been possible under the dictatorship, that period was over:

> But what outrage that this should happen in these times? ... We speak of the negligence of the Medical-Legal Institute. But also of the indifference of the authorities who would not listen to us. There are Presidents who would not listen to us – Aylwin, Frei and Lagos – but were prepared to listen to those proposing projects of impunity.[29]

---

27   Victor Orsorio, 'El Escándalo del Patio 29: Los errores de identificación' [The scandal of Patio 29: The errors of identification], Ercilla, No. 3293, 8–21 May 2006.
28   Pamela Pereira, in J.J. Ortiz, C. Uruza and H. Cossio, 'Dramatica notificación a familiares de DD.DD por error del SML: Anuncian acciones legales', La Tercera, 22 April 2006.
29   Alejandra Chacón, 'Patio 29: El dolor de verlos desaparecer dos veces' [The grief at seeing them disappeared twice], La Nación, 22 April 2006, pp. 1–10.

New revelations of government complicity in withholding critical doubts further tore the fragile relationships between the state and the families of victims. It emerged that as early as 1994, a team of forensic experts from Glasgow University, checking on progress, had urged drastic changes to the procedures of identification and the personnel – but the report had been quietly shelved. A second report by an independent agency questioned the qualifications of the Medical-Legal Institute professionals, warning that the staff had not been assessed or accredited by any international forensic organisation. It urged that any further identifications be suspended until the matter was cleared, another recommendation that was ignored. The 'Scandal of Patio 29', as it began to be called, threatened even to divide the once tightly knit human rights community. The focus of the accusations, some argued, should not be on the errors made by the Medical-Legal Institute, nor even on the remains themselves. Rather, it should be the failed responsibility of the state, past and present.

> Bones are not a person's most important thing. If there were no Law of Amnesty [prohibiting the prosecution or naming of perpetrators] and if they would name the people military officials involved, more exact information would be obtained, and we would be closer to reconciliation. The bodies don't give us that, [information] it's the political will to arrive at justice.[30]

***

Rogelio Rodriguez:

> Yes, I suddenly go to the cemetery, yes, I go there sometimes. To visit the *compañeros*. Yes, I go to see my dead friends that I'm telling you about, because I have faith in the dead. I know many people in the families of the detained-disappeared, they're for the most part, dead. Yes, I see people suffer greatly, mothers for their sons, several women for their husbands, for their fathers. It was very sad in all that time, to see lines of bodies waiting at my crematoria. Wanting information.

---

30 Javier Rebolledo and Luis Narvaez, 'Patio 29. Muertos sin nombre' [The dead without a name], *La Nación,* 29 April 2006, pp. 3–4.

Nena reflected in 2007:

> I wouldn't like to live through it again, I wouldn't want to see it again. Because I've got children, I have grown-up grandchildren, I have great grandchildren, little ones, so I wouldn't like to live through it because I get emotional easily, it moves me when I remember. I'd say it would have been better if they had left them there in the Patio, so they would recognise them with a Memorial, a nice thing to do would be to fix it. I'd like to see a square with a monolith with the name of everyone [disappeared] just to know if the bodies existed here or not. Of course. And I hate what I saw, what was done here, that I wouldn't want to see it again, but to me I'd like to see this beautiful square, I'd like to see it as a plaza like they've done in other parts where people were shot, when they were detained and disappeared they have done lots of memorials. So why don't they do it here when the bodies are here?

The story of whether Nena's vision has been fulfilled must await the last chapter.

4
Carved cherubs frolicking in a sunny stream: The National Stadium

Don Roberto Sanchez, first a worker, then a detainee, then a reinstated worker in the National Stadium of Chile, comes from Temuco. Born in about 1951, he recalls a strangely ambiguous relationship with his brutal stepmother. Once she floored him with a crack on the head with her shoe, then revived him in tears. Small, tough and nuggety, at 17 Roberto told her that he was off to seek his fortune, like so many young men for centuries before him, in Santiago. His stepmother cried and gave him a packet of money to look after himself. It was many years before Roberto saw her again, this time under circumstances even more unhappy.[1]

At about the same time as Roberto Sanchez changed his status from stadium cleaner to stadium detainee, another young man – we don't know his name because he will soon become a detained-disappeared – is frog-marched from the Victor Jara Stadium into a van that, crammed with 20 other prisoners, will take him to another stadium, a much larger holding centre. It is the 60,000-seat National Stadium of Chile. In the next two months more than 20,000 detainees will be processed here, some to be sent on to other torture and extermination centres, some to be released, some jailed in state prisons, some to die here. But the stay of this young man will not be long.

---

1 Roberto Sanchez, interview, 12 May 2014.

Roberto Sanchez.
Source: Photograph by Peter Read, editing Con Boekel.

On the 11th night of captivity, after a week of torture and beating, he curls up as usual into a foetal position in the changing room of the main stadium beneath the bleachers. It is known as the Coliseum, and the changing room as *camarín* no. 3. In the darkest hour of the night the lights snap on. Four guards enter, the officer shouts his name. The young man stands and tries not to trample any of the 40 other prisoners, now wide awake and apprehensive, jammed up on the cement or crouched on the wooden benches. Another torture session, as he supposes. Handcuffed, blindfolded, he is pushed up the wide staircase, upstairs towards the broadcasting studios and presidential viewing box where he has already been three times tortured. But on the first floor, instead of turning right, he is ordered left. Up another flight of stairs, then another to a metal ladder. The sounds of military boots echo oddly off the hard surfaces as he tries to reason where he is. A jangle of keys. A metal door opens. Pushed towards the sound he feels the chilly September night air on his face. *God, we're going outside. This must be the roof.* Sensing a new tension in the guards, he feels a rifle butt pressed deeper in his back. 'Keep going you filthy motherfucker.' Pushed forward, slow step by slower step. The open reverberations of the deserted amphitheatre, the distant hum of the sleeping city. *Ay mi madre, they're going to push me off.* Six more steps. The very last sounds this detained-disappeared hears in this life are 'Fucking communist'.[2]

***

The National Stadium of Chile, based on the Olimpiastadion of Berlin, is not just an Olympic-standard soccer field but a huge sports complex, holding the now 80,000-seat arena itself; swimming pool and change rooms; tennis, basketball and archery courts; velodrome and weights room; and a dozen training fields. It holds huge emotional significance as the first site to which the world's press was drawn immediately after the coup. It was the first, as well as the largest, of the major interrogation, torture and extermination sites in Chile. In cruelty, violence, intimidation and terror, as well as disorganisation, its enormities were quite the equal of anything that happened anywhere under state terrorism in South America. It was the first Chilean centre to practise on a large scale the systematic electrical torture developed in Algeria and Brazil for which some Chilean officers had received advanced training.[3] In March 1990 the National Stadium was the site where Patricio Aylwin, the first democratically elected President of Chile in 18 years, presided over a national exorcism of the recent past before a crowd of 80,000 people. A white horse galloped across the arena, a gigantic Chilean flag was unfurled, and the widow of a detained-disappeared danced Chile's national dance, *La Cueca*. Symbolically, she danced it alone – *la cueca sola*.[4]

Equally, since 1937, hundreds of thousands of Santiagans have held the stadium in quite different, and affectionate, memory. The home of Chile's national soccer team, it hosted the World Cup in 1957. Chileans have come over many decades to play or to watch their favourite sport. It is the nation's preferred concert venue. Rod Stewart, Cindy Lauper and Bon Jovi had each performed between the period known as the return of democracy and Aylwin's ceremony; since then the Rolling Stones, Paul McCartney, Elton John and Madonna are among dozens

---

2 Don Victor Peña identified the site where a body was found smashed on the wooden seating of the arena.
3 'The secret history of Brazilian torturers who brought terror to the detainees of this country in the National Stadium', 24 April 2014.
4 12 March 1990. Heraldo Muñoz, *The Dictator's Shadow: Life Under Augusto Pinochet*, Basic Books, Philadelphia, 2008, pp. 217–18.

of international stars to perform, often at the moments when the consultations as to the stadium's future were at their most critical.[5] In 1990 its status as memory site both for death and for entertainment made its future more contested and more uncertain. Some wanted it declared a historical monument, others that it move on. Why, asked the critics, should sport never again be played at the stadium simply because the state had used it for its own purposes, for just four-hundredths of its working life?

Between 11 September and 7 November 1973 a constant stream of at least 20,000 detainees were entering and leaving the stadium, transferred from the Stadium of Chile, from the factory precincts around the city, the universities, former Allende government offices, and the working-class government settlements called *poblaciones*.[6] In this time an unknown number of detainees, perhaps 500, were released. Execution estimates within its walls – again there are no certain figures – vary from 35 to 500. Most of the captives were transported to other centres – the state prisons, to 1367 José Domingo Cañas, Londres 38, Villa Grimaldi, or to the far north of Chile, to the mining town of Chacabuco.[7]

The most critical geography of the stadium as detention and torture centre is, first, the arena, known as the Coliseum. Trucks and vans carrying the prisoners enter through the least frequented entrance in the street known as Pedro de Valdivia. They arrive dressed as students, or ready for the factory, the office or in suits. Some tumble from the transport bloodied or with broken ribs, past a pile of bodies bound for Patio 29 estimated, on the first day after the coup, to be as high as a man.[8] Sometimes the detainees have to run the gauntlet of beatings and blows as they scramble, handcuffed or hands on necks, 40 metres towards the Coliseum main entrance by the ticket office. On this first night some find themselves sleeping on top of each other in the ablutions, others in the *escotillas*, the covered entrance

---

5 'Estadio Nacional Julio Martínez Prádanos: Concerts', Wikipedia.
6   *Poblaciones*, which we will investigate more fully in Chapter 6, were poor and often politically radical working-class settlements sponsored by government since the mid-1960s.
7   On 12 October 1973, in an effort to display the even-handedness of the regime, 327 detainees out of a group of 3,500 were released; Steve Stern, *Battling for Hearts and Minds: Memory Struggles in Pinochet's Chile, 1973–1988*, Duke University Press, Durham, 2006, p. 59.
8   The estimate of the height of the body pile was given by an Army officer, in Carmen Luz Parot, *Estadio Nacional*, DVD, 2002.

4. CARVED CHERUBS FROLICKING IN A SUNNY STREAM

ways into the arena, or in the corridors under the banks of seats, or in the changing rooms. Here they will remain crammed together in terror. On the fifth day, the restraining wire fence separating the seating from the main arena completed, they will be allowed out by day. From 16 September, 5,000 male detainees daily emerge to sit or stand on the wooden tiers of seats, unwitting subjects of photographs that will be reproduced round the world for decades. Every 15 metres stand armed guards – in front, behind, on every side of each enclosure. Some are conscripts just out of school, simply told to report for military service. One smuggles some fruit to a few detainees. *Don't reveal where you got it or I'm fucked.* Towards one end of the grassy central arena is erected a disc with a huge black centre. The chilling rattle of a machine gun splits the air. Three executed detainees fall to the grass. A hooded figure, known as the *encapuchado*, moves slowly on the outer lane of the athletic track beside the perimeter fence with his escort of four soldiers, peering closely at the detainees. Next he enters the seating area, up and down the aisles, between the benches. To hide one's head invites a closer scrutiny. The hooded one stops to point to a detainee. The guards seize him or take his name.[9] Esteban Carvajal recalls:

> The fear was a living thing. That day I didn't sleep. Nobody slept thinking that the *encapuchado* came. We consoled ourselves thinking that this could be a simple method of intimidation, but we were convinced that the *compañeros* chosen by the mysterious man would not return to see us. Everyone asked the same question. Who was the *encapuchado*? He seemed to know half the world.[10]

Early morning is perhaps the worst time, when names roll out from the PA across the arena and into the bleachers. When so ordered to attend, each individual must come instantly to the black disc. Each may then be taken to one of the administration offices upstairs to check registration. Each will be issued with a compulsory identifier, yellow, black or red. Red means marked for imminent execution. The interrogation is fast and brutal.

---

9 Evidence Esteban Carvajal 'Patricio' in Villegas, *El Estadio*, pp. 28, 38–39.
10 Esteban Carvajal, in Villegas, *El Estadio*, p. 30. One of the *encapuchados* was revealed to be the Socialist militant Juan Muñoz Alarcón, whose murdered body was found in Santiago in 1977; 'Estadio Nacional, Santiago', Memoria Viva.

Why are you here?
I don't know.
Tell us the names of three communists and you can go free. Be quick.
I don't know any.
Where have the Marxists hidden their arms?
I know nothing about them.

Each answer is followed by a blow. Or the torturers will run a metal instrument over his genitals, grind his toes into the floor with their boots or burn the tops of his fingers with cigarettes.[11]

Within a week the procedure shifts to interrogation in the chambers set up in the changing rooms of the velodrome, the cycling track, pride of the stadium, which stands 200 metres away at the southern end of the precinct. Here too stand the most feared buildings of all, two spiral-shaped concrete structures, the closed weightlifting arenas known as the *caracoles* (literally, 'snails').

On the summons to the black disc the prisoner's mates wish him well, knowing that if he returns at all, he will be very probably supported between two *compañeros*. It is unlikely that he will be able to walk. The detainee, his head covered with a blanket, is escorted outside the arena, turned left towards the velodrome. If this is his first time, the prisoner will stumble into the interrogation where the officer will tick him off the list of the day, the suspects who must be interrogated and in all probability tortured. Each of the 30 interrogators working in shifts generally knows no more than the officer as to the nature of the alleged offence. Most begin with 'Why are you here?' Frequently the detainee will not know either – perhaps he was seen flicking through a leftist tract in a bookshop before a zealous guard, himself no better informed, but warned that he had better arrest someone, orders him outside. Replying in a manner deemed to be unsatisfactory, the male detainee is ordered for torture in the south *caracol* adjacent to the velodrome. The queue lengthens with the day so he must stand, waiting at attention, under threat of instant death, for his turn at the *parrilla*. Still blindfolded, he absorbs the thunderous military music from the loudspeakers, or a burst of machine gun fire of a real or faked execution from the direction of the entrance way into the velodrome.

---

11   Of the many accounts of interrogation, see, for instance, Adolfo Cozzi, *Estadio Nacional*, Editorial Sudamericana Chilena, Santiago, 2000, p. 70 passim; and Samuel Riquelme, in Villegas, *El Estadio*, pp. 79–82.

4. CARVED CHERUBS FROLICKING IN A SUNNY STREAM

From inside the *caracol*, the screams of the tortured rise higher and higher until it seems his eardrums must burst. Sometimes he waits all day, and marched back again on the next. Those detainees who can bring themselves to revisit the *caracol* today recall a diabolical mix of hideous pain and mundanity. Seven times is the journalist Alberto Gamboa brought to the weights room: when he returns for the first time in 29 years with the filmmaker Carmen Luz Parot, he finds himself sweating, his throat fills with mucus, he can hardly breathe – exactly as if he is being tortured again. One session he recalls was shorter than the others: he hears the torturer tell his assistant, 'Let's make this a quick one, we have to finish early. I have to meet my wife at 5.20 to take her to that movie, the Godfather.'[12]

Barely alive, the detainee will be dragged back into the changing room of the main stadium, bones or teeth smashed, maybe deafened, half naked, electrode marks all over his body, the scrotum monstrously enlarged. All night he cries in agony on the freezing cement, to receive what comfort he may from his petrified comrades – who may now well suspect that he has been 'turned' informer.

Women detainees do not enter the Coliseum but jam into the men's changing room of the swimming pool. Some, it is said, are executed in its underground section, or against the outside wall, but most are tortured, or killed, on the *parrilla* in the northern *caracol* not far from that of the men.[13] Less is known about what unspeakable tortures they endure, for little is spoken about this north *caracol*, and their message to the world, when the survivors come to describe their experiences two decades later, is a different one.[14] Roberto Muñoz, standing outside the southern *caracol*, waiting to be thrown on the *parrilla*, could clearly hear their terrible screams from 50 metres away.

***

---

12   Luz Parot, *Estadio Nacional*.
13   Drawn from a number of sources, including Luz Parot, *Estadio Nacional*; Bill Vann, 'Chilean court re-enacts stadium execution of American journalist [Charles Horman]', World Socialist Web Site, 17 May 2002; and *Chronicle of Higher Education*, 2001, chronicle.com, Section International, p. A36; see also Cecilia Valdes, 'Torture charge pits professor v professor', *New York Times*, 8 September 2001.
14   See Chapter 7: 'Villa Grimaldi'.

By 2000, successive governments of the centre-left Concertación government, and the district mayor who held administrative control over the structure, remained undecided whether to demolish the ageing stadium structure altogether and sell the land for housing, build another in another location, or restore it. The outer cement walls of the main arena were peeling and dirty, the sports fields overgrown. Even seven years after the transition to democracy nothing was memorialised, until on the 28th anniversary of the coup, 2001, a somewhat unspecific plaque to the ordeal of the detainees appeared overnight, obscurely attached to the outer wall near the main entrance. It read:

> Between the 11th of September and the 7th of November 1973, the National Stadium of Chile was used as a concentration camp, and place of torture and death. More than 12,000 political prisoners were detained here without charge or process.
>
> In memory of all those who suffered within its walls and those who hoped, in the darkness, to see the light of justice and liberty.

Then followed a beautiful, though obscure, invocation of the dead by the poet Stella Diáz Varín, who had paid for the plaque herself:

> I demand from my dead
> That in their own day
> I will find them, I will transplant them
> I will undress them
> I will bring them up to the light
> Close to the ground
> Where their song
> Will be nestling, waiting for them[15]
>
> (Tr. Paula González Dolan)

Heroic words; but the plaque, the same colour as its surrounding wall, was easy to bypass, and mysteriously fixed so high that no one could read it without the aid of a stepladder.

---

15   Les obligo a mis muertos
     En su día
     Los descubro, los transplanto,
     Los desnudo
     Los llevo a la superficie
     A flor de tierra
     Donde esta esperándolos
     El nido de la acústica.

A more significant event towards serious remembrance came two years later, in 2003 in the stadium's Declaration as a Historic Monument. Seven years 'special protection' accompanied the declaration, not least as a gesture towards the country´s 200th anniversary of release from Spanish control.

The tour, 2009

Don Victor Peña is a senior official in the management of the stadium. He has carried out several impromptu tours before, mainly for investigators.[16]

He begins at the *escotilla* no. 8, the entrance way that leads into the arena itself. It is not surprising, given the stadium's doubtful future, that the area is cold, dirty and messy, and holds some modern graffiti. Hundreds of detainees were crammed into it on their first and subsequent nights. Although the walls have been whitewashed to conceal such traces, Don Victor's torch illuminates faint inscriptions carved by detainees with whatever was handy. One reads:

RJJ
12 IX 73[17]

Don Victor believes that up to a dozen such inscriptions may be recoverable. He leads into the main arena. Over there was the black disc at which prisoners had to gather when their name was called. The corpse of the detainee thrown off the roof landed just where he stands. Into the darkness again to enter a changing room known as *camarín* no. 3. This too is dirty, the windows so covered in dust to be darkly opaque. The basins and toilets, he explains, have not been touched since the detainees last used them. Covered in grime, dried calcium rivulets under the taps, they look a little like the bathroom porcelain recovered from the *Titanic*. The tattered remains of a temporary photographic exhibition are pinned to a frame in a corner. Don Victor unfolds some to reveal the exiguous detainees' sleeping space. The ceiling, which must have leaked at some point,

---

16   Don Víctor Peña, video interview and stadium tour, 2009, 2010.
17   For commentary, see Valentin Rozas, 'Tres maneras de explicar la presencia de graderias antiguas' [Three ways of explaining the presence of the old seating], Bifurcaciones revista de estudios culturales urbanos.

has been repainted but looks ugly and stained. This will be the only one of these changing rooms, he explains, to be preserved. Outside he points to a subsidence beside the outer wall of the Coliseum.

> We used to think it might be a mass grave, but it turned out not to be. Not one of the guards who used to guard the prisoners has ever talked publicly. Nobody knows what happened to the bodies of those killed at the stadium. We just don't know anything here, neither what happened nor what's going to happen.

The next point in this informal tour is the men's changing room at the swimming pool. Here some hundreds of women were held, but never, unlike the men, allowed outside except to be interrogated and tortured. The building looks in much better condition; no wonder, it began to be used as a changing room again in the 1990s.

At the pool Don Victor introduces Don Roberto Sanchez, foreman of the swimming pool precinct. He is short, dark and broad, wears a T-shirt inscribed 'Chileswimming', holds a tape-measure and looks busy.[18] On invitation to tell his involvement in the stadium on camera, however, he readily agrees to stop work. 'Nobody has ever asked me about this before.' Don Victor, the guide, has himself never heard more than that Roberto Sanchez had been a detainee here during the dictatorship. Before the coup, since 1970, he worked as a cleaner. Days after the coup, in mid-September 1973, walking with a mate near Santiago's main watercourse, the Mapocho River, he noticed three bodies floating in the current. While engaged in pulling them out they were overtaken by a dawn patrol, whose commander, in the dangerously fragile post-coup atmosphere, wrongly assuming that a pile of military clothing nearby must be connected to the two men, arrested them. Don Roberto found himself a despised detainee in the stadium in which he was an employee the day before. He spent his nights in the dreaded *galeria*, the cold and dark spaces under the wooden spectator benches enclosing the main arena. Several months incarceration brought violent beatings. Yes, he agrees, this was the inferno that journalists speak of, not least because, unlike a regular prison, no rules applied. No protections, no records, no charges, no accountability. The security forces were police, judge and jury. Some of the soldiers were kind, but most were not. The lowest ranks were

---

18 Don Roberto Sanchez, interviews, 2009, 2010, 2012, 2013.

generally the worst – but sadists are sadists at any level. Three times – he thinks – he was taken to the *caracol*, the weight-training room, to be tortured on the *parrilla*. Blindfolded throughout, he never saw his torturers, and was too nervous to remember their voices. 'One tries to forget these things'; but he can neither forgive nor forget. 'I know who some of the torturers are, yes. If I have to engage them in conversation, I would but will never be their friend.' Don Roberto will die with his memories, he says, but the pool and the stadium won't, they'll still be here. 'But you returned here to work?' 'Yes, because it is the people who are guilty, not the place.' He practically lives at the stadium, he says, six days a week, 7 am to 9 pm, 38 years in the job.

Don Victor continues the walking expedition, past the arena entrance, 200 metres towards what the prisoners knew as the Via Crucis, the way of the Cross, leading from the stadium to the torture chambers at the extreme end of the precinct. Here, on the left, is the velodrome where the major interrogations took place. In the passageway leading to the cycling track, Don Victor warns: 'Don't be deceived by these marks in the walls. People will tell you that all are bullet holes. Some are, most are not.'

From interrogation each detainee was led 30 metres to wait his turn in the weight-training room, the *caracol*. It is a windowless circular concrete shell, tiled floor, cement walls and ceiling. Inside it is empty, echoing, black, stained. A bird's nest balances precariously above the entrance.

***

The Declaration as National Monument with its seven years 'special protection' included the appointing of a team of experts to plan a process of further memorialisation. Their brief included the preservation and eventual restoration of the washroom *camarín* no. 3 and the entrance walkway *escotilla* no. 8, including the detainees' inscriptions. Crowds entering for football or a concert would be routed away from them. The draft protocol controversially excluded conserving the north and south *caracoles* of torture and other significant sites, but the swimming pool changing room would be barred from further use. Elsewhere, and little by little, the stadium's facilities were planned to come to life: first the sports fields, the running track, the pool. The women's torture chamber, the northern *caracol,* having been quietly leased to the University of Chile's sports facilitators, was surreptitiously set aside. No protocol determined the destiny of the 200-metre walkway, the avenue of death, the Via Crucis, that detainees had taken from the Coliseum towards the velodrome. The men's torture chamber site, the south *caracol*, would, by inference, remain unused, stained, filthy and neglected.[19]

The team of heritage consultants awarded the contract prepared its first meeting. Mindful of the recent recommendation of the Valech Report on Torture to create on-site symbolic monuments to the dead, the committee began considering demands for the conservation of the nation's prime Historic Monument of the misdeeds of the military regime.[20] At its head was Wally Kunstmann, President of the Metropolitan Region of Political Prisoners, leading a team that included historians, lawyers and architects.[21] She informed President Bachelet's heritage advisor that the team was drawing up plans for an 'Open Museum Site for Memory and Homage', and 'Educational Museum for Human Rights'.

Released only seven years later, Kunstmann's blueprint, acknowledging the twin tasks of memory and homage, was no exercise in fence-sitting. Her project aims were to preserve the integrity of the stadium as a Site of Memory, to commemorate the victims and survivors, to encourage the recognition of other memory sites, to make accusations against the perpetrators and to promote respect for human rights through compulsory education. She distinguished between the separate sites of detention, torture, shooting and disappearance, and envisaged, finally, the creation of a Journey of Memory that would take in every significant part of the detainees' journey from bloody arrival to torture or death. Her intention was to consciously relate human rights abuses

---

19 Information about the women's torture centre is elusive, for it has ceased to be part of the stadium's official remembrance; Don Roberto Sanchez, interview.

20 'Report of the National Commission on Political Imprisonment and Torture' ('Valech Report'), 29 November 2004, p. 1059, recommended commemorative monuments listing victims from both sides, and public parks for commemoration and places for 'recreation and for bolstering a life-affirming culture'.

21 The authors of the Heritage Report, entitled *Open Museum. Site of Memory and Homage*, were Wally Kunstmann, President of the Metropolitan Region of Political Prisoners; Alejandra Lopez, historian; Sebastián Insunza, lawyer; Carlos Duran, Aleksandra Buzhynska, Marcel Coloma, and Claudio Guerra, architects. This section is based on the document, *Proyecto Estadio Nacional. Memorial Nacional. Comité Estadio Nacional 2002–2007*, photocopy document in possession of the authors. See also Katherine Hite, 'Chile's National Stadium: As monument, as memorial', *ReVista*, Spring 2004, 58–61.

in the stadium to state transgressions worldwide. She embraced the principle that 'A people without memory was a people without identity'.[22]

In practice, this meant that visitors entering through the principal gate on Avenida Grecia would immediately turn left towards the women's detention site, the former changing room, near the pool. They would enter at ground level, and perhaps descend to the execution wall below ground. A plaque outside would explain its significance. They would then follow a marked path to the Coliseum to inspect passageway no. 8 with its permanent display of the best-known photographs of the detainees and a map of the precinct. The scratchings on the wall would be conserved, protected and where possible deciphered. Changing room (*camarín*) no. 3 downstairs would feature a depiction of a struggling fish beneath the caption 'Caught in the Net'. A detour would follow towards the detainees' entrance from Pedro de Valdivia Street. A 6-metre metal tree was to spring from a reinforced concrete symbolic depiction of the Coliseum walls. In the 50 metres between the detainees' entrance and the arena itself, the consultants planned to set thousands of ceramic tiles into the roadway leading to the Coliseum, each inscribed, 'I was here' followed by a name of a survivor and the date of arrival.

From this point the visitor would follow the 'Via Crucis', now known as the Pathway of Memory, towards the velodrome. The walking track would become a memorial avenue. Handsome trees set on each side would intersperse with sculptures relating to human rights and testimonies of survivors. Inside the south *caracol*, the torture chamber of the men, the consultants proposed a three-dimensional digital display, though of what was not specified. Of the tunnel leading to the velodrome, Kunstmann proposed silhouettes of detainees in shatterproof glass, arms raised, in the sections of concrete wall where the bullet marks are most obvious.

Stage Two of the project, the consultants designed as a Museum of Memory in a People's Plaza, four times the size and double the height of the weight-training room. It was to be sited alongside.

---

22   Kunstmann plan, 2008.

Not surprisingly, both the details of the 2010 Kunstmann plan, and the question of whether there should be memorialisation of any kind, were the subject of much unfriendly conservative comment. The manager of the national archery team complained that his competitors could no longer use the swimming pool changing room. They had nowhere to put their belongings, which were stolen when they left them outside. He denied that anyone had visited the changing rooms to say 'I want to remember where I was a prisoner'. The markings in the exterior wall, rumoured to be bullet holes of firing squads, he maintained could have been caused by faked executions to frighten the prisoners, and who could say if they were bullet holes at all? He suggested a memorial plaque, after which the team could go on using the facilities. That was refused, but so was Kunstmann's team refused permission to move the weekly candle-lit vigils outside the stadium onto the wooden bench-seating inside. A savage attack by the group called the 'Tenth of September Movement', dedicated to 'Those who brought peace' (i.e. the Pinochetistas), in 2012 denounced Kunstmann's group for 'trying to turn Marxists into martyrs'. They responded to her words

> Every enclosure, with its gardens, trees, its coliseum, absolutely every place in the National Stadium was used for torture.

with the sarcastic

> The prisoners had to be hung up on trees to be tortured?[23]

It now transpired that the obscure and (unless one stood on a ladder) unreadable plaque on the stadium perimeter wall had been fixed in 2001 without government permission. According to the radical journal *The Clinic*, Carmen Luz Parot, producer of the film *Estadio Nacional* in 2001, had written to the CEO of ChileSports, to suggest fixing two memorial plaques. One would be on the south *caracol*, and the other outside the main entrance. Receiving no reply, two members of the Association for the Politically Executed decided to do it anyway. Very few guessed that the plaque, following its mysterious nocturnal appearance, was unapproved, nor that the reason for it being placed so high was to avoid vandalism. Amidst the wrangling as to what kind of

---

23 'Marxistas tratan de imponer historia falseada de Chile' [Marxists try to impose false history on Chile], Movimiento 10 de Septiembre, 12 April 2012. Permission to hold the candlelight vigils was granted in 2010.

memorial the stadium should contain, the mayor of Ñuñoa, threatened to demolish the whole stadium, citing its age and decrepitude, 'The declaration of National Monuments is so subjective that the title is given to any sites where torture supposedly took place ...'

Don Roberto Sanchez – not that anyone asked his opinion – was bitterly opposed. 'I have been working here for 38 years, and was only tortured for two months. How could I not wish it well? It is the people that are guilty, not the place.'

The expected dissent, though, was no more bitter than what was had been going on amongst the memorialisers. Feuding, perhaps inevitable given the bitter memories and the government's tardy and cautious brief, was not long in coming. According to US observer Zachary McKiernan, hostilities between the memorialisers began immediately. Shortly after the first meeting in April 2003, the team fractured, unleashing, from what archival records and interviews indicate, a long war of suspicion and divisions between human rights activists, professionals, survivors, and the government planner.[24] Two architects expelled from the committee went on to develop their own proposal. Known as the 'Rodriguez' because of their close family connection to a detained-disappeared, they formed their own team of experts to produce a parallel model of remembrance. Kunstmann referred to them as 'robbers' who looked down on the rest of the group. An ugly quarrel followed a suggestion to invite the popular artist Sting to perform at the stadium whereby spectators would wear Pinochet masks. The 'Rodriguez' team objected, and also to the proposal to include the whole 60-hectare precinct in an Open Museum.[25] Into the midst ChileSports jumped in to propose a different redevelopment altogether, a sports precinct of parks and lakes, but with no protection of the special sites like *escotilla* no. 8. Kunstmann announced that in a dream she had seen the south *caracol* and the swimming pool changing room destroyed, which, since not much had been actually conserved since the declaration, were still in some danger of destruction. She alleged that the Rodriguez team had disappeared with the plans for both sites. The government's heritage adviser asked that all the plans, including

---

24   Zachary McKiernan, 'National Stadium, national memory: A personal letter', Public History Commons.
25   For another version of the dispute, see Veronica Torres, 'Los Escritos de los presos politicos del Estadio Nacional: El pergamino, la lápida y la canción de Bebo' [The writings of the political prisoners at the National Stadium], *The Clinic* online, 10 November 2010.

that of ChileSports, be put on show. Tensions culminated in a tense meeting with Bachelet's human rights adviser in 2008 that resulted, according to McKiernan, in 'piecemeal and spotty historical work', such as the preservation but lack of protection of the inscriptions in passageway no. 8.

The Rodriguez alternative, in contrast to Kunstmann's walkway, was a series of eight 'memory tunnels' situated at eight 'stations' placed at the sites that everyone agreed were the most critical.[26] The government adviser ordered a meeting between the two factions, which ended in a former detainee exclaiming, 'I was in the changing rooms – you have nothing to do with any Project'. Exhausted, the Rodriguez faction withdrew. In 2010 Kunstmann's plan was finally approved. The battle of wills was over. Which was more important, asked the executive secretary of the Monuments Advisory, the person who did the monument, or the monument itself? Such jealousies and envy threatened that nothing would be done.[27]

The government had at last approved the memorial in principle, but when would work begin? Apparently, not very soon. The release of the Kunstmann plan opened a period that the critic and journalist Veronica Torres called not 'Open Memory' but 'Spineless Memory'.[28] ChileSports, whose approval of any memorial project remained necessary, remained more interested in getting the stadium ready for the South American Games scheduled for 2014, and seems to have been ready to use the dissent among the memorialists as an excuse to further its own program.[29] Nobody in government seemed ready to take charge of any part of the project, preferring, in Kunstmann's opinion, stalling tactics like a program to list every tree in the whole precinct.[30] At length the silhouette figures in the velodrome and south *caracol* were agreed upon, but without resolution if or how the inscriptions in *escotilla* no. 8 were to be conserved. Torres wondered if Chileans really deserved a national memorial, for neither government nor people

---

26 'Proyecto de memoria y educación en el Estadio Nacional de Chile: "Museo Abierto, Sitio de Memoria y Homenaje"', Archives Audiovisuelles de la Recherche.
27 Veronica Torres, 'Los escritos de los presos políticos del Estadio Nacional: El pergamino, la lápida y la canción de Bebo' [The writings of the political prisoners at the National Stadium], *The Clinic* online, 10 November 2010.
28 Kunstmann to Read, 7 July 2014.
29 Hernán Rivera Mejía, 'Estadio Nacional de Chile: Un museo abierto', Archivo.
30 Kunstmann to Read, 7 July 2014.

4. CARVED CHERUBS FROLICKING IN A SUNNY STREAM

showed the required sensitivity. All the same, she concluded, successive Concertación governments in the early years after the transition to democracy had seen the horrors close up, and Pinochet remained head of the Army. Torres might have added to the mix the Chileans who opposed outright any form of memorial; those who acknowledged the terrible deeds of the stadium that had occurred only within a space of two months at a site that also represented secular history, sport, enjoyment, concerts, drama and national pride for more than for three quarters of a century; and those who demanded the entire precinct be destroyed or never used again.[31] Torres, and all Chileans, may well have asked if such cross-cutting emotions, desires and agendas could ever be accommodated within a single memorial, if at all. In 2010 the Chilean state was facing almost as many difficulties as it had seven years before if it wished to use the stadium as the principal memorial to the victims of the Pinochet regime.[32] Indeed, it was not until the four-year term of the centre-right government of President Sebastián Piñera in 2008 that work finally began on the 'Greek Memorial' near the main entrance, the part-restoration of the Pathway of Memory to the velodrome, the 'protective shield' round the women's prison, and a 'homage' to the workers of the industrial zones near the entrance gate from Pedro de Valdivia. But that entrance was not planned to include an information plaque.[33]

In truth the differences between the Rodriguez plan, with its tunnels and stress on education, and Kunstmann's vision of a rather more emotional Via Crucis, might be considered minor. More was at stake,

---

31 Quotation and article, Torres, 'Los escritos de los presos políticos del Estadio Nacional: El pergamino, la lápida y la canción de Bebo': 'Rescatar la memoria en democracia ha sido complejo. Pero no menos de cómo ha sido en Alemania, o en otros lados. Villa Grimaldi fue el primer sitio de conciencia recuperado en América Latina y Bachelet la primera Presidenta en hacer una visita de Estado a ese lugar.

En un bar de Providencia, tomando unas cervezas, Carolina Aguilera, 36 años, socióloga que trabaja en la Corporación Villa Grimaldi, me explica cómo ha entendido – a pesar de las críticas que comparte – el actuar de la Concertación.

Me puedo poner en la cabeza de ellos y entender el miedo que tenían. El '99 fue el Boinazo, a Pinochet lo tomaron preso en Londres. Y después de la dictadura la gente empezó a portarse bien. Racionalmente, se puede decir que se debería haber hecho más. Pero en concreto los que gobernaban vieron el horror de cerca y Pinochet seguía siendo el comandante en jefe del Ejército. Esa cuestión no hay que olvidarla nunca.' (*The Clinic*, 28 October 2010).

32 The authors have heard this view expressed on several occasions; see also Katherine Hite, 'Chile's National Stadium', *ReVista*, Spring 2004, 58.

33 In fact it does. The Pedro de Valdivia entrance memorial was completed according to the Kunstmann plan in 2015.

though, than egos and jealousy. At the heart of the tensions were the central questions of public memorialising: who, in the end, could claim first privilege in determining the form of the memorial – the survivor, the relative, the human rights advocate, or, as the principal financier, the state itself? And to what extent should a memorial to terrible deeds be intended primarily to evoke the emotions of pain, sympathy, horror, rage, or instruct in the historical circumstances and civil morality, or prevent a repetition, or to encourage national reconciliation, or even to apportion blame?

Yet for all the criticism that those who had been detained in the stadium should have the right to decide on its representation, Kunstmann's team had got it right in emphasising a visitor's walking tour that was more emotional than instructional. The movement of visitors must always be a central decision for the museum curator. Effective exhibitions answering both curatorial design and visitor preferences must follow a logic that may be temporal, factual, emotional or cumulative, to ensure that the visitor will stay to be informed or moved; he or she should not wander off to another part of the display distracted by an interesting photograph or exhibit. In the Kunstmann plan the visitor would follow a quasi-chronological logic beginning at the women's prison, proceeding past a major informative signage at the 'Greece Memorial', detour to the sculpture at the prisoners' entrance at Pedro de Valdivia, confront the emotive, dust-ridden chambers of the changing rooms and *escotilla* no. 8. Lastly, the visitor would proceed up the prisoners' Via Crucis to the velodrome and torture centre of the highest emotional level. The museum sited here would carry the information the 'Rodriguez' group planned to impart on its version of the visitor walkway. The view from the top floor would dominate and belittle the *caracol* beneath.

4. CARVED CHERUBS FROLICKING IN A SUNNY STREAM

The principal memorial, main entrance, National Stadium of Chile.
Source: Photograph by Peter Read, editing Con Boekel.

The smaller structure at the left is the swimming pool changing room, National Stadium of Chile, occupied by the women detainees. The larger, more modern structure attached to it is the display area opened in 2014.
Source: Photograph by Peter Read, editing Con Boekel.

Roberto Sanchez, released finally from prison in 1976, returned to Temuco, his birthplace, and to his foster mother, to find a large photograph of Pinochet in the family home and a cousin in the police force. He found himself treated 'worse than dirt, as if I was a communist traitor', served another brief jail term, and returned to Santiago. Here for a time he lived rough, drinking heavily. By 1990, though, he was a casual worker at the stadium, and in 2000 he became permanent.

Don Roberto Sanchez is still happy to talk to visitors whom he trusts, recount his life, show them the space under the seats where he spent the first night of detention. In all his years as foreman he has only visited the *caracol* once, when it was used as a storeroom during the dictatorship, and that was to clean it. He found himself sweating, his arms covered in goosebumps, his breathing laboured. It was an experience he is unwilling to repeat. Hearing the national song 'Libre', which was sung by detainees to those who were being released to return to their families, will always reduce him to tears.[34]

His central concern is for the stadium precinct itself. In the unique viewpoint of the insider/outsider, Roberto is determined that it should not be damaged, harmed or punished for actions taken by others within its walls. Memorialisation should be minimal. He is angry that the washbasins and changing rooms are still in their original condition rather than being reconstructed and re-used. He refused to put his name forward to the Valech Report as one of those tortured in the stadium: 'too many just jumped in for the money, who hadn't been tortured at all'. He is uneasy at the endpoint of the visitor's journey to the *caracol*, and its planned People's Plaza.

What form, then, should the memorialisation take for him? Just a little monolith, just a plaque perhaps, a little fountain and a quotation. 'But it should not be for us victims, there are not many of us left, and we'll take our memories to the grave.' Make it symbolic, and certainly not ideological. He doesn't want future generations to remember the pain, or carry the struggle into the future, only to know what happened. The punishment for the perpetrators should come not from the courts but from God. He doesn't like the monument and list of names outside José Domingo Cañas 1367 – much too cold and impersonal. Even the climax at the end of the Pathway of Memory, he thinks, should in no sense be grand or monumental nor display long lists of survivors' testimonies. So just a little memorial, then, a pretty little fountain with little angels, that's all. Others had it worse than me. Keep the stadium. Use the stadium. It was bad here only for two months in 71 years. Just a pretty fountain by the south *caracol*, just a little plaque, no names, no accusations, just water flowing gently over the stones, and carved cherubs frolicking in the sunny stream.

---

34   Roberto Sanchez, interview, 21 June 2015.

5
Last stand of the MIR: Londres 38

Londres 38 – the English equivalent would be '38 London Street' – is the only chapter in which no single individual carries the narrative. The reason is that, whatever divisions existed amongst the survivors and families about the future of the building, by 2008 the dichotomy that had emerged was between the Bachelet-led centre-left coalition and the Allende-era radical left; and in particular, the remnants of the revolutionary party known as the MIR. The struggle to memorialise Londres 38 is a different kind of struggle to the others.

Towards the end of 1973, the dictatorship government realised that the occupation of the National Stadium must soon be ended. The international press remained unconvinced that the detainees were not maltreated. Two weeks after the coup the Archbishop of Chile, Raúl Silva Henriquez, demanded entry from the colonel in charge and spoke to many of the detainees, amazed to confront several people whom he knew and respected.[1] Several days later, he founded the Comité de Cooperación por la Paz en Chile (Committee for Cooperation for Peace in Chile) and oversaw what was at first the clandestine, later the principal, clearing house of information about the disappeared.

---

1   Roberto López, 'Cardenal Silva Henríquez en el Estadio Nacional (1973): "Vengo a ver a mis hermanos en desgracia"', [I come to see my brothers in misfortune], *Cambio 21*, 27 September 2007.

It was known as the 'Vicaría de la Solidaridad', the Vicariate of Solidarity, and was the destination for people like Nena González to pass on their secret news.[2]

On 21 November, the Chilean national soccer team was scheduled to play a World Cup semi-final against the Soviet Union. The world governing body of soccer visited the stadium. Concluding that no detainees were present (they were being held clandestinely in the changing rooms) it insisted the game proceed. Unsurprisingly the Soviets refused to play in a country that had overturned its elected Marxist government; the Chileans turned out to kick a solitary goal into the net unopposed. Chile moved to the final but much of the soccer press was scandalised.[3] Week by week sporting groups asked to resume use of the training facilities or the main arena. The stadium would have to be vacated, and soon.

To minimise further accusations of torture and executions in the international press, by November some hundreds of detainees had already been moved to the far northern mining encampment of Chacabuco. At the same time, the just-established security force, the DINA, began planning a series of secret bolt holes, generally private houses seized from the arrested, where detainees could be taken quickly, interrogated and tortured before being trucked to the larger and already overcrowded former civilian prisons like Tres Alamos.

One of the first new clandestine sites to be chosen for the interrogation, torture and possible execution of detainees was an elegant nineteenth-century mansion in the middle of Santiago's CBD. Only metres from the capital's principal thoroughfare and opposite a busy hotel, its address was Londres 38. Until 11 September, when the military seized it, Londres 38 was the headquarters of the Santiago branch of the Chilean Socialist Party. From mid-November it became the first of the Santiago post-stadium torture and extermination centres. How many detainees passed through Londres 38 is unknown, but it probably surpassed

---

2   Initially the Committee for Cooperation for Peace in Chile, see 'Comité de Cooperación para la paz en Chile', Arzobispado de Santiago, Fundación Documentación y Archivo de la Vicaría de la Solidaridad.
3   'The soccer match that disgraced Chile', PRI Public Radio International, 11 September 2011.

1,000. Of these, 96 were known to have been killed, including 13 young women. The DINA called its new centre 'Yucatán'. It closed in September 1974.[4]

The first purpose of the initial detentions, apart from pre-empting the imagined counter-coup, was to extract the names of known subversives, and the whereabouts of the supposed arms stashes. Most of all, DINA interrogators wanted the identity and the whereabouts of the leaders, already hidden in their safe houses, of the Movimiento de Izquierda Revolucionaria, the Movement of the Revolutionary Left, known as el MIR. The dismemberment of the MIR by the security forces, and the subsequent attempt of its remaining membership to establish itself within Londres 38 after 2005, is one of the themes of this chapter.

The MIR, whose members were known as MIRistas, was a political party new to Chile. Tracing its foundation only to 1965, it was of a notably different caste to the other leftist parties. Its leadership was drawn mainly from the upper classes, the well educated, students and professionals. It differed, for example, from the Communist Party, founded in 1922, which had emerged from the Chilean factory and rural workers' movements and stood for the democratic exercise of workers' power. Before the coup the Communists were tolerated, if not respected, throughout Chilean society. The MIR never enjoyed that status.

In other ways also, the MIR did not sit comfortably anywhere on the continuum of the left. All that lot, the MIR claimed, had prostituted their revolutionary essence by leading the workers into an electoral and parliamentary swamp.[5] Indeed, on Allende's election, debate raged whether the MIR should support him or oppose him.[6] Describing itself as Marxist-Leninist, the party was to lead 'the working class and the exploited masses towards socialism and its national emancipation'. Its self-conception was never less than lofty: it held (again in its own judgement) 'a revolutionary audacity capable of opposing cynical imperialist violence with the virile and proud response of the armed masses'. Its belligerent stance and assumption of elitist leadership made

---
4 'Recinto DINA – "Londres 38"', Memoria Viva.
5 Cited, ibid., p. 5.
6 Lucía Sepúlveda Ruiz, *119 de Nosotros*, Colección Septiembre, LOM Ediciones, Santiago, 2005, pp. 29–30.

it analogous to a religious 'elect', and not necessarily popular with all factory workers or rural communists like Victor Jara; but conversely, its call to arms and its attractiveness to the younger and articulate urban generation helped to make it the first target of Pinochet's security forces.

Elitist though the party was, all levels of the MIR structure paid a terrible price for their rhetoric. Though many escaped or went into exile, hundreds did not. By October 1975, 347 MIRistas had been executed or disappeared. A MIR commander, Andres Pascal Allende, estimated that between 1,500 and 2,000 MIRistas were killed overall, of a total membership of some 10,000 at the time of the coup, equalling between one-half to two-thirds of all Chileans killed during the Pinochet period.[7]

In September 1973, the MIR's head was the charismatic but elusive Miguel Enríquez Espinoza. Like Che Guevara, on whom he modelled himself, he had once been a physician. Now, from a succession of 'safe' houses, he led the resistance of his party against Pinochet until October 1974, when he and several other MIRistas were killed in a spectacular firefight.[8]

Those MIRistas who survived the focused persecutions on the streets, in safe houses and at the National Stadium were among those first to be held in the just-opened Yucatán (Londres 38). In this way was the connection between the MIR and Yucatán established. Indeed, such was the persecution of MIR that, unlike other major parties like the Socialists and Communists, by 1990 the party had ceased to function even as a political force. After the transition to democracy, the remaining membership struggled to establish themselves in Londres 38 as soon as they were able, as much memorial to what the party had endured as signifier of its very existence. But we shall see how a succession of centre-left governments, 1991–2010, were unimpressed by its attempts. Similarly unimpressed were the other Allende-era parties of the left.

---

7 'Los Allende: con ardiente paciencia por un mundo mejor' [With burning patience towards a better world] by Günther Wessell, cited in 'Revolutionary Left Movement (Chile)', Wikipedia.
8 For a number of sources on Enríquez, see www.archivochile.com/.

5. LAST STAND OF THE MIR

In 1993 survivors led by Roberto D'Orival Briceño, brother of a detained-disappeared, formed a collective, which they named 'Colectivo 119', to press the memorialisation of a particular group of mainly MIRista detained-disappeared. The '119' were particularly connected to Londres 38 through 'Operation Colombo', a brutally clumsy attempt by the DINA to account for some of the many hundreds of the left who had disappeared in the first year of the coup. In June 1975 the DINA published its infamous list of 119 'missing' Chileans whose bodies had been supposedly discovered in Argentina, through the preposterous claim that they all had fought and killed each other.[9] Conveniently, the bodies were so mutilated that they could no longer be identified: even fingers or hands were missing from many of the bodies. Such a statement, as obscene as it was ludicrous, was soon exposed as the lie it was; yet it allowed the DINA to continue to take refuge in the claim that it had no information on those missing people whom it had, of course, detained, tortured and killed. Ninety-four MIRistas were listed among the 119, of whom at least 47 are thought to have been killed within Londres 38 itself.[10]

***

The first detainees of Londres 38 arrived, mostly from the stadium, in sealed refrigerated vans or other vehicles, bound hand and foot, bundled into the formal entrance hurriedly turned into a makeshift docking bay. Unlike at the stadium, at Londres 38 they remained bound and blindfolded, day or night, dumped on chairs by day and the floor by night, from which movement at all times was forbidden. Food and toilet visits twice a day were the only collective movement allowed, though shortages of chairs and blindfolds ensured that everyone soon discovered where they were. The sound of the bells of the well-known Church of St Francisco were easily recognisable, while Socialists, familiar with the building, recognised the black and white tiles of the entrance way by peering below their blindfolds.[11] Nor did they need to be told what was in store for them. A detainee was thrown in amongst them so badly injured that he died retching in front of them, invisible but diabolically audible. Every day (except Sunday), every hour, seemingly every minute, came echoing down

---

9   'Londres 38', Wikipedia.
10 Ruiz, *119 de Nosotros*, p. 29.
11 'Recinto DINA – "Londres 38"', Memoria Viva.

the stairwell the names of those next to be summoned upstairs to be interrogated, punctuated by screams from those already bound on the *parrilla*.[12] Several times a day came roll-call, that at least ensured that every detainee knew who had arrived, or left or died. Patricio Rivas, a leading MIR official held in Londres 38 for 72 hours in late December 1973, recalls his arrival at the torture centre:

> A kind of infernal choir filled the place. I heard screams of different tones, from different mouths, which blended with the summons of the agents. They were screams of horror that bit the air and which, even when they ended, still vibrated in space. They weren't screams of fear, they were of loneliness in the face of the incomprehensible. The voices of those young people remained there forever.[13]

Raimundo Belarmino Elgueta Pinto, former MIRista, recalled:

> The principal method consisted of applying an electrical current on the 'grill', for which I was made to take all my clothes, they would tie me by the hands and feet to the electric bed, and connect cables to the fingers of my hands and feet and also to the penis and/or testicles and left a 'floating' cable which they applied to the different parts of the body. The 'sessions' were of variable duration, some very prolonged and others very brief.[14]

---

12 The Londres prisoner Erika Hennings, public address, 10 December 2009, recording in possession of the authors.

13 Quoted, Peter Read and Marivic Wyndham, 'The day that Londres 38 opened its doors: A moment in Chilean reconciliation', *Universitas Humanistica. Revista antropologia y sociologia*, no. 71, January–June 2011, p. 200: 'Una especie de coro infernal llenaba el recinto. Oía gritos en distintos tonos, desde distintas bocas, que se mezclaban con las órdenes de los agentes. Eran gritos de espanto que mordían el aire y que al terminar seguían vibrando en el espacio. No eran gritos de miedo, eran de soledad frente a lo incomprensible. Las voces de esos jóvenes quedaron ahí para siempre.'

14 'Testimonio de Raimundo Belarmino Elgueta Pinto', Memoria Viva:

> En Londres 38 fui torturado diariamente, con excepción del domingo que en aquella época era todavía descanso obligatorio, mediante golpes de puños y pies y aplicación de corriente eléctrica sentado en una silla, acostado en la 'parrilla' o colgado de una barra metálica. El método principal consistió en la aplicación de corriente eléctrica en la 'parrilla', para lo cual era obligado a desnudarme, me ataban de manos y pies al catre metálico, me conectaban cables a los dedos de las manos y de los pies y también al pene y/o testículos y dejaban un cable 'volante' que aplicaban en diferentes partes del cuerpo. Las 'sesiones' tuvieron duración variable, algunas muy prolongadas y otras muy breves…

5. LAST STAND OF THE MIR

Despite its rapid occupation, the DINA soon found the building unsatisfactory. The loud symphonic music played in the street could not conceal the screams from the top floor. While local residents could be intimidated into avoiding the area, Londres was an important thoroughfare in the heart of the city through which passed observers, foreign officials, reporters or even the tourists of the Pinochet years. Thus even while the ordeal of the detainees continued, the security forces were busy preparing larger and better concealed torture facilities ready for use by the end of 1974.

***

Thanks to its high status, physical elegance and prime location half a kilometre from the seat of government, Londres 38 was not levelled by the dictatorship, as were many of the other major torture and execution sites, to conceal its atrocities. Rather, in 1978, the building was made over by Pinochet to the politically reactionary and quasi-military organisation known as the O'Higgins Institute, whose membership contained a significant number of former Army officers. They were still entrenched in the building after the transition to democracy, well able to summon deference in each of the centre-left governments elected after Pinochet's departure. Ten years later, in 2001, the O'Higgins members objected strongly to any reference to the brief but terrifying role of their headquarters as the first of Pinochet's specifically created torture centres. They aggressively denied knowledge to any enquiry and, to deceive strangers, changed the number of their institute from 38 to 40. For a decade the centre-left Concertación governments, implicitly acknowledging the potential of the O'Higgins Institute to encourage a further military coup, resisted any attempt at an official recognition of the building's past.[15]

For as long as the O'Higgins Institute remained in control of the building, commemoration of the site by mourners was as necessarily restrained as at the stadium. By day physical protest was impossible, but from 2003 peaceful and silent demonstrations began outside on the narrow pavement between the building and the hotel. Sorrowing families, and a few survivors, would gather once a week to place candles on the footpath in a *velaton*, or vigil. They might read aloud one or

---

15 Steve Stern, *Reckoning with Pinochet: The Memory Question in Democratic Chile, 1989–2006*, Duke University Press, Durham, 2010, pp. 270–71.

two testimonies, or paste photographs of the detained-disappeared on the walls. Father, mother, daughter, son, husband, wife, *Donde está?* Where is he? Where is she? Early next morning the O'Higgins workmen arrived to pull the posters off and whitewash the wall. The despairing cries to the disappeared had themselves disappeared. All that remained, to careful observers, were a few whitewashed corners of posters too hard to remove, and the tiny marks at ground level where the vigil candles had discoloured the once elegant white façade.

The front façade, Londres 38, showing the marks of burning candles resting against it during the vigils held for the detained-disappeared.
Source: Photograph by Peter Read, editing Con Boekel.

The silent reverent vigils did not remain so for long. The government's actions, though founded in sensible deference to the O'Higgins Institute, only served to focus attention on a building so easily accessible by day, and where dozens of pedestrians walked past or stopped at the evening vigils. By 2005 the mourners' numbers at the vigils were swollen by young people intent on changing the meaning of the once silent ceremonies. They began to call a rhetorical roll to demonstrate an improbable solidarity between Chile's old political left:

The Socialist Party of Chile?
Presente!
The Communist Party?
Presente!
El MIR?
Presente!
El MAPU? [The small Popular Unitary Action Party that formed a part of Allende's coalition]
Presente!

In 2004, news spread that the O'Higgins Institute members would be invited to find a new site for their headquarters. It was no coincidence that at this point the unity between the collectives advocating a memorialisation of Londres 38 – in a form as yet undecided – began to fracture. At least two collectives demanded a distinct voice. One was Colectivo 119, already created to honour the 119 murdered political prisoners, whose members were almost all MIRistas or their families. Naturally, their first demand was the recognition and memorialisation of the 119. A second collective, confusingly named the 'Friends and Families of the 119' (Amigos y Familiares de los 119) occupying a lower socioeconomic place, and with no direct links to the victims of Londres 38, nevertheless believed themselves to be more genuine inheritors of working-class struggles than the elitist MIR. Indeed, it was they who began to shift the solemn weekly witnessing to the dead towards the political soapboxing and noisy critiques of the Concertación governments that from 2005 marked the evening gatherings. Londres 38 was acquiring the new status of protest site in addition to its role as historical actor.[16]

A second tension to split the collectives Colectivo 119 and Colectivo Amigos y Familiares de los 119 was whether to accept the government as partner in memorialising the building. The inexperienced and often belligerent 'Friends and Family', unused to negotiating with the state at any level, held that no one associated with the building should deal with a government that had prevaricated and compromised with the military. The leader of the Colectivo 119, Roberto D'Orival Briceño, whose brother Jorge was among the 119 disappeared, understood that their connection to the building, apart from through his own

---

16   Marivic Wyndham and Peter Read, 'The disappearing museum', *Rethinking History. The Journal of Theory and Practice* 18(2), April 2014, 165–180.

group, was tenuous.[17] His collective of former MIRistas was better educated and more confident in negotiation, which only increased the opprobrium directed at it. Even though it had established itself on the coat-tails of the 119, the Friends and Family Collective thought its attempts at negotiation to be counter-productive, or worse. Where was the leadership of the left, it asked, when the rank and file began to be rounded up, tortured and killed? Why had so many abandoned their posts and gone into exile, to return only when it was safe, while the workers had suffered most? In return, Briceño's collective hammered at the theme that the working-class distrust of the 'establishment', of whatever political colour, was destructive and stupid. Privately, some held that the ignorant left would probably destroy places like Londres 38 should they be allowed to build workers' houses on the site. Only peaceful protest and patient negotiations would persuade – not force – the government to act. As the gap between the collectives widened, the footpath activities became more discordant. Songs, recitals and theatrical roll calls for worldwide oppressed minorities began to replace the fewer personal testimonies at the evening vigils. Vigil candles were overshadowed by displays and puppet shows, amplified music and denunciations – not of Pinochet's regime, but of Bachelet's![18]

It was in the context of the 2004 Valech Report's multiple testimonies of torture at Londres 38 and elsewhere, and in the expectation that the O'Higgins Institute would be prepared to move to new quarters, that Bachelet's centre-left government finally declared the building a historic monument.[19] A somewhat obscure bronze tablet sunk into the pavement outside the building revealed only a few details of what atrocities had occurred inside:

> Londres 38 Secret Centre of detention, torture, disappearance and execution 11 September 1973 – September 1974. It is estimated that more than 2,000 people were detained in Londres 38, 96 of whom were executed, are currently disappeared or died later as a consequence of the tortures; 83 were men and 13 women, two of whom were pregnant. Declared a Historic Monument in 2005.

---

17   The Friends and Family Collective, led by Ximena Muñoz, has been renamed 'Collective 119 for Human Rights'.
18   Read and Wyndham, 'The day that Londres 38 opened its doors', pp. 202–3.
19   'Report of the National Commission on Political Imprisonment and Torture' ('Valech Report'), 29 November 2004.

5. LAST STAND OF THE MIR

The restrained language and the position of the plaque on the pavement, rather than on the wall, indicated that the Department of Historic Monuments was anxious not to offend the powerful and the threatening. Behind closed doors the Bachelet government continued to negotiate with the O'Higgins Institute, not to resume the building, but to offer several attractive sites elsewhere in the city to exchange for Londres 38.

Dissent among the memorialisers, exacerbated by rumours, continued to widen. Most of the Socialist members of Colectivo 119 split to form a new but not unfriendly group, Colectivo Londres 38, to look after their own party's interests in the building. Both rejected the endless Friends and Family mantra of 'No negotiating with the government'. Only peaceful protest and patient negotiations, they reasoned, would convince the government that the institute should be persuaded to leave. Trying to smash in the front door of Londres 38, as some extremists in the Friends and Family were demanding, would be highly counter-productive. Keep this up and everyone would finish up with nothing. The Friends and Family Collective sidetracked the demand for memorialisation by a separate agenda of free education and health benefits that should be granted not only to the children of victims of repression, but to all working-class children. Discussion intensified: if there was to be a central archive of historical research installed in the building, rumoured to be the government plan, what would be its purpose? Should the planned memorialisation inside be specific to the building, sombre and contemplative, or should it confront visitors with torture instruments? Who would control it? In the last resort, should the leftist groups work with the government towards reconciliation and, if so, at what price to justice and truth?

Unexpectedly, in February 2006, the O'Higgins Institute put the building up for sale. The collectives claimed victory, but the government forestalled discussion as to who would own it by announcing that it, not the collectives, was already the owner of Londres 38. It confirmed its plan to install on the site a yet-to-be-established Institute for Human Rights.

At last here was something that could unite the collectives. Almost everyone, it seemed, opposed the government's plan. In March 2007, Colectivo 119 invited all interested parties to a meeting to decide the preferred purpose. The Colectivo Londres 38, dominated by Socialists, demanded that the building should be dedicated to the history of the Pinochet repression and the memories of all those who had suffered within its walls – by implication, *not* just MIRistas, and *not* just the 119. A participatory process should define its uses, after which the state should have no role beyond ensuring that its management was public, democratic and participatory.[20] Meanwhile, the building remained locked and bolted and the government gave no indication when it would allow public entry.

Stymied, the collectives planned their own exterior memorialisation, to be much more obvious and informative than the Department of Historic Sites' understated and obscurely placed plaque. The collectives agreed that in the pavement of the public street outside the building, 300 black-and-white granite tiles would imitate the floor inside the building that victims had glimpsed through the bottom of their blindfolds. A further 98 bronze placards would list the names and ages of the 85 men and 13 women believed politically executed in the building. As significant as the name would be a statement of political affiliation. One would read, for example:

> Abundio Alejandro Contreras González
> 28 years old MIR

The government agreed that this (slight) further memorialisation of the detained-disappeared might proceed.

No sooner had the divisions closed in opposition to the government's plans, than they reopened on the alternative agendas for the conservation and memorialisation of the building. Now that the plaques and memorials were in place outside, what should be interpreted inside, and how, and when? One end of the spectrum of possibilities stood for an empty, silent building, bare and darkened rooms for quiet contemplation. What would be the place of the MIRistas? The centre-left and moderate Bachelet Cabinet was by no means enamoured of memorials to a pro-Cuban revolutionary party that did not believe in democratic rule; and it was this vision of a specific, MIRista-dominated memorial House of Memory that the state's agencies would

---

20   Colectivo Londres 38, 'Londres 38. Un Espacio Para La Memoria', pamphlet, 10 December 2007.

progressively thwart. The state would tolerate no memorialisation of a particular site at the expense of its plans for its own wider, and more diffused, account of the recent past.

It was at the official opening and reoccupation of the building, scheduled for International Human Rights Day, 10 December 2007, that the point at which the divisions between the three collectives, as well as the interests of general state and the localised victim, at last became unedifyingly manifest.

What would the day bring? Colectivo 119 wanted a solemn and respectful ingress by which only its own members should first be admitted to begin to exorcise their memories and conduct their rituals. Tensions rose as the Ministry of National Assets announced that, contrary to the wishes of seemingly everyone else, it would take charge of the formal opening as a major media event. The collectives debated whether to boycott the event; most people decided that it was in their best interests to attend. But during the morning, rumours spread that the Minister, hearing of a planned counter-demonstration by the Friends and Families Collective, had postponed the formal opening until further notice. By three in the afternoon, few in the crowd gathering outside knew what was to happen, or when. By four, 200 people stood outside awaiting developments, debating, listening to speeches and performers. The building's windows and door on the bottom floor were wide open, but representatives of the Communist-dominated Friends and Families Collective stood outside barring entry to all but their own members. By half past four, the number of people being allowed to walk in and out of the main entrance was increasing. Suddenly a spokesperson for the Friends and Families Collective, showing its customary contempt for all things governmental, announced defiantly that since the Minister had forbidden entry, those present should 'force' their way in.

> We must repudiate the Ministry, *compañeros*, for [all] government still represents the long repression of the workers. The entry of we urban unionists will be like a vigil, but something more. Treat it with the utmost respect, but move in.

Swept aside were the Colectivo 119's plans for a dignified, formal opening by the Minister, invitation-only, ritualised, ecumenical, sombre, ethical and poetic. The chance to impress upon the Minister how important was the site to the MIR and to the families of the 119 was lost.²¹ Two hundred people, denied entry for 34 years, pushed forward.

Those in the first dignified surge found themselves bypassing a man weeping uncontrollably, just inside the interior entrance, comforted by a woman while a video photographer held them in close focus. His sobs, momentarily, were the only sounds to disturb the reverent silence. Little by little, silences became hushed conversations. At this still point, each traumatised family was claiming a space for its own truth. A voice from somewhere asked what a room was used for. On the second floor a weeping woman disclosed to a friend that her disappeared son and a journalist detainee had been paraded together in this very spot. They could hear their footsteps on the wooden floor; through their blindfolds, they could see the light of day filtering through the wooden shutters. The journalist had survived, her son was disappeared. His photograph hung from her neck. *Donde está*? She turned to the back wall and wept afresh. Other mourners took an incense stick and made their way to the upper floors, those of interrogation and torture, to pore minutely over their walls and floors in search of painted-over messages. A man searching above the picture rail in the *parrilla* chamber found, perhaps, what he had been looking for: a tiny potpourri of flowers, dated 2005.²² In the basement, a couple were earnestly examining the tiny mosaic of colour tiles in the pantry, evidently searching for something they expected to be there.

Meanwhile on the first floor, in the largest room of the mansion, once the drawing room, then the main holding cell, a discussion was beginning. First respectful, then noisy, soon heated, it centred on the future of the building. The drama of the afternoon was precipitating a climax of tensions years in the making: to express individual grief, to give voice to national workers' movements, to bind the site to international human rights, and to further the cause of national reconciliation. Boiling over here were not only the emotions of the terror but the years of frustration at the institute, at the government,

---

21   Roberto D'Orival Briceño, interview, 11 December 2010.
22   The date probably referred to an entry into the building by some former detainees and judicial investigators.

5. LAST STAND OF THE MIR

at the other collectives, at each other in a divided political left with nowhere to go. Roberto D'Orival Briceño bellowed at the Family and Friends Collective:

> Why do you keep excluding us? We are constantly being discredited but this sort of exclusion and behind-the-hand criticism has got to stop. We need to combine not only to decide the building's future but the whole future of the left in Chile.[23]

A proposal to set up a café, proposed by the Friends and Family, was furiously shouted down. 'You haven't suffered with us.'[24] A woman asserted that her sister had been disappeared upstairs in this very building and that she would never, ever, allow the place to become a coffee shop for tourists.

Who had the moral rights to the building – intellectuals or workers, survivors or supporters, professionals or well-meaning supporters? Was it the MIR? Or was it the families of the 119? Would the opening of the building be a victory for local activism and the current struggles of Santiago urban workers – the present; or a victory for local memory, truth and justice set in a context of international human rights – the past; or the Concertación's developing national agenda of investigation of victims (not perpetrators) and reconciliation – that is to say, the future? In the broadest terms, the question was: Who in the end holds the emotional and moral rights to this building, and to Chile's immediate past?[25] Perhaps fortunately, the debate was terminated by the arrival of Erika Hennings, former tortured detainee of Londres 38, widow of a detained-disappeared, expelled to France in October 1974, and articulate spokesperson for the Colectivo 119.[26] To an audience at last hushed, she related that her teenage daughter, standing white-faced beside her, had never before entered the building. Though beatings took place in the room where she stood, her worst memories were footsteps echoing up and down the wooden staircase all day, waiting to be called to what she called the extermination room. *When you were called, you knew.* Her husband Alfonso defied orders to creep across to her by night to touch her. *It was an act of love I'll never*

---

23 Roberto D'Orival Briceño, interview.
24 Ibid.
25 Discussion based on informal conversations by the authors with members of rival factions while waiting for the doors to open.
26 For biographical details see, for example, 'Alfonso Chanfreau', Wikipedia.

forget. Someone had been thrown from – she pointed – that window. Some detainees had been hanged from – that staircase. She glanced up and whispered, 'I can't go there'. She asked to be alone with her daughter for a few minutes.

The tour, 2010

The opening of the house was a year in the past, and the first guided official tour was still 18 months in the future when Michele Drouilly, sister of a detained-disappeared MIRista, allowed the authors entry to the silent site.[27]

These first interpretations of the terror were personal, precise and agonising. From perhaps minutes of the building's opening, tiny ornaments and drawings had begun unobtrusively to appear. In a cramped and windowless cell (probably originally a storage pantry) a drawing depicted four blindfolded, handcuffed individuals jammed together on the floor. On the landing outside the torture chamber – originally a bedroom – another tiny drawing showed the infamous interrogators Miguel Krassnoff and Moren Brito, flanked by a guard, sinister and threatening. A blindfolded, naked detainee hung upside down suspended by the knees and hands from a pole. A naked man was shown plunged by two guards into a barrel, probably sewage. Some of the reproductions were attached by three corners, or hung crooked or slightly torn. Their positioning was unmistakably urgent, neither decorative nor informative, indeed, since each picture was only some 8 by 12 centimetres, they seemed more analogous to flowers on a grave than to a public display. Each depicted a specific torture in its precise location: the drawing of the figure in the barrel hung in the upstairs bathroom, in the part of the building now closed to visitors. Each of these locations had become a private altar for perhaps a solitary mourner. While some of those experiences were not specific to Londres 38, their reproductions memorialised the exact and unspeakable events that had occurred not anywhere else, but *here*. On the ground floor, in another bathroom, someone had glued an image of a young man's face on an inlet valve that served poignantly to frame it.

---

27   See Chapter 7.

5. LAST STAND OF THE MIR

Throughout the building, still closed to the public, the mood of the impromptu signage was one of barely restrained horror and grief at what had happened *here*, not there, and to *this* person, not that.

To this point in late 2010, neither the Department of National Assets nor the collectives had agreed on the direction of any historical display. It was to be another full year before the first indications of the shift from the minutely particular to a general statement about the building themselves took form.

The tensions were neatly displayed in a wordless exchange between collectives and individual in what had once been the reception area of the building. That the collectives were prepared to work together was apparent in a rather bureaucratically worded sign – the first inside the building – propped against the chimney above the marble mantelpiece. Note the prioritising of the achievements of the different collectives:

> Had it not been for the actions of the ex-detained [Collective 119], the families of the victims [Collective Londres 38] and the social organisations [Families and Friends of the Collective 119], this site would still remain ignored. Virtually 'erased' from the city.

During the year an unknown mourner had placed five photocopied cards, mostly representing victims of a single MIRista family – Alberto Gallardo, Roberto Gallardo, Catalina Gallardo, Rolando Rodriguez and Monica Pacheco – arranged against the wall of the first room that one entered. Beside each card was propped a paper rose. Below each photograph was typed:

> Executed by the DINA 9th of November 1975.[28]

The poignant memorials were arranged propped against the first signage in the building, partially, though no doubt deliberately, obscuring its message.

***

---

28 These were placed by Alberto Rodriguez Gallardo, infant survivor of the deaths of many of his family in 1975, at the hands of the DINA. All were members either of the MIR or Communist Party; Alberto Rodriguez Gallardo, 'The truth is I don't know the word "justice", and even less the word "pardon"', *El Irreverente*.

During 2011, though the building was not yet formally open to the public, favoured members of the collectives might find their way into the building to impose their own vision of what the memorial should become, while several judicial enquiries asked survivors such as Erika Hennings to accompany them on inspections. But what now appeared to be the first state-sponsored signage in the building indicated that the agonised recognition of certain sites was giving way to a creeping generality. The largest space on the ground floor, where the detainees were held handcuffed and blindfolded, was the only room whose purpose to the DINA was identified. It was here that Patricio Rivas had absorbed the 'infernal choir, those screams of horror that bit the air' that 'when they ended, still vibrated in space'; here Alfonso Chanfreu had crept across the midnight floor to touch his wife Erika Hennings for the last time. The signage, in contrast, was prosaic and flat.

> DETENTION ROOM. Common room in which during the day the male and female detainees remained seated and blindfolded. During the night the chairs were removed and they slept on the floor.

At the same time, other signage was appearing in different rooms, directed by a more poetic hand, but one which also eschewed both precision and location. It was not clear who had written them, nor for whom. This caption seemed to reflect the horror that Rivas could not forget:

> The problem was not, nor is, only to speak or tell of what was experienced, rather to find ears that want to listen.

This caption appeared on a door on the first floor:

> The ear allowed them to see without eyes, identify the house and its surroundings, recognise days and nights and hold in their memory the voices of friends and comrades.

And prominently inscribed on the walls of another room:

> How does one fill this void so full of entrapped memories? This is a past that continues to be part of our present.

Finally, the visitors, even if making their own way in, could reflect upon this wall signage, first scribbled on a cigarette packet by a woman prisoner, the MIRista Muriel Dockendorff Navarrete. She wrote it to her friend Sandra Machuca, fellow detainee in another Santiago interrogation and detention centre, Cuatro Alamos. Muriel died, Sandra, and the precious message, survived.

> I remember when I met you in the house of terror ... In those moments in which a light was a dream. Or a miracle, however, you were light in those darknesses. We were one in one misfortune. Today thousands of misfortunes. Later I see you as before, as I know you will be today, in some other place, always looking to windward. We will meet through the mists that we will dispel.
>
> Do not forget me.[29]

Heart-stopping as Muriel Dockendorff's farewell message was, the explanation below introduced a new element into the display. It indicated for the first time that the Concertación Government's interpretation of Londres 38 might not only compromise the minutiae of every room, but the particularity of the building itself.

> Letter written by Muriel Dockendorff Navarrete – today a detained disappeared, to her friend Sandra Machuca, 10 October 1974, while both were detained in the camp [now Site of Conscience] Cuatro Alamos.

At the time of signage, no certain evidence existed that the MIRista Muriel Dockendorff had ever been held in Londres 38 at all. Yet in the decade that followed, it was such heroic statements that reminded MIRistas of what they had once been, and why. Though the party was in ruins, the visionary ideals that bound them demanded an honoured remembrance.

It was towards the end of 2011 that the purposes of the building, which the government had first signalled in 2005, became more obvious. Londres 38 opened officially with an exhibition and guided tour in 2011. Dominating and beginning the display was a historical timeline that marked the annual course of the dictatorship. It began with the story of the 119 disappeared radical leftists – while noting that such psychological warfare was practised by other dictatorships of the time! In the account of succeeding years, even Londres 38 did not always figure. The text for the year 1983, for instance, noted only

---

29 'Muriel Dockendorff Navarette', Memoria Viva; see also, Berenice Dockendorff Navarrete, *Homenaje a Muriel*, self-published, Santiago, March 2008.

the first of the widespread nationwide strikes against the dictatorship. The caption for 2005 noted the year in which Londres 38 was handed over to the collectives. For 2010, the year in which the government assumed a more direct control over the historical interpretation, the signage traced the state's own role precisely. A laboriously worded sign explained that, 'meeting the will of the current government', a working group had been formed of the three collectives, along with representatives of the Presidential Assessors Commission of Human Rights, the Program of Human Rights of the Ministry of Interior, the Metropolitan Regional Administration, the Executive of Architecture of the Ministry of Public Works and the Council for National Monuments. 'Amongst others'!

Guide Leopoldo Montenegro reminded visitors of the significance of this new agenda: the building should not be allowed to remain a thing of the past but must develop the means of educating future generations and develop a pedagogy. Only state funding could repair the damage to the house; indeed, he reminded his every audience, the Rettig Report had stressed that sites like Londres 38 were the state's responsibility.[30]

Equally significant was what, by 2011, had vanished. The drawings of the detainees cramped in a tiny cell, the photocopies of the Gallardo family members obscuring the entry signage, the depiction of individual tortures, the tiny photograph of the young man in the lower bathroom – all were gone. Leopoldo Montenegro was unable to explain their disappearance: he did not know that they ever had been there. To the question as to why, for example, there was no physical evidence of torture instruments such as the *parrilla*, as the Museum of Memory and Human Rights was displaying at this time, he replied that such an object would be 'contrary to the aesthetic of the display'. Indeed it would.[31]

By 2012 the displays had assumed a new irony. The most dominant voice when the building was still in the hands of the O'Higgins Institute, that of the Colectivo 119, was now altogether absent inside the building, its displays relegated to the pavement outside.

---

30   Leopoldo Montenegro Montenegro, guide, video recording of tour of Londres 38, 30 November 2011. The Museum of Memory and Human Rights was inaugurated by President Michelle Bachelet in 2010.
31   Leopoldo Montenegro Montenegro, interview, 3 December 2012.

In September this took the form of a nine-panel temporary exhibition, packed away each night, presenting a photograph and biographical information on each of the detained-disappeared.[32]

In 2012 the years of struggles to rescue Londres 38 as a specific Site of Conscience of the MIR, especially of the 119, appeared to have come a full circle. The same spatial tensions of the time prior to that day in 2007 when Londres 38 first opened its doors, between the public and private, the outside and the inside of the site, still held. The years of vigils and pasted photographs of victims of Londres 38 outside, when the building was occupied by the O'Higgins Institute, had answered only their immediate purpose. Now the physical and metaphorical spheres of interior and exterior had imposed themselves: the state in control over the politics and interpretation of the interior of the building, and the collectives in charge of the various public spaces staged outside. The extent to which some members of the collectives have resigned themselves to these divisions of space and power was reflected in an anonymous justification of the status quo that argued, in phrases as cumbersomely opaque in English as they are in Spanish:

> [W]e aim to go beyond the traditional concepts of museum or commemorative space, privileging the relationship with the community, in pursuing a collective and participatory conception. This means that the memories related to the site involve other groups and sectors of society, whose participation is necessary in order to generate processes of elaboration of those memories and the construction of collective knowledge a constant and always inconclusive dynamic. Therefore, the realisation of the project necessarily meets in the convocation of other social sectors, creating new links and networks which facilitate the process of the recuperation and elaboration of memories.[33]

What had gone wrong since the optimistic days when the O'Higgins Institute finally left the building? Like the equally emblematic National Stadium, the political left had been routed by the Concertación's own interpretative purposes. Bedevilled by internal divisions between its many claimants, the grieving families had been outmanoeuvred. By 2012 it seemed evident that the decade-long negotiations between state and collectives had been settled decisively. The history and

---

32 For Erika Hennings's comment, see Ramona Wadi, 'The right to memory in Chile: An interview with Erika Hennings, President of Londres 38', Upside Down World, 2 May 2002.
33 Cited, María José Perez and Karen Glavic, 'La experiencia de la visita y la visita cómo experiencia: memorias críticas y constructivas', Londres 38 Espacio de Memorias, 2011, p. 2.

politics of memorialisation of Londres 38, reflected so eloquently in the constantly changing signage, pointed to how that state had been able to turn the divisions in the left to its favour.

George Orwell wrote of the Spanish Civil War, 'No one who was there in the months at a time when people still believed in the revolution will ever forget that strange and moving experience'. MIRistas believed in a version of that same revolution that, similarly, failed. Deprived of both physical home and physical memorial, the MIR thereafter took refuge in rehearsing its pride in the stirring ideals and selfless comradeship of a generation prepared to die for its beliefs, a brief flowering of a conviction that the world could be and should be changed by dedicated young people. By 2012, though, that matchless time seemed another universe.[34]

---

34 Orwell to Cyril Connolly, quoted, Valentine Cunningham, *British Writers of the Thirties*, Oxford University Press, Oxford, 1989, p. 422.

Londres 38 with its message of November 2015, 'Break the pact of silence'. On the darker flagstones are inscribed the names of the detained-disappeared believed held here, and their political affiliation.
Source: Photograph by Peter Read, editing Con Boekel.

6

The chosen one: 1367 José Domingo Cañas

In the district of Ñuñoa, 10 kilometres from the CBD of Santiago, stands a former House of Torture known by its street address '1367 José Domingo Cañas'.

Our exploration of the memorialisation of this site turns, far more than any other, on the relationship between the only person known to have been tortured to death within its walls, and the maternal aunt of that victim. She was Lumi Videla Moya and her aunt, Dr Laura Moya Diaz. The museum and display located on the site of what was, before the coup, a substantial suburban house is very largely the product of Laura Moya's unshakeable dedication to the memory of her niece.

This discussion also takes in, for the first time, the Chilean housing estates known as *poblaciones*.[1] Industrial unemployment following the decline of the saltpetre mines after World War Two, then rural unemployment in the 1960s, brought large numbers of unskilled and semi-skilled workers to the capital. Generally they settled in shanty towns (*campamentos*) anywhere there was available land, often enough on the edge of canals, but apt to be washed away during the Andean springwater melt. In answer to the mushrooming urban

---

1   Laura Moya, Ricardo Balladares, Claudia Videla, Akison Bruey, Hervu Lara, Andres Carvajal, Mario Aballay, Marcelo Alvarado, *Tortura en Poblaciones del Gran Santiago (1973–1990)*, Colectivo de Memoria Histórica Corporación José Domingo Cañas, Santiago, 2005, p. 131; see also Jorge Ojeda Frex, 'Las Batallas de La Legua', Alterinfos, 5 June 2008.

slums, President Frei in the late 1960s accelerated a program by which the state resumed or bought sizeable areas near the declining factories to establish officially recognised encampments called *poblaciones*. Here the immigrants were settled with a minimum of state-provided amenities – perhaps half a dozen working taps, street lighting and communal ablutions, even if individual dwellings went unconnected.

Poster, 1367 José Domingo Cañas, featuring Laura Moya Diaz (left) and Lumi Videla Moya (right).
Source: Photograph by Peter Read, editing Con Boekel.

6. THE CHOSEN ONE

The excitement of the anticipated Allende victory, then the Allende social program itself, introduced more positive associations than the drugs and delinquency with which the *poblaciones* had been habitually linked by the Santiago upper classes. For many of the residents, *poblaciones* offered the chance of exciting workers' collectives confidently predicted by Che Guevara. Here was a chance to remake Chilean society in Cuban-style worker-livings. Such hopes and dreams were not, of course, unnoticed by the conservatives. The North American correspondent James Whelan overstated the reputation of *poblaciones* as 'lawless bastions of armed terrorists',[2] but they certainly stood high on the military's hit-list at the moment of the coup. And at the top of that list was the *Población* Nueva Habana (New Havana).

New Havana was established in 1969, and during the Allende years took a decidedly radical direction. Instead of the disorganisation usually associated with the *campamentos*, the ad hoc stop-anywhere settlements, the *poblaciones*, like New Havana, were self-constructed blocks composed of 60 families under a delegate who represented the residents in the directorate, the legislative body for the whole *población*. Above the directorate stood a body of seven officials elected in rotation by universal suffrage. The 'General Assembly' was the body of directors who defined the major projects.[3]

Middle-class Santiagans feared and avoided the *poblaciones*. Allende applauded them while his opponents despised them as seedbeds of Latin American communism, if not a precursor to a new Cuba. Plans were laid to strike at them even earlier than the assault on Allende himself. Very early in the morning of 11 September 1973, two war planes made low-level flights over New Havana; all day helicopters flew about menacingly and at night shone their powerful lights into the *población* dwellings. Troops arrived on the 13th to systematically kick in the doors and seize workers and leaders known to them; during the night, patrols shot their guns into the air to intimidate the residents.[4]

---

2   James R. Whelan, *Out of the Ashes*, Regnery Gateway, Washington, 1989, p. 580.
3   Moya et al., *Tortura en Poblaciones del Gran Santiago*, p. 131.
4   Ibid., evidence of José Moya Paivo, director of the founding group of New Havana, pp. 131–32.

Linking the House of Torture 1367 José Domingo Cañas and the *poblaciones* is the redoubtable figure of the Professor of Psychiatry at the University of Chile, Laura Moya. She had helped to plan and develop the poblaciones, she had applauded and encouraged them, she had worked with their residents, and during the dictatorship, she had suffered with them.

Laura Moya Diaz

A convinced and unreconstructed Marxist, Laura Moya was fond of displaying her hand 'that shook the hand of Fidel [Castro]'. Though positioning herself firmly within the intellectual vanguard of the workers' movement, as a psychiatrist she sought ways to give the community of workers 'tools and capacities to communally confront health issues, including mental health'.[5] Though she published books on 'peoples' doctors' murdered by the regime, the last 15 years of her life were directed almost obsessively at preserving a personal memory of her niece Lumi, the memorialisation of the site where she was tortured and died, and in seeking justice for those who had killed her.

In the 10 years before her death in 2013, Laura Moya wrote four short books. The first, *1367 José Domingo Cañas: An Experience Not To Forget,* related the story of the site and its victims, detailed the history of the centre, the role of the DINA and brief biographies of 42 'Detained Disappeared' known to have spent some time within its walls. The second, *1367 José Domingo Cañas: More Memories,* provided interviews with survivors, more biographical information and future plans for the memorialisation of the site. The victims were presented not in the random order of the first book but now under categories beginning with 'Married People'. So Lumi (and her husband Sergio Perez Molina) came first, as she had in the first book. Moya's third book was most unusual in stressing the relationship between a House of Torture and its local community: *The Repression in the District José Domingo Cañas During the Dictatorship (1973–1990): Memories of the Neighbourhood.* Its epigraph announced the guiding principle

---

5 'Chile: Fallece Laura Moya, ejemplar luchadora de los DDHH' [Laura Moya dies, exemplary fighter for Human Rights], Kaos en la Red, 26 October 2013.

'To incorporate the repression of the suburb in collective memory is the best homage to those who suffered at the hands of the DINA for fighting to make a better world'.

Moya's fourth book was dedicated to Lumi herself: *Lumi Videla Moya: Her Life, Her Struggle, Her Heroic Death*. Very shortly after this labour of love in 2013, her homage complete, Laura Moya died.

There is no doubt that although the people of the nearby *poblaciones* contributed much energy and passion when they climbed over the wire barrier fence of José Domingo Cañas for the first time in 1995, it was Moya's Marxist passion that brought the site to what it is now. Her social connections with the political elite, her understanding of how to work the bureaucracy, her persistence and her considerable wealth very largely saved the site from being turned into a factory. Her dominating personality won her admirers, but not many friends and not a few enemies. At the time of her death, she had driven away many of her former supporters, but acquired others. Her insistence on advancing the particular memorialisation of her niece above the detained-disappeared believed held in Cañas was at times resented, but in the end Laura held the trumps. The third book in the series, on the repression in the whole district, presents a striking 1995 photograph on its front cover. There stands the house in ruins, burnt, and in process of demolition. A man returning after illegal entry jumps back over the gate. The poster signage reads:

> Former Torture Centre 40 Detained Disappeared
> For 21 years we've been after the truth and justice.
> Yesterday terror protected the killers. Today the justice system does the same.
>
> I don't forget. Do you?

A large named photo of Lumi completed the signage outside the house. Did anyone object? It was Laura who had conceived the topic, researched and written the book, paid for the printing and, in all probability, supervised much of the signage on the day of the demonstration.[6]

---

6   Carlos Espinoza, dir. and prod., *Las Luciernagas* [The Glow-worms], DVD, 2006.

Some Chilean left intellectuals, while paying lip-service to the needs and desires of the working classes, can be dismissive of their supposed lack of education or assumed naïveté. Laura Moya, putting herself in the Che Guevara-style intellectual vanguard, perhaps stood among them, out of a sense of *noblesse oblige*. From the time she was first able to enter the site in 2000, she encouraged the participation of the *poblaciones* of the precinct, La Legua and La Victoria, in the memorial; one of the first inscriptions on the dividing wall between the house site and its neighbour was the Cuban slogan 'Always Onwards to Victory'.

A picture of Dr Laura Moya, psychiatrist and intellectual revolutionary, begins to emerge. In her third book on José Domingo Cañas she wrote:

> The act of giving testimony transforms into a relationship between the giver and those who listen and absorb the testimony. In this sense, if we understand the testimony as a construction of memory, we realise that we are confronting many voices of the heard, the lived, the process of the time, which we recognise as a form of truth of a particular past, which in another form reflects the collective.[7]

Through the somewhat turgid prose we hear the voice of one who never ceased to demand structural change, societal reform from the bottom, and was irritated when the search for the truth of what actually happened at José Domingo Cañas in 1974, and punishment of the perpetrators, was sidetracked into contemporary issues of international human rights. The search for truth was, and should be, unending. To allow the wounds to be silenced, she wrote, was to become complicit in impunity. *We cannot live in a city that forgets its history.*[8]

The information of what had occurred could only, in 2000, be drawn from the people themselves. That year Moya founded the candlelit vigils, each candle representing a victim, outside the site every Wednesday night. At that time very little was known about who had been held in José Domingo Cañas or what had happened to them. Passers-by were invited to join the little groups sitting in a semicircle with their candles, round the list of names of the

---

7   Laura Moya, *La Represión en el Barrio José Domingo Cañas Durante la Dictadura (1973–1990): Memoria de los Vecinos*, Fundación 1367 José Domingo Cañas, Santiago, 2013, p. 10.
8   Moya, *La Represión en el Barrio...*, p. 16.

detained-disappeared, on the pavement outside the deserted site. Through many interviews over many months Moya began to systematise and compare the growing dossier. She reflected:

> The majority of passers-by to whom we handed a flier explaining the motive of our meetings gave us suspicious looks on first contact. But after we were there every Wednesday without a single absence for ten years, they came to salute us and came closer. Finally many of them became integrated in these vigils, participating in conversations, showing their satisfaction in the warm and sincere ambience that gave them confidence. It was ringed with candles that faintly lit up the place making them feel more secure. The ambience was certainly between us when the cold forced us to light a big brazier in the centre of the circle around which we gathered. Sometimes a maté or a coffee went round the circle from hand to hand.

A participant, surely another Marxist, drew this second word picture:

> Little Laura and her gang were in circles chatting and a tasty and excited murmur made a spiral, or better still, a black hole of humanity. They told stories and passing by the fire, looked after it. At this time, to me, the story was the meta-story, the circular set-up and the context of seats, candles and bodies/disappeared human beings. The gesture towards human rights was *text and pretext*.[9]

Rather more poetic was a verse dedicated to the 'curious glow-worm' Laurita:

> Your brilliance attracted new glow-worms
> Clearly invading the dark cold nights
> Of winter
> And the hot dusk of summer.[10]

Week by week, month by month, Moya's dossier enlarged. In the darkness she never stopped asking questions. She wanted dates and facts from everyone who came to participate: 'Why are you here?' 'Were you detained in this place?' 'What happened?' 'What else do you remember?' 'Did you speak to anyone also held here?' 'Do you know anyone who was?' 'When?' 'Who?' 'What political party did they belong to?' The chilling picture emerged: DINA trucks would

---

9   Ibid., p. 18.
10 Roberto Castro, 'Luciernaga Curiosa', in Roberto Castro, *Puerto Futuro*, Edición Luciernaga, Santiago, 2007, p. 35.

back into the building during curfew hours while screams resounded into the street. Neighbours well understood what they had to do: talk about the screams and trucks only behind closed doors and windows. Walk past on the other side of the road. Avoid eye contact with anyone connected with the building.[11]

Maria Cristina Lopez Stewart

Moya's first book of her series, *An Experience Not To Forget*, relates that it was the mother of the detained-disappeared Maria Cristina Lopez who first contributed to the mystery of her daughter's disappearance.[12] Maria Cristina was a member of the MIR, arrested at the age of 21 by the DINA in a house in the upper-class suburb of Las Condes. Maria Cristina had dreamed, in her adolescence, of parties and clothes, but during her years as a trainee history teacher, she became more serious in her dedication to the helpless and the poor. Maria, her mother continued, was known as a rebel in college, especially in highlighting the different clothes worn by rich and poor. She dressed down to match the poorer students. On completing her last exams, she asked if she could graduate in the college uniform, as the poor were forced to do, and not in the regulation white dresses that upper-class girls wore: permission refused, she stayed at home. The young idealist used to say that she would not sleep on a night in which a child was homeless. Maria Cristina's zeal intensified when, at about 19, she enrolled at the University of Chile to study history, but spent most of her time in trying to alleviate the lot of the poor in the *poblaciones*; it seemed, to her mother, that her greatest happiness lay in being with them and hanging out in their homes.[13]

After the coup, her hiding place betrayed, the DINA came for her on 22 September 1974. For a month her family heard nothing, before receiving an anonymous message, then a call from Maria Cristina herself, on her birthday, 22 November, telling them she was okay, but unable to say where she was nor even whether she had been detained.

---

11 Espinoza, *Las Luciernagas*.
12 Corporación José Domingo Cañas 1367 [Laura Moya], *Una Experiencia Para No Olvidar*, Corporación José Domingo Cañas, Santiago, 2001.
13 'Maria Cristina Lopez Stewart', in ibid., pp. 41, 57–63. Moya's second volume, *Más Memoria* [More Memories], added that Maria Cristina was always happy, of soft voice and loving smile, a tall and beautiful lady, with skin the colour of honey.

Constantly blindfolded, very probably she did not know that she was being held at José Domingo Cañas. Her health, according to a woman detained with her, began to deteriorate from anaemia exacerbated by the pitiful detainee ration. In all probability she was tortured by beating and electricity to make her reveal the whereabouts of the MIR leader, the charismatic Miguel Enriquez.[14] Though her mother never doubted that she was taken by the DINA, the authorities always denied it, probably to quell the outrage at the disappearance of so many young leftist militants. Nobody knew where she was. Knowing nothing, but suspecting that she might be being held in the better-known detention centre Tres Alamos, Maria Cristina's sister and mother visited it several times a week to be rudely told that nobody was held there by that name.[15] Several survivors remember seeing Maria Cristina in José Domingo Cañas, but nobody has reported seeing her anywhere else. Thus it seems probable, though not certain, that she had died in José Domingo Cañas itself perhaps in late 1974, as a result of malnutrition, anaemia and the effects of torture. Even now, no more is known about her than that Maria Cristina Lopez Stewart is a detained-disappeared.

Whatever the circumstances, in June 1975 the military government published the list of 119 missing militants, mostly members of the MIR, whose bodies had been supposedly discovered in Argentina. The name of Maria Cristina Lopez Stewart was included among them.[16] Several years later, but away from the Cañas vigils, more information about Maria Cristina was coming to light whose ambiguous nature accentuates again the agonisingly fragmentary scraps of information enacted by a policy of 'night and fog'.[17] According to a youthful admirer, Luis Muñoz González, Maria Cristina Lopez immediately following the coup went into hiding and resisted all attempts by her family to persuade her to seek exile. Instead, she threw herself into the resistance. In the months before her detention she asked Luis to

---

14 Whether she did so is another matter. Few MIRistas, for obvious reasons, knew the location of his safe house, and the identity of the betrayer remains uncertain.
15 Corporación José Domingo Cañas 1367 [Laura Moya], *José Domingo Cañas 1367: Más Memoria*, Corporación José Domingo Cañas, Santiago, 2007; 'Caso de los 119, operación Colombo', Exilio Chileno.
16 'Maria Cristina Lopez Stewart', Memoria Viva.
17 'Night and fog' was the policy fostered by the Nazi leader Wilhelm Keitel, who believed it more effective in intimidating the civilian population than publicised executions.

find her a safe house where he could contact her rapidly.[18] His brother Hernán clouded the mystery of her disappearance as late as 2013. He related how, in April 1975, Maria Cristina, looking terrible, very pale and speaking slowly, arrived escorted by DINA troops at his parents' house. They demanded to know the whereabouts of his brother Luis, whom they must have suspected of MIR membership. On being denied, they ransacked the house and threatened to take Hernán away for 'further questioning'. Luis's father was on the point of confessing Luis's whereabouts when Maria Cristina stepped forward and taking him by the hand said, 'Tell them nothing. To resist is the only thing that remains for a proud people'.

Luis Muñoz González did not reveal this curious information publicly until 40 years later, in September 2013. Such were common elements in the life of the detained-disappeared after kidnapping and detention that the candlelight vigils or visits to detention centres could never uncover. If the story is accurate, Maria Cristina was alive and in the hands of DINA five months after it was reasonably assumed that she died. Where had she been? In José Domingo Cañas? Was she being kept alive in the hope of extracting information? Why was she brought to this house? Had she been dragged there in the hope of persuading Hernán to cooperate? Was she killed after this failed attempt, after her heroic advice to reveal nothing? It was only a month later that Maria Cristina's name was published among the 119 left militants who had supposedly fought each other to a fatal standstill in Argentina. The news, though, never reached her sister. Safe in France, racked by the guilt of the survivor, she wrote to Maria Cristina who, unknown to her, had been executed some six years previously:

I am proud of you
Today Cristina, you are a prisoner, a disappeared
I am free and safe
I can speak, I can say whatever I think
I was fearful, Cristina, and abandoned my country and left you there a prisoner
I had to search for you, guiding my steps and my letters
They watched our house
And I escaped
Now I'm in an immensely rich country

---

18   Raúl Caviedes, 'Memoria Historica. Detenidos Desaparecidos. Los Familiares'.

Where there are no *poblaciones*, Cristina!
New friends help us
There is no danger here
Except the immense danger in living securely
Without the constant fear of failing in the task
The work of denouncing your prison
Of [keeping on] meeting more *compañeros* who understand us
To meet new friends who'll support us right now
2500 *compañeros* are prisoners
without trial, without conviction ...[19]

Lumi Videla Moya

On 4 November 1974 the naked, mutilated body of Lumi Videla Moya was thrown over the wall of the Italian Embassy during the hours of curfew. The grotesque and crude attempt to blame the 250 refugees crowding the embassy grounds for killing her in a Marxist orgy soon backfired amidst hostile international publicity.[20] Among all the martyred opponents of the regime Lumi thereafter became, in no small measure thanks to the efforts of Aunt Laura, a larger-than-life cult hero of the Chilean resistance. Her name has become synonymous with the torture centre in which she died.

Laura Moya's last (and posthumous) tribute to her niece, *Lumi Videla Moya: Her Life, Her Struggle, Her Heroic Death*, added to the considerable amount that she had already written.[21] Laura claimed that Lumi's grandmother Livia founded the Chilean Socialist Party (though her name is not mentioned in some accounts of the birth of the party) while all of her family were leftist militants. By adolescence – we can hear the voice of Auntie Laura so clearly here – she was 'stimulated to learn about nature and its dialectics, to observe human behaviour ... to see the characteristics of different social groups to

---

19 Composed in about 1981. Maria Cristina's sister does not name herself; 'Maria Cristina Lopez Stewart', Memoria Viva; see also Lucía Sepúlveda Ruiz, *119 de Nosotros*, Colección Septiembre, LOM, Santiago, 2005, pp. 321–27.
20 'Quienes y por que mataron a Lumi Videla y arrojaron su cuerpo en la Embajada Italiana de Santiago?' [Who killed Lumi Videla and threw her body into the Italian Embassy, and why?], Villa Grimaldi.
21 Corporación José Domingo Cañas [Laura Moya], *Lumi Videla Moya, Su Vida, Su Lucha, Su Muerte Heróica* [Lumi Videla Moya, Her Life, Her Struggle, Her Heroic Death], Corporación José Domingo Cañas, Santiago, 2013.

gradually come to understand the system of domination by which a social minority exploited the larger'. We can read both the atmosphere of her household, and of the 1960s student experience in which everything seemed possible, in a friend's message addressed to her on her 15th birthday wishing her 'a revolutionary salute from a comrade who always has valued you. May all your ideas always triumph and when we are in the Socialist Republic of Chile, may we know how to fulfil our obligations and accomplish our ideals.'[22]

Lumi and her friends continued to take themselves just as seriously in the years before Allende's election. Before leaving secondary school, she had enrolled in the Young Communists in demonstrations against the US role in Vietnam and Cuba. A friend remembered her there as being combative, a hardened warrior, tremendously daring, brave and audacious, who used to shout out slogans 'like a man' because women students were too genteel.[23] But it was not long before, according to Laura, Lumi found 'contradictions' in the thoroughly working-class orientations of its programs. She shifted her allegiance to the party of the revolutionary left-wing intellectual elite, the MIR.

At the University of Chile, like Maria Cristina Lopez Stewart, Lumi threw herself into the leftist politics of the poor. She spent much time at the radical New Havana *población*, where in 1970 she joined a vigilante group taking 'direct justice' (whatever that meant) against alcohol-sellers and brothel-keepers within the precinct.[24] By 1971, she had become head of the 'Political Militant Group' charged with the organisation of the MIR in Santiago.[25] While at university, too, she met Sergio Perez Molina. They married in 1960; in 1970 Lumi bore a son, Dago Emiliano Perez Videla.[26] While Sergio spent the whole of 1972 in Cuba learning the strategy and tactics of an urban revolutionary,[27] Lumi was at the forefront of another MIR initiative, the Revolutionary Workers Front.[28]

---

22 'Mireya', quoted, Moya, *Lumi Videla Moya*, p. 20.
23 Nora Astica, quoted, ibid., p. 25.
24 Moya, *Lumi Videla Moya*, p. 31.
25 'Lumi Videla Moya', *Punto Final*, 19 December 2013.
26 Moya, *Más Memoria*, pp. 34–35.
27 Testimony of Dago Perez Videla, *La Memoria Rebelde*, p. 71.
28 Moya, *Lumi Videla Moya*, p. 33.

From this point Lumi Videla's story is intertwined with that of Sergio. Like all MIRistas (following the edict that MIRistas should not and did not seek exile) the couple went into hiding, and for a year sheltered in a safe house. Following a request made to the clandestine but still hierarchical leadership, the parents stepped back from the struggle for a few months in order to care for Dago Emiliano. But not for long. Aunt Laura revealed a poignant moment during Dago's fourth birthday 'hot chocolate' party, to which the neighbouring kids were invited. Drawing Laura aside, and looking through the window into the distance, Lumi and Sergio told Laura that they had decided to resume the struggle of resistance to the dictatorship. Recognising the risk of torture and death of the child as well as themselves, they asked her to look after him. Thereafter their contacts with Dago were confined to Laura's reassurances, from her own safe house, that the child was safe from DINA persecution and the threat that if the child was found he might well be tortured in front of his parents to force confessions.

No Santiago safe house was really secure. The parents must have known that any wanted leftist, especially MIRista, might be recognised and betrayed, even while walking or cycling in the street. Lumi and Sergio undertook that if one of them were detained, as would be apparent by their failure to return home, then that partner would do their best to hold out against torture for 24 hours in order give the other time to escape. This was exactly what should have happened: spotted walking in Gran Avenida by the informer Marcia Merino Vega, Lumi Videla was detained. She was supposed to be home by 1 pm. By 9 that night Sergio was 'very worried' about her. Inexplicably, he did not take her absence to be the sign that clearly, in retrospect, she had been detained. He remained at home and was himself detained the next morning. Lumi had begun 43 terrible days of detention, and had presumably resisted the first 24 hours of torture within the walls of José Domingo Cañas.

The capture of Sergio Perez Molina shortly afterwards was taken to be a particular coup – as a senior member of the MIR he was savagely tortured to reveal the names and whereabouts of its leadership, especially that of its elusive general secretary Miguel Enriquez.

Lumi's period of detention in José Domingo Cañas is better known than that of any other detainee. One story relates that, comforting a young detainee who had been returned to the holding cell horrifically tortured by electricity, she remarked 'this boy has become a man'. The biographical listing 'Memoria Viva' lists depositions of several people associated with her, including several who saw and talked with her in the house of torture. The online archive reveals that the initial beatings and torture of Sergei failed to extract any information about the MIR leadership.[29] Cañas commandant Contreras resorted to more desperate measures. In the expectation that other MIRistas held in Cañas would be sufficiently overcome by the sight of the tortured Sergio to reveal Enríquez's hideout, several, including Lumi, were brought to him to find him savagely tortured. They were told that medical attention would be sought for him if they revealed the address. Next day the detainees were again brought in to find Sergio in a worse state than before, vomiting blood and with a new bullet wound in his leg. Even when Lumi was removed from his cell, his terrible screams and pleadings to be killed went echoing round the whole building. Later Lumi asked to say goodbye to him, which she was allowed to do for a minute.[30]

Sergio Perez, now very near death, was then driven to one of the DINA's 'clinics', where, according to the infamous torturer Osvaldo Romo Mena, in the sinister Spanish idiomatic phrase 'le dieron duro', 'they gave it to him hard'. It was here that he died. Perez, like Maria Cristina Lopez Stewart, remains officially a 'detained-disappeared'.

At this point the curious personage of Luz Arce Sandoval enters the story. A militant Socialist during the Allende years, Luz Arce was first arrested and tortured in 1974. She consented to act as informer for the DINA, at first to provide names and addresses, later to pose as a detainee in several houses of torture.[31] Yet on finding herself sharing the same cell as Lumi Videla, doubtless having been placed there to report conversation, she seems to have been overwhelmed by the calm and resolute presence of her cellmate. In her book, *The Inferno,* she claims to have confessed to Lumi her role of agent provocateur. Lumi replied, if Arce is to be believed, that she too was trying to curry favour with the guards in order to find out as much as she could, presumably to be revealed later on her hoped-for release. From this distance it seems more likely that the DINA officers were playing with

---

29 'Lumi Videla Moya', Memoria Viva.
30 'Videla Moya, Lumi', Centro de Estudios Miguel Enriquez.
31 'Lumi Videla Moya', Memoria Viva.

6. THE CHOSEN ONE

Lumi to gain information, rather than the reverse. Whatever the truth, Luz replied, 'Lumi, don't trust any of them. It is one thing for any one of them not to beat you and give you a cigarette, and another thing altogether for them do something for you, something that would go against the DINA.' In an affecting moment, perhaps exaggerated in the light of Luz Arce's later confession and public contrition, the terrifying circumstances brought the two women closer. Lumi told her companion:

> You're from the Socialist party and I'm from the MIR. We are both trying to do something. I realise that we can't both win. We are doing two very different things. I can't do anything else. I've thought about it and I can't.

Luz replied, 'Lumi, you're acting with a short-term goal. And you'll die whether you achieve it or not. You're committing suicide.'

On their last meeting, when Luz Arce was suffering from fever, Lumi Videla insisted that she swap her own, elegant brown leather jacket for Luz Arces's miserable and holey knitted sweater. *When we aren't together any more, it will be like a hug from a friend.* She was already destined for terrible torture and death within a few days. One authority represents the moment as Luz Arce seeking 'a kind of absolution from a woman destined for martyrdom'. Whatever the truth, Luz Arce says that she received the first intimation of the death of her new-found soulmate when she saw two of the guards rolling dice as to who would get her clothes.[32]

It was not until 2001 that it was officially confirmed that Lumi had been asphyxiated, perhaps even accidentally, to stifle her screams. Her body had been thrown over the embassy wall as a reprisal for an attack on a DINA agent shortly before, and to punish the Italian ambassador for taking in so many refugees.[33] Laura Moya claimed that such was the international revulsion at the DINA's actions that not

---

32   Luz Arce, *The Inferno: A Story of Survival and Terror in Chile,* tr. Stacey Alba Skar, University of Wisconsin Press, London, 1984; see also Jean Franco, foreword to *Luz Arce and Pinochet's Chile,* p. xiv.
33   Jorge Escalante, 'Asesinato de Lumi Videla: El "Guatón" Romo contó que el general Garín le pagó por su silencio' [Murder of Lumi Videla: 'Pot Belly' Romo reveals that General Garin paid him for his silence], *La Nación,* 25 July 2007.

only was torture within Cañas reduced, but was instrumental in the abolition of the DINA the following year, to be replaced with a new, though similar organisation, the CNI.[34]

Removed from the embassy, Lumi Videla's body was hurriedly buried in a family tomb, and in no little danger to the mourners. Flowers arrived anonymously, a few friends arrived in cars without identifying licence plates. In 2004 Lumi was reburied, the cortège halting while tributes were paid at the famous Memorial to Victims of the Dictatorship in the General Cemetery, some 200 metres from Patio 29. Only two people were required to carry the box containing her bones. They were Lumi's aunt Laura and her son Dago. *You left dead. Now you return alive.*

Legal proceedings began in 2006, initiated by Laura Moya and Dago Videla. In 2007 the Court found that Lumi had been murdered, and that Sergio Perez Molina had been kidnapped by DINA officials, which constituted a crime against their human rights. For the murder of Lumi Videla, Manuel Contreras received a sentence of 15 years and a day, Krassnoff Martchenko received 10 years and a day, and the officer who held her down while she suffocated, Willeke Floel, five years.[35]

Another sign of passing times were the reflections of Dago Perez Videla, the little boy who only saw his parents together for a brief four years before both were captured and tortured to death. On the 40th anniversary of her death, he tried to resolve his emotions in broken phrases that seem just a little wistful:

> I want to thank my mother Lumi Videla and my father Sergio Pérez, because thanks to them I have looked straight, always hold my head high to carry a blazing heart, and having the strength to demand justice and follow their lead. They gave me the best example that a son can follow and I want to thank them the best example that a son could have, and I give thanks to them in front of all your compañeros.[36]

---

34 The new organisation, founded in 1977, was the CNI, the more euphemistically named 'National Information Centre'; interview Laura Moya by Marivic Wyndham, August 2013; Whelan, *Out of the Ashes*, p. 736.
35 Moya, *Más Memoria*, pp. 36–37; see also Escalante, 'Asesinato de Lumi Videla' [Murder of Lumi Videla…].
36 Quiero agradecer a mi madre Lumi Videla y a mi padre Sergio Pérez, porque gracias a ellos he podido mirar de frente y tener siempre la frente en alto, tener un corazón ardiendo y tener la fortaleza para pedir justicia y para poder seguir su camino, ellos me dieron el mayor ejemplo que un hijo puede tener y yo tengo que agradecérselos delante de todos sus compañeros.

***

Meanwhile, a law of 1990 provided that houses seized by the military should be returned to their proper owners. The empty house soon was reoccupied by drug dealers and petty criminals; some of the homeless saw the ghosts of the disappeared. Tiles cracked, a window broke, the garden went wild. Neighbours, some concerned about the deterioration, souvenired bits and pieces and wondered how the decay could be stopped.[37] Some time in 1999, workmen paid by the owner of the toy store next door arrived to begin the destruction of Casa Domingo Cañas 1367. Within a week the site was empty, the pool filled in, the door constructed by the DINA to allow secret ingress from the house next door was blocked, and a steel fence erected outside.

Since Lumi's death Laura Moya had never once visited the site, nor barely mentioned her niece. The destruction of the House of Torture seemed to have galvanised her into active memorialisation. From 2000 she became, as she put it, 'la persona indicada'– the chosen one. In December she began the foundation that would, more than a decade later, in part fulfil her vision of what she termed a collective memorial – an evocation designed to 'disturb the present time through the collective actions lived by the people in the past'.[38] The Wednesday evening vigils began. On behalf of the foundation she began involved negotiations with several ministries to acquire the site and establish a House of Memory. Under her direction, students from Ñuñoa produced a maquette of a remarkably ambitious precinct incorporating not only 1367, but the blocks each side. A splendid five-storey building on the left, Laura explained, would be for 'accommodation', but who would live there, or who would pay for it, was far from clear. Despite the misplaced optimism there came some tangible successes.[39] In 2002 the Cañas site, after vigorous lobbying, was named a National Historic Monument. At least the site could no longer be built over nor demolished by the toy shop owner. In 2006, in answer to Laura Moya's ceaseless lobbying, several government departments agreed to acquire the site, construct the House of Memory and ultimately cede ownership to the corporation. The House of Memory itself, though far from Laura Moya's hopes, was opened in April 2010.

---

37   Espinoza, *Las Luciernagas*.
38   Moya, *Memoria de los Vecinos*, p. 69.
39   Moya, *Más Memoria*, pp. 105–7.

In what was probably her last interview before her death, Laura Moya confessed to a little disillusionment. The structural changes to society that she, as a dialectical materialist expected, had not occurred. Nor was anyone even demanding them any more. Truth and justice for the detained-disappeared seemed as far away as ever. Young people seemed too sceptical to take part in political protest, and those involved seemed less dedicated to defending the rights of the working peoples. They were militant for a while, then went off to pursue their own desires. Human rights? How could there be talk of human rights when classes were still not equal. Without drivers like 'justice' and 'truth' the future was empty. The local communities, which had done so much to protect the Cañas site even before Laura was involved, were less interested than they had once been; the neighbourhood was becoming more middle class. She had donated her Marxist-inspired library to the people, and sold her magnificent architect-designed home in Las Condes to fund early construction, and jumped in whenever money was needed urgently; but the state had not fulfilled its share of the contract. Her last words recorded in this interview concerned how she saw the future: 'I see [it] as very grey. I won't say black.' Her last words, after turning off the recorder were, 'You know, I am totally the boss of this place. Just me.'[40]

What remains today of Laura Moya Diaz's vision of the complex she dreamed of we will consider in the final chapter. At this point, we turn to 2006 after the House of Torture itself had been destroyed, the grounds desolate and dusty, not even locked any more. The presence of Laura Moya is already everywhere, but does not yet overwhelm the voice of the *poblaciones*. Anyone can do 'the tour' just by entering the unlocked gate and walking about. Though the walls on each side carry much signage and political exhortation, the principal space where stood the house, its garden and swimming pool is barren, neglected and overgrown and depressing.

---

40 Laura Moya, interview, 2012.

6. THE CHOSEN ONE

The tour, 2006

In front, between the footpath and the road, stands a monument listing the names of the 42 detained-disappeared. The name of Lumi Videla, politically executed, is not, of course, among them, she's on the more prominent other side. Carved thus on the side facing the road is the inscription:

> In this House, José Domingo Cañas 1367, in the year 1974 during the Dictatorship 1973–1990, 42 compañeros became Detained Disappeared.
>
> And murdered under torture
>
> Lumi Videla M.

Lumi Videla Moya's name is the only one to appear on this side of the memorial stone at José Domingo Cañas. The names of others believed held here but who may have been killed elsewhere are on the other side, facing the pavement.
Source: Photograph by Peter Read, editing Con Boekel.

On the right-hand side, the dividing stone wall between the site and its neighbour, is painted an arresting mural of four naked men and women suspended, in obvious agony, by ropes tied to their hands. The protruding, unnaturally wide rib cages and the elevated position of the women's breasts on their bodies suggest that this depiction is by no means imagined. Some years after production, apparently on request by one or two neighbours, the genitals of the figures were painted over with loincloths as well as the women's faces. The painting is now restored, but that first urgency to communicate something truly terrible is no longer evident. Beside the depiction are the words:

> They murder the flesh
> But not the idea

On a neighbouring wall is a proud mural painted by the *población* 'La Victoria' depicting women, men and children waving or bearing arms and flags. It reads:

> For You. Always Were Are and Will Be (*Población* La Victoria).

Another nearby painting depicts two arms emerging from a pool into which a stream flows. On it are inscribed the words:

> The fallen...
> Eternal springs of life

An unsourced plaque:

> And if on the other hand
> they were to survive
> in the truth
> of a fellow man
> in the broken voice
> of a spokesman
> of the people

The most poignant and poetic of the markers is a poem by the Uruguayan leftist exile poet Mario Benedetti:

> Then if they return as birds
> To perch once again
> On the ruins of the future
> As a good omen
> To meditate on the earth
> And its divisions.
>
> (Tr. Paula González Dolan)

6. THE CHOSEN ONE

Bureaucratically destroyed signage, José Domingo Cañas. Originally the message read, 'Here were committed the/Most ferocious violations/Of human dignity/For this reason we demand/JUSTICE AND PUNISHMENT'.
Source: Photograph by Peter Read, editing Con Boekel.

The last and most visible words painted on the wall on the left, and opposite the graphic images of the suspended detainees, are inscribed by the people of La Legua.[41]

> Here were committed the
> Most ferocious violations
> Of human dignity
> For this reason we demand
> JUSTICE AND PUNISHMENT

It is signed 'Brigada Pedro Rojas. [*Población*] La Legua'.[42]

The voices of the *poblaciones* were not entirely broken by the coup. We will find no stronger public statement by onsite victims of the regime in all of Chile.

---

41 'La Legua', Wikipedia.
42 La Legua is another of the *poblaciones* that, like La Victoria, has contributed to the signage of Cañas. It was the first of the *poblaciones* to be created, in 1947, following the closure of several saltpetre mines. The allusion to 'Brigade' may allude to a brigade dedicated to a particular purpose commonly formed within the Chilean Socialist Party.

7
A garden of horror or a park of peace: Villa Grimaldi

Jacqueline Paulette Drouilly Yurich lived with her family in Temuco, southern Chile, for much of her short life. Hers was a comfortable, middle-class family that followed a life of sensibility and poise. French as well as Spanish was spoken at home. Her father was a member of the Socialist Party, her mother rejoiced in graceful soirées.

In 1971, in what was to prove a fatal act, Jacqueline joined the MIR in part through the encouragement of her boyfriend, later husband, Marcelo Salinas Eytel. Her younger sister believes that her heart was never quite in the cause. In 1973 she returned to university and resigned from the party. She did not realise that in the eyes of the security forces, the DINA, nobody ever resigned from the MIR but remained a dangerous suspect forever.

During 1974, while still at school, Jacqueline rented a room that she shared with Marcelo and a friend. Their mother Norma Yurich recalls:

> On August 2, 1974, she married Marcelo Salinas Eytel at the Civil Registry in Ñuñoa. Soon after they moved to Decombe 1191, occupying the second floor, which had its own entrance. The house belonged to a fellow social work student. Five days before her arrest, my husband and I visited and had dinner with them. At 6 pm we returned to Temuco. That was the last time we saw them.

> On October 30, 1974, close to midnight as she was completing an assignment for school in the first floor of her classmate's house ... men dressed as civilians arrived in two vehicles and began asking for Marcelo. She told them he was not there, that he would arrive soon and that she was his wife. They then proceeded to interrogate her, roughly forced her to the second floor, harassing and hitting her and committing every sort of abuse to obtain the whereabouts of her husband ... After barely putting on a wool coat and hat, they threw her in one of the vehicles and told the people in the house that they were taking my daughter as a HOSTAGE until they had my son-in-law 'if he arrives' (it was already past curfew).[1]

Jacqueline's sister Michele, then in her early teens, shudders at the memory of that night, 30 October 1974, when at about 10.15 pm the DINA burst in looking for Marcelo. Identifying Jacqueline, they dragged her upstairs and ransacked her room while searching for evidence of party connection. In the bedlam, at 14 minutes to 11, Jacqueline's alarm clock fell to the floor and smashed. Today the clock and the shards of its glass face are among Michele's most treasured possessions.

Within days Michele's father escaped to Algeria, taking Michele with him. Michele, deeply traumatised, or as she puts it, in 'a neurosis of anguish', was deeply unhappy in Algeria. Two years later she had to travel to Spain to renew her passport, but unknown to her, militant exiles had established themselves in her country of refuge. Francoist Spain was all too willing to comply with Pinochet's request to deny any Chilean further refuge. Michele crossed to France where she sought asylum and remained until 1993.

---

1   'Jacqueline Paulette Drouilly Yurich', Memoria Viva; 'Jacqueline Paulette Drouilly Yurich', Las Mujeres de Villa Grimaldi, 19 May 2007; Arturo Alejandro Muñoz, '¿Quién asesinó a Jacqueline Drouilly?' [Who murdered Jacqueline Drouilly?].

7. A GARDEN OF HORROR OR A PARK OF PEACE

Michele Drouilly Yurich.
Source: Photograph by Peter Read, editing Con Boekel.

Since then, like others mourning a detained-disappeared family member, the family continues to mark Jacqueline's absence not on the unknown day in which she was murdered, but on the day she was disappeared. Today they still do not know where she died, nor if she was pregnant at the time of her death.[2] All they know is that she was held progressively in Tres Alamos, José Domingo Cañas and finally in the best-known site of all the Chilean sites of torture, extermination and disappearance: Villa Grimaldi.

***

Villa Grimaldi is the most infamous, nationally and internationally, of all the Chilean sites of torture, extermination and disappearance. It was the first such site to be rescued for memorialisation, then held at arm's length from government interference. Its supporters formed the earliest, best organised and most closely community-controlled collective so as to make Villa Grimaldi the first such site in Chile to be

---

2   Paz Rojas, María Inés Muñoz, María Luisa Ortiz, Viviana Uribe, in *Todas Ibamos a Ser Reinas* [We were all to be Queens], Colección Septiembre, Santiago, 2002, p. 13, maintain that Jacqueline was three months pregnant at the time she was disappeared, but not all of the family agree.

recognised as an International Museum of Conscience.³ The display and the Park of Peace is the only one to have retained any hard-won degree of independence, and the only one to enter a second and different phase of self-presentation. It was the first site in which serious alternative models of memorialisation were debated and acted upon by survivors and their families. It is still the only Santiago Site of Conscience capable of accommodating a large gathering of survivors or mourners.⁴ For a time it seemed that it might become *the* national archetypal site-memorial. Theorists of national culture, national reconciliation, public history, public culture, visual communication, torture, semiotics, feminism, dark tourism, representation and sociology have all found fertile ground here for discursive exposition, through site visits, theses, books, articles, symposia, seminars and films.⁵ The 'Corporation Park of Peace Villa Grimaldi' itself has produced dozens of publications, films and pamphlets and maintains an archive and oral history library.⁶ Perhaps more academic and social comment has been focused on the Villa's Park of Peace than on all other Chilean Sites of Conscience put together. It was here that from 1974 some 4,500 persons were detained and tortured, and where at least 229 were murdered or disappeared.⁷ To the tortures of beatings and electrocution, already familiar to detainees transferred to the villa,

---

3   'We are sites, individuals, and initiatives activating the power of places of memory to engage the public in connecting past and present in order to envision and shape a more just and humane future.' www.sitesofconscience.org/members/.

4   Carolina Aguilera and Gonzalo Caceres, 'Signs of state terrorism in post-authoritarian Santiago: Memories and memorialization in Chile', *Dissidences, Hispanic Journal of Theory and Criticism* 4(8), article 7 of digitalcommons.bowdin.edu/dissidences.

5   Site visits: Nelly Richard, 'Sitios de la memoria: Vaciamiento del recuerdo', *Revista de Crítica Cultural* 23, 2001; Mario I. Aguilar, 'El Muro de Los Nombres de Villa Grimaldi: Exploraciones sobre la memoria, el silencio y la voz de la historia', *European Review of Latin American and Caribbean Studies / Revista Europea de Estudios Latinoamericanos y del Caribe*, no. 69, October 2000, 81–88; 'Experta norteamericana Katherine Hite visitó Villa Grimaldi', Villa Grimaldi; Thomas Larsen (transcript), 'The Anatomy of Torture – Villa Grimaldi', *New Letters* 74(1), Fall 2007–08.

Films: Germán Liñero, *El Muro de los Nombres* [The Wall of Names], 1999; Quique Cruz, *Archaeology of Memory*, 2014; Carmen Rojas, *Memorias de una MIRista* [Memories of a MIRista], edición mimeografiada, Jose Miguel Bravo, Santiago, 1995.

Oral history: Mario Garcés, 'Archivo y Memoria. La Experiencia de Archivo Oral de Villa Grimaldi', *Cuadernos de Trabajo Educativos* 3(VI), n.d., c. 2010, n.p.

6   For example, National Monuments Council, *Parque por la Paz Villa Grimaldi*, documentary, n.d., c. 2006.

7   Villa Grimaldi, villagrimaldi.cl/victimas, accessed 13 May 2013.

was added a new method of detention. They were jammed, sometimes four at a time, into tiny cells constructed in a wooden tower standing near the swimming pool at the rear of the site.

In deep and unresolved mourning for Jacqueline, Michele was from 1993 a member of the collective seeking to preserve the site, and for more than a decade threw her formidable efforts into the prolonged and tense debate as to what should be memorialised within the site, and how, and by whom. She insisted that the lives of the victims before they were brought to Villa Grimaldi should be revered, held as precious to the educational program or, indeed, to the story of what happened to them afterwards. Today, though unacknowledged by name, her mark on the Park of Peace is profound.

***

Villa Grimaldi really was a villa constructed by an aristocratic family in the nineteenth century on the eastern edge of the city, so far out that, even in the 1960s in the heyday of American westerns, it was known to taxi drivers as 'western town'. Famous or notorious for its imported Greek columns and Carrara marble, by the 1960s weekends at the villa had become spacious languorous afternoons for Santiago's literary classes, poetry, good food, red wine and music amidst surroundings inevitably matched in purple prose.

> This capricious Mirror of Water, one of the three which exists in the Villa, holds in its centre the Cornetín of Fontainebleau, from which they say on nights of the full moon comes forth the music of dreams. Created in bronze and iron, no one can describe its beauty.[8]

In 1974 the DINA acquired the building, it is alleged, by arresting the daughter of the owner and holding her in captivity until the title deeds were made over to them. Installed, DINA kept the principal building for administration but destroyed most of the garden while constructing wooden prison huts and converting the water tower into tiny confinement cells reserved for those regarded as most dangerous. The Italian marble and the Greek columns disappeared and have

---

8   'Villa Grimaldi, Historia y Características de las Grandes Mansiones', tourist brochure, n.d., c. 1960.

not been seen again.⁹ Vacating the site in 1978, the successors of the DINA, the CNI, began seeking ways to conceal evidence of the crimes committed there. Seizing the moment, the last commander of Cuartel Terranova, as the DINA had renamed the villa, began proceedings to purchase the estate as a profitable housing precinct. In 1987 a section of the press, human rights organisations and local supporters, survivors and mourners managed to prevent the sale to save the site.¹⁰ Too late: by the time it had become the property of the state, almost all the buildings had been razed. In 1991, just a year after the transition to democracy, the Rettig Report recommended the creation of public memorials and parks to honour the victims of the dictatorship. In 1993 the moderate Aylwin Government, the first elected government after the transition to democracy, was seeking ways to placate the left without antagonising the right. Funding the restoration of the precinct and the erection of a wall of memory answered both Rettig's recommendation and practical politics.¹¹

Furious debates, neatly encapsulated in Spanish as 'polémicas intensas', centred on the kind of memorial the precinct should become.¹² The torture survivor Pedro Matta recalled the positions:

> The group was divided in their opinions: part of the group wanted to rebuild the former torture centre as it was during the time of its functioning (which proved to be impossible as there was not enough funding to do that); another part wanted to demolish everything that remained there and build a beautiful park to the memory of those who disappeared or were killed at the site, and finally, another group, in which I counted myself, proposed that all the artefacts and buildings

---

9   Jorge Escalante, Nancy Guzmán, Javier Rebolledo, Pedro Vega, *Los Crímenes que Estremecieron a Chile* [The Crimes that Shook Chile], CEIBO Ediciones, Santiago, 2013, p. 156.
10   Unusually in Santiago, a leading force in demanding recognition of the site was a local citizens' group, La Asamblea Permanente por los Derechos Humanos de Peñalolén y La Reina [The Permanent Assembly for Human Rights of Peñalolen and La Reina]; Macarena Gómez-Barris, *Where Memory Dwells: Culture and State Violence in Chile*, University of California Press, Berkeley and Los Angeles, 2009, p. 51.
11   'Report of the National Commission for Truth and Reconciliation' ('Rettig Report'), 1991; Victoria Baxter, 'Civil Society Promotion of Truth, Justice and Reconciliation: Villa Grimaldi', *Peace and Change* 30(1), 2005, p. 127; Stern, *Reckoning with Pinochet*, pp. 169–71.
12   Michael Lazzara, 'Tres recorridos de Villa Grimaldi', in Elizabeth Jelin and Victoria Langland, eds, *Monumentos, Memoriales y Marcas Territoriales*, Siglo Veintiuno, Madrid, 2003, cited by Gilda Waldman, 'La "culta de la memoria": problemas y reflexiones', *Politica y Cultura*, no. 26, 2006, p. 5; Katrien Klep, 'Tracing collective memory: Chilean truth commissions and memorial site', *Memory Studies* 5(3), 262–63.

that were not destroyed by the dictatorship should be preserved for the memory of this country and a park should be built round them. This was the proposition that was hammered out.[13]

The unexpressed agenda of the government was assumed, as later turned out to be the case at Londres 38, to homogenise memories, to hold any discussion of those responsible to the broadest terms, to neutralise the horrors of the site, to minimise both the influence and funding of the Cuban Government, and to recast the site as a springboard of national reconciliation.[14] The strength of feeling against the latter can be felt, even a decade later, in the words of Viviana Diaz, executive secretary of the Group of Families of Detained-Disappeared:

> [T]ime has passed, but the violations of human rights are still an inexcusable aberration; the truth of the deeds has always been here. Those of us who lived the terrible experience needed to claim these spaces, first to convince and later to sensitize our own compatriots that were confronting a situation never seen before, that people after detention, disappeared. Many did not want to know, others not even want to find out ... [We want] a society that does not mortgage justice for fear of powerful factions, a society which dares to look us in the eyes and whose authority gives us, at the least, the audiences which we seek. A society which does not believe that all that is written in the Rettig Report is the culmination of all the searches and which now leads us towards a reconciled society.[15]

Memories, the Corporation of the Villa Grimaldi Peace Park insisted, should be personalised and precise. Osvaldo Torres, a member of the corporation, argued passionately against what was taken to be the state agenda:

---

13 Matta in Baxter, 'Civil society promotion of truth, justice and reconciliation', p. 129.
14 Signage formerly displayed (2008) at Villa Grimaldi referred to the Cuban Government's financial assistance in establishing the Park of Peace.
15 'El tiempo ha transcurrido, pero las violaciones a los derechos humanos siguen siendo una aberración inexcusable; la verdad de los hechos siempre ha estado aquí. Quienes vimos la terrible experiencia tuvimos que ganar los espacios, primero para convencer y luego sensibilizar a nuestros propios compatriotas de que estábamos frente a una situación nunca antes vista ... [Lo que decimos es una] sociedad que no hipoteque la justicia por miedo de los poderes fácticos. Una sociedad que se atreva a mirarnos los ojos y cuyas autoridades nos otorguen, al menos, las audiencias que solicitamos. Una sociedad que no crea que todo lo escrito en el Informe Rettig es la culminación de las búsquedas y que ahora caminamos hacia una sociedad reconciliada'; Viviana Diaz, 'Chilean society of today in the light of human rights violations in the past', in *A Museum in Villa Grimaldi: Space for Memory and Education in Human Rights*, International Seminar, August 2005, Corporación Parque por La Paz Villa Grimaldi, Municipalidad de Peñalolén, Santiago, n.d., c. 2006, pp. 23, 25.

> [A] museum of memory and human rights is of a different nature. The memory is ours, the testimonies are ours, the multiplicity of interpretations flow through our communication channels, different types of schools and family chats. In this sense it is not a museum of the republic which sets out epic lectures on the construction of representative democracy, but rather a piece of history which contains unshakeable truths and various interpretations.[16]

Clear enough; but very frequently, in the next decade, the rights to express the 'various interpretations' would overshadow the meaning of the 'unshakeable truths' themselves.

Throughout the planning of 1992–94 ran the constant themes of trauma, resentment, anger, frustration, nightmares and agony of those most closely associated with the Villa's Pinochet years. What should be displayed? How should the horrific events they had suffered be presented, if at all? Initially, all the guides were to be survivors, on the understanding that they would limit the accounts of what they and other detainees had suffered to generalities.

In this way, and amidst much controversy, Villa Grimaldi was by 1995 becoming a haven of peace, tranquillity and reflection: rolling lawns, a fountain, flower beds and a plaza open to concerts and plays would gesture towards the beautiful garden that Villa Grimaldi once had been. A facsimile wooden tower, from which detainees could hear the shrieking of the guards' children in the pool, would be rebuilt. A 2-metre model would reproduce the proportions of the original villa, later the headquarters of Cuartel Terranova. Among the few objects to survive the scorched-earth CNI destruction were the pool itself, a small shed nearby once used for manufacturing fake documentation, the rose garden and a huge Argentinian pampas tree, an ombú. None of them, however, could ever symbolise tranquillity, for each bore particularly anguished memories. A young man had been drowned in the pool and, when empty, a dozen people had been crammed into it and covered with blankets during an international inspection. Detainees squeezed into the tower could smell the roses; and a guard had been beaten to death hanging from the ombú. But amidst the internal dissent, one principle remained firm: for all its financial support, the state must

---

16   Osvaldo Torres, in *A Museum in Villa Grimaldi: Space for Memory and Education in Human Rights*, International Seminar, August 2005, Corporación Parque por La Paz Villa Grimaldi, Muncipalidad de Peñalolén, Santiago, n.d., c. 2006, p. 132.

be kept away. When, in 1998, the government officials learned that they were not to be admitted to the opening ceremony for the Wall of Memory – which the state itself had paid for – they sent in a truck to carry away all the support they had set up the day before – chairs, dais, public address system, even the refreshments. 'But you can keep the carnations, fellers.'[17]

From within the corporation, almost every aspect of the planned design continued to be challenged. Yes, the destroyed tower would be rebuilt. But surely, asked the critics, this was inauthentic. Unsupervised children might frolic about and tourists use it just as a good viewpoint for photographs.[18] Similarly, a solid line connecting the former detainee entrance to the rebuilt tower, intersected by a second line connecting the new entrance way to the Wall of Memory, was designed to form a cross signifying 'Nunca +', a graffitist's abbreviation for 'Nunca Más' (Never Again).[19] But critics again asked: might the cross so formed be mistaken for a Christian cross, or worse, imply or encourage reconciliation between victims and perpetrators?[20] Good intentions are ever apt to misinterpretation. In West Germany in 1992, a sculpture of a grieving mother nursing her dead son was unveiled as a crucial element of the Central Memorial for the Victims of War and Tyranny. Officially it signified that death erased all differences, but to some it suggested the possibility of honouring German soldiers in the same place as Holocaust victims. Confronted with the prospect, in 1993, of adding a reconstructed watch-tower to a section of the Berlin Wall, German critics called it Disneyland.[21]

Joining the discussion in 1993, Michele Drouilly could see the force of the arguments to find out the truth: in case any murdered detainee had been buried near the brick front wall of the precinct, she thought it best to excavate it to find out, even if it meant its destruction. She also understood the museological significance of the original structures and disapproved of later changes. Building the concert and convocation area she thought a mistake because it required the destruction of one

---

17 Roberto Merino, guided tour, 2008.
18 The predictions were noted by the authors on several tours, and by Gómez-Barris, *Where Memory Dwells*, p. 53.
19 Ibid., p. 62.
20 Rodrigo Artegabeitía, 'Corporación Parque por la Paz Villa Grimaldi: una deuda con nosotros mismos' [A debt to ourselves], Ministerio de la Vivienda, Santiago, 1997, cited by Waldman, p. 5.
21 Knischewski and Spittler, 'Competing pasts', pp. 168, 175.

recently constructed arm of the 'Nunca Más'. Behind the modern bathrooms, someone had unearthed a plaque erected in the early 1990s containing a very incomplete list of the detained-disappeared. It was thought to be out of date rubbish. Out it went. A radio communications tower had once stood above the detainees' entrance. Out that went too. 'The trouble is, we Chileans are such amnesiacs.' The curatorial committee affirmed the decision to erase any remaining evidence of the Pinochet past, not least because the corporation wished to create a Park for Peace, which preservation of the remains of the tower was seen to work against.[22] Within weeks even its tiled floor had vanished. Yet 10 years later, the discovery of the grand stairway used by the CNI to enter their old headquarters was hailed as the most significant discovery of all the artefacts remaining from the time.

Positions polarised further after the park was formally opened in 1997. Photographs showed the much-respected Father Aldunate leading the procession through huge piles of concrete, rubble and waist-high weeds.[23] The tensions between the most basic issues of public memorialisation continued to bubble. The guide Roberto Merino Jorquera in 2008 summarised the three dominant views as those supporting either the reality of blindfolds and the *parrilla*, or a park of peace and beauty, or an invitation to civil society to participate in new plans for the villa including a children's play area and a football field![24] Corporation members were – and are – weighing the relative values of memory, memorialisation and education to ensure the safe future of Chilean society, the kind of emotions they wanted aroused in visitors, how to deliver justice to the victims, as an international demonstration of what Chileans had learned from the dictatorship, as a continued investigation of the past as suggested by the Rettig Report, as a reaffirmation of the values of life and peace fundamental to Chilean society, as emblem of hope, or as artistic statement![25]

---

22 Mario Aguilar, 'The ethnography of the Villa Grimaldi in Pinochet's Chile: From public landscape to secret detention centre, 1973–1980', paper presented at the Latin American Studies Association conference, Dallas, Texas, 27–29 March 1973; cited Gómez-Barris, *Where Memory Dwells*, p. 68.
23 Discussion by writers and speakers in Dante Donoso and Coral Pey, eds, *Villa Grimaldi. Un Parque por La Paz*, Asamblea Permanente por los Derechos Humanos, Santiago, 1996.
24 Roberto Merino Jorquera, recorded guided tour of Villa Grimaldi, November 2008, video by authors.
25 Discussion by writers and speakers in Donoso and Coral, *Villa Grimaldi*, 1996.

Roberto Matta, who had summarised the quadrants of opinion back in 1997, believed that the interests of reconciliation slid all too easily into self-censorship among the tour guides. In 2000, amidst disapproval of some other members of the Corporation of the Villa Grimaldi Peace Park, he devised a tour as both guide and author that firmly placed him among those wishing to present the blindfold and the *parrilla* in their full horror.

The first tour, 2000

Matta's tour began with a statement of condemnation of the state's efforts at reconciliation:

> From the time of the Pinochet dictatorship, with its ironclad policy of cancelling freedom of the press, by putting into effect a brutal censorship in the name of 'Christian Civilization' or the 'Occidental Way of Life', there has existed a simultaneous and parallel effort of many people to ... cover over the crimes committed over a seventeen year period, to the years of the Political Transition, during which several regimes have constantly reminded the citizenry of this country of the need to 'forgive and forget', and to 'look ahead and not back'.[26]

After showing his visitors the position of the administrative headquarters and the entrance gate, Matta led them to the detainee point-of-arrival in words very far from tranquillity, meditation or forgiveness. One such visitor was Diana Taylor, teacher of Performance Studies and Spanish at New York University. She noticed that at the start Matta spoke only in the third person, kept his eyes downcast and his emotions restrained. Matta began:

> Agents of DINA kidnapped people off the streets and from their homes, work, and schools ... On being arrested, the person was pushed into the back of the truck and forced to lie down as three agents climbed in. While one pointed a machine gun at the prisoner, another fastened the canvas cover [of the light truck] shut, while the third quickly pulled the victim's wrists behind and tied them and then the ankles. The eyes were taped shut and a blindfold tied tightly. On the ride to Villa Grimaldi, the victim endured the 'softening' during which they were punched and kicked. Hard blows were aimed at the solar plexus

---

26 Pedro Alejandro Matta, 'A Walk Through a 20th Century Torture Centre Villa Grimaldi, Santiago de Chile. A Visitor's Guide' (written in English), 2000.

of the male and the breasts of the female. Kicks went everywhere. Stopping inside the gate of Villa Grimaldi and in view of the main house, the canvas of the truck was opened and the victim pushed out, falling to the ground. With ankles untied, the blindfolded victim was made to stand for the 'welcoming committee', in which six or eight agents punched and kicked him or her round the circle and into semi-consciousness, then to be dragged to the first session of torture. It happened to thousands where you now stand.[27]

Proceeding anticlockwise from the main gate, Matta's next point was 30 metres to the right:

Here the torture began at this place of the first *parrilla* (grill). In a shack with an iron bedstead, a desk with a tape recorder, a chair, and an electric shock device, the victim, still blindfolded but with hands free, was ordered to undress. Clothes were torn from the resisters. Forced to lie naked, the victim was tied to the bedstead with legs apart and arms at the sides. Electric shocks were then administered to the genitals and other parts of the body with increasing intensity, frequency and duration. Between the applications of electricity, the group of four to six torturers barked questions about the victim's activities and those of friends and relatives. The session could continue for two to three hours but seldom longer, because human resistance has its limits.[28]

Taylor observed how, several minutes into the tour, Matta began to re-enact the scenes he was describing. The personal pronouns changed from third to first, the emotions more overt. In her analysis of Matta's performance she wrote:

Being in place with him communicates a very different sense of the events than looking down on the model – it brings the past up close, past as actually not past. Now. Here ... I too am part of this scenario now; I have accompanied him in here. I am suddenly rooted to the place restored as practice. My eyes look straight down, mimetically rather than reflectively, through his down-turned eyes. I do not see really; I imagine ... I participate not in the events but in the transmission of his affective relationship to place by listening to his voice and following his steps. My presencing [being present] offers me no sense of control, no fiction of understanding. He walks, he tells, he points.[29]

---

27 Ibid.
28 Ibid., pp. 9–10.
29 Diana Tayor, 'Memory, trauma, performance', *Aletria* 1(21), January–April 2011, p. 70.

At this point, for reasons that became clear later, Matta stopped his anticlockwise tour to divert across to the eastern side of the precinct. At his site 22, he stopped at a concrete slab to explain that it was:

> [the] [a]rea that was used for parking the pickup trucks and other vehicles after their human cargo had been dumped on the ground in front of the main house. Prisoners were brought there after all the other techniques of torture had failed to make them 'talk'. Naked, bound and blindfolded, they were thrown down, and a truck driven over their legs, fracturing and crushing the bones. The excruciatingly painful injuries would add to the dehydration produced by weeks of torture, especially on the *parrilla*. With the meagre diet, absence of medical care, and the filthy conditions in the cells, gangrene usually developed, sentencing the prisoner to be 'disappeared'.[30]

Next he came to the rebuilt water tower and its minute detention cells reserved for the 'uncooperative'. Taylor continues:

> The isolation cells, he says, were one metre by one metre – five men were squeezed upright, into that space. There is an original small brick semi-circle there where the captives were allowed to sit each day for a few minutes. He sits. Remembers. He says nothing.[31]

Matta's tour now doubled back to reach its climax, following the rear boundary across to the memorial wall naming the 229 detained-disappeared from Villa Grimaldi. In contrast to the busy, noisy memorial to Pinochet's victims at the Santiago General Cemetery, the Wall of Names was intended by its designer to encourage just such personal reflection by installing it in the quietest part of the grounds, amidst shady trees and seats for contemplation.[32] Mario Aguilar found its textuality 'open, waiting, luxuriant, inconclusive, disturbing, demanding'.[33] Others, though, have found the wall, and the whole site, uninformative: 'Here came workers, artists, academics. Who were they?'[34] Matta, however, had a third purpose. Taylor continued:

---

30 Matta, 'A walk...', p. 18. Modern signage makes no reference to this site beyond 'Aquí se torturaron con vehiculos' [Here they were tortured by vehicles].
31 Taylor, 'Memory, trauma, performance', p. 70.
32 Gómez-Barris, *Where Memory Dwells*, pp. 63–65.
33 Aguilar, 'El Muro de Los Nombres de Villa Grimaldi', 2000, p. 84.
34 Antonio Traverso and Enrique Azúa, 'Villa Grimaldi: A visual essay', *Journal of Medical Practice* 10(2&3), 2009, 218.

When he gets to the memorial wall marked with the names of the dead (built twenty years after the violent events) he breaks down and cries. He cries for those who died, but also for those who survived. 'Torture', he says, 'destroys the human being. And I am no exception. I was destroyed through torture'.[35]

Taylor learned later that Matta repeated this tearful performance — for performance was what it was — as part of each of his tours. Far from condemning him, she understood his reasons, while reflecting that by such emphasis on individual trauma, the risk remains that:

> [the] politics may be evacuated ... Standing there, together, bringing the buildings and routines back to life, we [should] bear witness not just to the personal loss, but to a system of power relations, hierarchies and values that not only allowed but required the destruction of others.[36]

Such, indeed, is a common criticism of the major reports into the violation of human rights by Latin American governments that tend towards story rather than explanation, narrative rather than forensic, privileging and validating the individual experience of trauma and healing, away from the inequities of the social structure.[37] Survivors, especially from the highly articulate and educated MIR, have been aware of and been worried by the disjuncture.

It is true that since Matta's tour of 2000 much oral history collected by the corporation has reflected the same diabolical personal experiences. Paz Rojas:

> They brought us again to Villa Grimaldi. This time the place and the situation according to prisoners was a true inferno. Every ten minutes they dragged prisoners out for interrogation. At the end of an hour or more they returned destroyed by the tortures.[38]

---

35   Taylor, 'Memory, trauma, performance', p. 70.
36   Ibid., p. 71.
37   Read, 'Reconciliation without history', p. 282; Greg Grandin and Thomas Miller Klubock, Editorial Introduction, *Radical History Review*, no. 97, Winter 2007, 3–7.
38   Paz Rojas, María Elena Ahumada and Juanita Méndez, *'Segundo Informe. Testimonios de tortura en Chile. Septiembre de 1973 a marzo de 1990s'*, Archivo CODEPU, Santiago, 2003, pp. 126–27, quoted in Gabriel Salazar, *Villa Grimaldi (Cuartel Terranova). Historia Testimonia, Reflexión*, Villa Grimaldi, Corporación Parque Por la Paz, Santiago, 2013, p. 112.

Conversely, others have speculated on the wisdom of such a performance. Claudio Durán, was concerned that different experiences were represented neither in the 'blindfold and *parrilla*' theme, nor in the Park for Peace itself. Where was comradeship? Where was resistance? He reflected that, though the blindfold was the military's first weapon of control, he and others could see below it. On trips to the ablutions, he could physically feel others in the line. *Beneath the blindfold, we were clearly and definitely us.* After torture he could comfort another victim: *Compañero, tranquilízate.* On occasions when the men were placed in a larger cell, the feeling was stronger still, especially among the recently tortured:

> This is ours. It was really yours, mine, everybody's. Pure undisguised humanity. Real love, without formalities. Sharing bread or the shaky bed with new arrivals, or a cigarette passed through the bars by a guard, the gaze of the one who gave it to you, just for that, Just for that. Two puffs each, hand it on. Gestures flying about on a sea of humanity.[39]

Roberto Merino Jorquera recalled that prisoners who were ordered to sit on a bench would rub against the skin of another, unidentifiable, detainee. He felt the sensation of two bodies close together. *It was a wonderful sensation of closeness even though we didn't know who it was.*

> To be received back into human shelter and comfort after electrical torture, unable to stand, bleeding, and broken. And it was incredible, after everything that happened, while a minute later, they'd ask you in a low voice, 'How are you, comrade, are you OK?' And get you to bed, cover you with something, because you'd be trembling. 'Comrade, take it easy. Rest. Don't have any water.'[40] And some would stroke your hair as well. Treated you as a child. Little by little you felt surrounded by a human warmth, of men, of women, of what was outside but slowly you'd relax. Is it because you're breathing the return of humanity? But you remain sceptical and suspicious. How could it be that barely five metres away you've passed from a chamber filled with inhumanity to one recharged with humanity? How to die and be reborn in such a short time?[41]

---

39 Claudio Durán, 'Autobiografía de un ex-jugador de ajedrez', in Salazar, Gabriel, Villa Grimaldi (Cuartel Terranova). Historia Testimonia, Reflexión, Villa Grimaldi, Corporacián Parque de la Paz, Santiago, 2013, pp. 44–46.
40 Drinking water after electrical torture was thought to be sometimes fatal.
41 Claudio Durán, *Autobiografía de un ex-jugador de ajedrez* [Autobiography of a ex-chess player], pp. 44–46, reproduced in Salazar, *Villa Grimaldi (Cuartel Terranova)*, pp. 209–11.

To the intellectuals of the former MIR like Roberto Merino, fresh from a sociology PhD at the Sorbonne in 2006, the defeated blindfold was more than just a way of outwitting the guards. The blindfold was a symbol of the state's attempt at hegemonising its absolute power to subjugate the body of its subjects. Detainee initiatives like peering below it, comforting a tortured victim or feeling the touch of skin, manifested resistance to that absolute power of the state. Resistance took many forms. The detainees never stopped trying to communicate with each other: one could pull the threads of the blindfold one by one so that the guards would not notice, the intention not so much to survive to tell the story, simply to get through the day with the support of one's fellow humans ranged against absolutist power. Shortly after he completed his thesis, Merino wrote an article for a multi-authored volume significantly entitled *Memories in Search of History: Further Explorations in the Political Uses of Memory*:

> When we try to comprehend 'what has happened to us' it is not to explain what happened to us from analogies and generalities that have appeared a multitude of times. To comprehend the meaning we have to start from the beginning with scientific rigour but at the same time to sound deeply in order to disentangle what has been hidden and objectified within the society, and searching for the deepest significance of what has occurred.[42]

After he completed his thesis, Merino became a tour guide in 2008. In discarding Matta's litany of evils presented to tourists, he used his Foucauldian theorisings to *shape* the experience, to give meaning to the inexpressible, somehow to comprehend that the experience went *beyond* guards and torture, to enrich the compendium of human sociology.

This meant, Merino explained to 15 somewhat bemused tourists on a hot November afternoon in 2008 that we should recognise the epistemological rupture (he meant dwelling on the emotions) that speaks of pain, suffering and torture, and utilise the more objectified terms of punishment, internment and extermination. 'Besides, I cannot transport the pain of torture to you, for pain is individual. All I can do is explain the meaning of suffering.' Furthermore, the description of

---

42   Roberto Merino, 'Memoria, olvido y silencios de un centro secreto de secuestro', in (unnamed editor) *Memorias en Busca de Historia, Más Allá de Los Usos Políticos de la Memoria,* Universidad Bolivariana, LOM Ediciones, Santiago, 2008, p. 91.

pain meant returning the observer to the state's absolute power over its victims, its disciplining of the body, its Panopticon control over its citizens. Detainees could be thought of not just as prisoners but 'that forming a social-political category'. The park itself was both aesthetic and symbolic. Beneath the violence of imperialism lay the structure of everyday violence outside the walls of the institution. Torture took place, yes: 'just here was where the flesh was thrown onto the *parrilla*'. The 'mercantilist production of social relations' allowed an array of possibilities for every individual, such as the solidarity of rubbing one's skin against an unknown fellow detainee. The traitors, the informers, the turncoats, the collaborators negotiated their own place in the social structure. Even the memorial wall, without the necessary sociological profile of the victims themselves, tended to objectify the experience. Tours such as these could return but little of the experience. *Only we can do that. If you want more, get it from the archives.* 'The essential point that I want you to remember', he concluded to his audience, 'is that in the end it is pain inflicted on bodies.'[43]

It was an extraordinary performance. Only occasionally had Merino referred to his own experiences as a MIRista detainee as part of 'ours'. Only a brief pause or a moment's faraway expression had signalled the prodigious attempt to drain his discourse of personal remembrance. He had every reason not to do so: Roberto Merino Jorquera, unknown to his audience, in 1998 was one of seven individuals who brought an indictment against the dictator Pinochet himself. It was Merino's own flesh that had been thrown on the *parrilla*. This man had been tied to a chair for several days and had a plastic bag tied over his head with the constant menace of asphyxiation.[44] In circumstances infinitely more agonising than anything proposed by the social scientist on whose

---

43   For an interesting discussion on Chilean trauma testimony, including the objectification of self by use of the third person, see Jaume Peris Blanes, 'Testimonies of Chilean exile: Between public protest and the working through of trauma', in Colman Hogan and Marta Marín Domine, eds, *The Camp: Narratives of Internment and Exclusion*, Cambridge Scholars Publishing, Newcastle, 2009, pp. 298–319.
44   'Roberto Francisco Merino Jorquera', in 'Auto de Procesamiento de 10.12.98 contra Augusto Pinochet Ugarte', [Indictment against Augusto Pinochet Ugarte], Puro Chile.

principles Merino's thought was rooted, for a full 90 minutes he had guided his audience on a tour of Villa Grimaldi without ever having used the singular personal pronoun.[45]

A counsellor may seek to equip the storyteller to make meaning of their experience.[46] Historians may hold that part of the explanation process is finding someone to blame, to transfer responsibility, generally to a higher authority, or to bring a violent past into such a state of order that no longer burdens the present.[47] It was as if, to the Villa Grimaldi intellectuals, there had to be more to the experience than a tale of hope, bonding, disappointment, capture, pain and catastrophic political defeat. *There must be a further meaning*. Michele Drouilly, ever the subversive, disagreed with Merino's interpretation. She thought it a misguided attempt, rehearsed by many others studying overseas, to make Latin American history fit European models. Once, she relates, she asked Merino to mend a teapot lid. He did so beautifully, but it would no longer fit the teapot!

Several women detainees at Villa Grimaldi took their reflections in quite different directions. Carmen Rojas found herself in a cell of some 20 square metres with 30 women for close company. Some she described as hostile, indifferent or bewildered, those whom Rojas supposed to have betrayed information or whose partners had done so. But she warmly recalled smiles and kindly gestures by other women. In low voices the women discussed what had gone so wrong with the socialist experiment. Had they adopted the wrong tactics? Or had the implementation of the tactics been wrong? Everyone took part; anyone who did not ran the risk of being accused of capitulating.

---

45   Michel Foucault, *Discipline and Punish: The Birth of the Prison*, Vintage, New York, 1975/1995.
46   David W. Peters, 'A spiritual war: Crises of faith in combat chaplains from Iraq and Afghanistan', in Cave and Sloan, *Listening on the Edge*, Oxford University Press, London, 2014, p. 234.
47   Taylor Kruass, 'In the Ghost Forest, Listening to Tutsi Rexcapés', in Cave and Sloan, *Listening on the Edge*, Oxford University Press, London, 2014, p. 99; Mark Cave, 'What remains: Reflections on crisis oral history', in Cave and Sloan, *Listening on the Edge*, Oxford University Press, London, 2014, p. 4.

Having been kept, often, in larger numbers, the women's experience seems to have been both more collectively shared and openly reflected upon than the men's.[48]

Gladys Díaz Armijo was a MIRista and well-known journalist who reportedly spent more time in Villa Grimaldi – three months – than anyone else. Immediately on arrival at Villa Grimaldi she was beaten. An unidentified voice snarled, 'Leave this bitch for me'. Her blindfold was caked in old blood: 'Don't worry about it, you won't be getting out alive anyway.' Strapped to the *parrilla*, she once regained consciousness to recognise the same man, by his voice, raping her. During each of the several sessions on the *parrilla*, her screams were so high-pitched and continuous that she could not recognise her own voice. After each session she bled from every orifice, including her breasts and her navel. 'I didn't give myself permission to feel the pain ... So much electrical current that it's hard to understand that the body can resist it.' She was forced to watch her partner being tortured. Some of her many bones smashed by beatings have never healed. Afterwards Gladys Díaz, like Rojas, reflected a humanism similar to that of Claudio Durán or Roberto Merino. 'The worst part of torture is not the physical pain that you suffer – I think that the worst part of torture is to have to realise in such a brutal way that human beings are capable of doing something so aberrant to another person as torturing them.'[49] From Díaz's experiences grew a love of humanity: 'I believed, and still believe, in humanity despite such unbelievable crimes ... I gained a profound admiration of the human being. I felt such a capacity of love so unconditional that I had never felt before. And that remains.' Like several other women detainees, she also carried her humanism into a more feminine sensibility. She found that 'the ways that one finds to defend oneself are unlimited. I sometimes dreamt about beautiful things ... I remember having awakened to the sound of a little bird that was outside, and how I was able to keep the sound of that bird's singing in my ears for days ...' Díaz was one of few survivors of detention in the tower, after which, having been unable to stretch her legs for so long, she was quite unable to walk.

---

48 Carmen Rojas, *Recuerdos de una MIRista* [Memories of a MIRista], edición mimeografiada, Jose Miguel Bravo, Santiago, 1995, pp. 56–57; see also 'Chile's Villa Grimaldi remembers horror of Pinochet years' (interview with Lelia Pérez), *Santiago Times*, 7 July 2013.
49 Thomas Wright, *State Terrorism in Latin America: Chile, Argentina, and international Human Rights,* Rowman and Littlefield, Lanham, 2007, p. 65.

Even more significant to her was the collective experience. She found that 'after using an almost bald toothbrush shared by 20 other women, one lost all one's arrogance'. The women formed their own resistance groups. They made domino tiles out of the tiny bread ration. Less restricted than the men, they celebrated each other's birthdays and explained the recipes they would use for celebration feasts. If no guards were present in the cell, they removed their blindfolds to greet old friends. 'You had a friend. A special friend at the absolute limit of the capacity and full sense of friendship.'

> Humanity, in this confused situation, there was no recognising hierarchies. Only comradeship. Only solidarity. Wasn't it this, precisely this, the essential truth of our life project for our society? Wasn't it here, in these moments? In this place, in a chemically pure form, the supreme reason for our struggle? To feel this here, right here, was to take the elixir of life.

Díaz 'worked at continuing to develop myself and to find inside the feminine soul, my own soul. I had always worked with men and then I wanted to recover the best of the feminine soul.' Together many of the women became collectively stronger than ever. They embroidered a handkerchief with the dove of love and peace from threads pulled out of brooms or prison blankets. They passed from mouth to mouth a cigarette butt thrown away by a guard. They shared the remainder of a guard's pudding 'spoonful by spoonful, mouth by mouth'. They sang the Angel Parra children's song 'The three peaks'; one Saturday night they danced without music.[50]

---

50 Drawn from Díaz, interviews, in Luz Carmen Castillo, *La Flaca Alejandra*, documentary, 1993; see also Tamara Vidaurrázaga Aránguiz, *Mujeres en Rojo y Negro*, Ediciones Escapararte, Santiago, 2006, pp. 302–314.

7. A GARDEN OF HORROR OR A PARK OF PEACE

Fragment of electrified barbed wire, one of the few remaining artefacts surviving from Cuartel Villanova (Villa Grimaldi).
Source: Photograph by Peter Read, editing Con Boekel.

***

At this point, Michele Drouilly re-enters the story of Villa Grimaldi as a major curator of its current displays. For years, as a corporation member, she had chafed at the lack of any obvious humanising impulse in the displays. The Wall of Names provided no more than a date of death, even less than the pavement inscriptions outside Londres 38. In about 2002 she began to persuade the corporation, first, to establish a 'Memory Room', to portray the lives of the victims before incarceration – and to allow her to begin work on it.

The objections of the management rested on one of those aching dichotomies that we have encountered so often, between the survivors and the relatives of the disappeared. Jacqueline's death, like that of every person taken into Villa Grimaldi and never accounted for, was unconfirmed, nor her body found. She was merely 'missing'. Apart from the Wall of Names, she and the rest of the detained-disappeared were nowhere. Passionately but coolly Michele analysed the precinct. 'You survivors', she told the committee,

> are the victors. I represent the vanquished, the detained-disappeared. *Where are we represented? We have nowhere to go. Nowhere.* If you want it never to happen again, then you must allow people to empathise, and the most direct way to do this is through the objects of their daily lives.

The mostly male committee gave in, not least, in Michele's view, because they had been thus shamed by a woman.[51]

Michele's 'Memory Room' was to be as personal and individualised as the rest of the display was not. Eighteen months later, installed in what had been probably a store room for the swimming pool nearby, her collections were ready and the queues to see the objects enormous. On the outside wall, she invoked the emotions of her visitors in majestic Spanish rhetoric impossible to render in English:

> Today, this room is a testament to the men and women who disappeared from here or who were executed here.

---

51 This section drawn mainly from Michele Drouilly, interview, 4 April 2015.

7. A GARDEN OF HORROR OR A PARK OF PEACE

The objects on display here are the originals providing evidence of the past of women and men which are so simple that they are often forgotten. Today they are the Detained Disappeared or Executed in this place.

The people who disappeared from here or who were murdered here loved, created, sang, prayed, cried, wrote, read and above all, fought for a better world ... In other words, they lived, like you and the people you love do.

We invite you to enter with respect, so that you may learn something of their lives.

Out of the more than 200 victims eligible to be represented, Michele Drouilly chose some 30 based on a sample of each major political party of the left. To the family of each she wrote appealing for objects and memorabilia, which she would then display, with their personal history, in glass cases. Each family responded differently, some ignoring the request, some sending the objects, some inviting Michele to visit them. The wife of a detained-disappeared was so traumatised that she had never visited Villa Grimaldi, and asked a friend to deliver the objects. One procrastinated so long that her disappeared, and famous, father is not represented even now.

Several of Michele Drouilly's captions reiterated the authenticity of each of the mundane objects: no archetype, no substitute, but each artefact of precious everyday significance *because* it belonged to each of the disappeared. Again and again she had to stress to the donors that she did not want their own testimonies or poems. 'This is their space, not yours.' Several she had to return to them. Objects, though, were sacred. Letters, a belt, a passport photo, *Treasure Island* in Spanish, a razor, the spoon someone always stirred his maté tea with. The exception to her insistence on original objects was the cabinet containing some found objects: beach sand, shells, a thimble, a hair ribbon and photographs provided by the family, and a letter. Its author was Marta Lidia Ugarte Román, a senior member of the Communist Party arrested on 24 August 1976 and held, briefly, in the Villa Grimaldi tower. Her broken, tortured and mutilated body, thrown from a security forces helicopter, washed up on a beach 182 kilometres north of Santiago. Evidently the piece of railway line tied to the sack holding her body had become detached, allowing the body to float to the beach.[52] Some 15 years after Marta Ugarte's death, Michele collected these objects from the very beach where her body had appeared. Another victim whose death meant much to the survivors of Villa Grimaldi was that of Carlos Alberto Carrasco Matus, known as Mauro, a 21-year-old conscript with leftist leanings, unfortunate enough to be detailed to the guardroom at Villa Grimaldi.[53] He is known to have spoken kind words and smuggled extra food to the detainees. Discovered, he was tied to the ombú tree that survived from the gracious pre-Pinochet era and flogged to death with chains. From his family Michele collected half a dozen photographs, his army insignia, and the shirt he was wearing the day he was arrested.

Naturally it is the section dedicated to her sister Jacqueline to which Michele has dedicated her most loving, sorrowful attention. Above her name she reproduced an epigram of Benedetti:

> They are somewhere, in cloud or tomb,
> They are somewhere, I am certain of that
> Over there far beyond the reach of the soul[54]
>
> (Tr. Paula González Dolan)

---

52 'Marta Lidia Ugarte Román', Memoria Viva; Mark Ensalaco, *Chile Under Pinochet: Recovering the Truth*, University of Pennsylvania Press, ebook, 2010, pp. 87–88. Similar to the obscene scenario invented by the DINA following the murder of Lumi Videla Moya, the conservative press speculated that she had been dismembered by a sex maniac, even by her lover.
53 'Carlos Alberto Carrasco Matus', Memoria Viva, www.memoriaviva.com/Desaparecidos/D-C/car-mat.htm; Steve Stern, *Remembering Pinochet's Chile: On the Eve of London, 1988*, Duke University Press, Durham, 2004, p. 79.
54 Estan en algún sitio/nube o tumba
    estan en algún sitio, estoy seguro
    allá en el sur del alma

7. A GARDEN OF HORROR OR A PARK OF PEACE

The Ombú tree, Villa Grimaldi. No signage attaches to it. Only Michele Drouilly's 'Memory room' gives an account of what happened here.
Source: Photograph by Peter Read, editing Con Boekel.

Under the caption 'Jacqueline Paulette Drouilly Yurich', Michele began:

> The objects contained in the case are the originals and belonged to her. The colour and texture of the paper underneath evoke the pullover knitted by her that she wore on the day she was taken to an unknown destination.
>
> The fragment is part of the pillowcase on which she would have laid her head on 31 October, if she had not been detained.
>
> The fragments are the remains of a ceramic vase which she cherished dearly, and which was found broken on the floor of the house, in the days after her detention.
>
> The book [*Treasure Island*] Jacqueline read with great enthusiasm when she was studying at the German College in Temuco.
>
> The embroidery threads remained held in her sewing box until now.
>
> The little flowers are the remains of a dress from the time when she was a little girl.

> The photo of her with her arm raised, has written on the reverse, 'For Marcelo, on the slope at Lastarria, like the Statue of Liberty'.
>
> And the photo of her as a little girl is the only one remaining, a little photo of a happy little girl.
>
> Jacqueline, you are always with us.[55]

Not displayed, however, is the clock with its shattered glass, its hands set at 14 minutes to 11 in the evening. That remains with Michele.

Yet her work of mourning and remembrance she believed was not yet complete.

Beside the ombú tree, the major survivor of the original Villa was the rose garden. The Cuartel Terranova commandant retained the roses because his weekend visitors to the swimming pool liked them. Ironically they meant even more to the detainees, especially those in the tower nearby, whose scent they could discern when all other sensory faculties were fading. Again Michele saw her opportunity and put it to the corporation that not only should the garden be preserved but the families of each of the 36 known female detained-disappeared of Villa Grimaldi be invited to place a rose within it in her honour. Someone suggested a tree instead: no, she countered, there would be too much dissent about whose was taller. Once accomplished, the families of other women killed or disappeared elsewhere in Chile up to 1980 she invited to take part, followed by those killed or disappeared in the whole period of the dictatorship.[56] More than 150 roses of every hue and bloom now waft their scent only metres from the little artefacts contained in the glass case of Jacqueline.

Jacqueline was now memorialised with the other women in the rose garden – but where was her body? The only hint was the ghastly fate of Marta Ugarte, whose body had freed itself from its lump of railway line, designed to make it sink, before floating ashore. Rumours that the mass disposal of drugged or dead bodies at sea had continued until 1978 were sensationally confirmed after underwater investigations

---

55 See also the extensive entries of the life of Jacqueline Drouilly online, such as Memoria Viva, www.memoriaviva.com/English/victims/Drouilly.html.
56 See the rose garden in Carmen Gloria Soto Gutiérrez, 'Hoy un parque para la paz... ayer, un lugar para la muerte. Villa Grimaldi, ex Cuartel Terranova. Chile, 1974–1978: Un espacio para la memoria colectiva', Revista Sans Soleil – Estudios de la Imagen, No. 4, 2012, 224–242.

uncovered fragments of rusty iron at the bottom of Quintero Bay, near Valparaiso. Although not initiating the project, Michele took part in framing the requests to the Ministry of the Interior to have the remains placed in the care of the Villa Grimaldi Corporation for conservation and display. In these days before the National Museum of Memory and Human Rights, it seemed that no one in the ministry knew what to do with them: they arrived at Villa Grimaldi one day by courier, wrapped in a parcel.[57] The remains were at length housed in a copper coloured cube-shaped structure balanced on one corner, perhaps to make it seem that it has been dropped from a great height. Visitors entered no more than eight at a time. The silence of the darkened interior was broken only by the recorded sound of the sea. Gradually to the visitor the subdued lighting revealed the rusty fragments, some no bigger than a matchbox, some larger and recognisable pieces of railway line. In a humanising gesture of which Michele Drouilly undoubtedly approved, a button rested on a piece of iron, lying just as it had been supposedly found many metres beneath the surface. For the new exhibition Michele wrote in the brochure still given to each visitor, 'the unique evidence of this monstrous form of annihilation applied to hundreds of prisoners of the dictatorship'.[58] It was not difficult to imagine that Jacqueline had shared the fate of Marta Ugarte.

The flame burns, but Michele Drouilly, like all the older corporation members, feels her age. Someone wrote to her suggesting a new rose garden in remembrance of the disappeared men. 'Good idea. Go and do it.' She abandoned an attempt to organise a 40th anniversary of Jacqueline's disappearance among her sisters: too much trauma, too much dissent, too many unlaid memories of family conflicts that had flourished not before 1974, but after. 'I just didn't have the heart to do it.' And the most sacred object of all, Jacqueline's broken clock, remains firmly in her possession.

Michele's efforts to humanise those whom she called 'the vanquished', that is, the detained-disappeared and politically executed, had quietly subverted the priorities of all the memorials we have so far considered. Her Memory Room demanded that Jacqueline and the others be recognised not as ideologues, victims, heroes, martyrs, MIRistas,

---

57 The Museum of Memory and Human Rights was opened in 2010, www.museodelamemoria.cl/.
58 Anon [Michele Drouilly], 'Testimonio Rieles' [Testimony of the railway lines], Corporación Parque de la Paz Villa Grimaldi, pamphlet, n.d., c. 2008.

Communists or Socialists, but as ordinary people with extraordinary dreams, a long life of promise before them. Her display depoliticised, then recreated, their lives to be treasured as individuals, not exemplars. Unnoticed at the time, her insistence pointed to a new direction of memorialisation that would be much more apparent five years later.

8
A memorial destroyed: Loyola, Quinta Normal

This chapter sets in opposition not so much two women, nor even their two different ideologies, but their two differing conceptions of how life should be lived. The two conceptions encompassed conflicts in housing, family values, politics, memory and, above all, in memorialisation: who should be remembered, and why, and where – and if at all. The ideological as well as physical conflict occurred in 5 hectares of what, in the early 1970s, had been a primary school, then an Air Force maintenance depot, then a base for the state security service, the CNI.

***

Josefina Roxana González Rodriguez grew up in the 1970s in the commune now known as Lo Prado.[1] Hers was a childhood of pitiless poverty, but it is not that which, in conversation, she emphasises. Rather, it was a childhood to be cherished. She is proud that her parents were married, not simply living together, and that they stayed together. She rejoices that she and her five brothers were raised in 'strong moral values': to know good from bad, to help the needy, work

---

1 'Lo Prado', Wikipedia. The information on Josefina Rodriguez is drawn from a number of discussions and interviews, principally 12 April 2015.

hard, earn a living. Rice and eggs was the staple dish. If a special guest came to dinner, her mother might buy a small bottle of coke from which everyone was served not much more than a thimbleful.

In the year of the coup into which she was born, the family was living in a new and radical *población*, or Cuban-style commune, of the type with which Lumi Videla Moya and other idealistic young MIRistas were so familiar – regular and uniform apartment blocks, 30 self-built dwellings in each.[2] Amongst the stable families lived several hundred *pobladores*, the poor and dispossessed shipped out from the *campamentos* of wealthier suburbs where they had been living rough in out-of-sight locations beside the city's canals. These newcomers formed a patrol of 25 rostered guards to protect the community, kept informed of daily events by loudspeakers. To at least one journalist, (the *población*) Che Guevara, despite its provocative name, was not marked by the drugs and violence such sites were often associated with. No beggars, drunks, vagrants or drop-outs here, but rather, a *población* marked by 'a dignity, a self-confidence, a certain fighting spirit and a sense of order never seen in the mushrooming *poblaciones* 10 years earlier'.[3]

Josefina Rodriguez's upbringing and her own sense of morality made her ambitious, upwardly mobile, distrustful of any extreme political party such as the MIR, yet deeply sympathetic to the oppressed. Her rules for life, in fact, were as close to practical Christianity as they were to moderate state socialism. Her mother was prepared to take in anybody in need of whom she approved. During the first and most violent year of the dictatorship, two cousins enrolled at the radical university USACH (Universidad de Santiago de Chile, formerly the UTE) sought shelter with her family. Josefina's mother took them in, shortly followed by DINA soldiers kicking in the door, but missing the cousins by searching everywhere except above the ceiling. Josefina

---

2 A *campamento* was an illegal settlement formed by the unemployed or homeless moving to the city, generally carrying the reputation of lawlessness and political radicalism. In the 1960s, Chilean governments began a program to legitimise and provide basic services to the *campamentos*, called *poblaciones*. A *comuna*, by contrast, was (and is) a legal entity forming part of a municipality.

3 'Una dignidad, una seguridad en sí mismos, un cierto ambiente de combatividad y un orden que jamás ví en las poblaciones callampas de diez años atrás', journalist's comment in *La Prensa*, 3 January 1971, p. 2, quoted by Boris Cofre Schmeisser, 'El movimiento de pobladores en el Gran Santiago: Las tomas de sitios y organizaciones en los campamentos. 1970–1973' [The movement of the poor in Greater Santiago 1970–1973], *Revista Tiempo Histórico*, no. 2, September 2011, p. 18.

Rodriguez's account of her early life, and the journalist's report about Josefina's *población*, speak loudly of firm but conservative moral values both within the family and, at this time, the community.

Josefina Rodriguez in her home at Renacer, Loyola.
Source: Photograph by Peter Read, editing Con Boekel.

In about 2000 Josefina took her firm principles and her young family to a more central area of Santiago known to be poor but upwardly mobile, the municipality known as Quinta Normal. Here she took residence close to the junction of two streets, Loyola and Neptuno. Hard by stood a forbidding though abandoned Air Force maintenance facility, later CNI depot, occupying some five hectares of unused real estate in a district that held its share of small businesses, private property, the homeless and urban slums.

In 2002 Josefina, ever alert to changing priorities in national social programs, followed with interest the announcement of a slum-clearance program in remote towns in the Atacama Desert known as 'Renacer' (Rebirth), sponsored by the Department of Housing and a large mining company. The scheme provided existing residents with brand-new dwellings for which they could compete and which they might eventually own. The program was to be extended into urban areas for which expressions of interest were now invited. Should approval to proceed on a particular site be granted to any group, they should then form a management committee, arrange building plans, draw up a list of potential local residents consistent with good character and existing humble circumstances.[4] Thus encouraged, Josefina Rodriguez gathered a team of four or five friends to see if such a housing scheme might be possible in Quinta Normal. Nobody in the mayoral administration raised any fatal objections. Her group researched possible sites to discover that the depot was no longer owned by the Air Force or the CNI, but by the municipality of Quinta Normal. Three years later, the housing department announced that the empty site, known for convenience here as Loyola, would be made over to Renacer to be managed by its own residents. During 2005 the Department of Housing and the municipality approved the construction of 72 new residences. They would be small, two storeys, two bedrooms, almost identical to each other, but clean, bright, strongly built, and a huge step away from the dark and decrepit dwellings in which the potential residents, including Josefina, were living. Here Josefina Rodriguez could continue her life's ambition to continually better the life of her family and the community, not through public welfare or armed rebellion, but through her own values of compassion and hard work.

These same values help to explain why she would shortly find herself in conflict with the first president of the Loyola Renacer, Julieta Kruskaya Varas Silva.[5] It was Varas, a member of a political cell even more dedicated to armed revolution through acts of urban terrorism than the MIR, who in 2007 declared Renacer a Site of Mourning and installed a memorial to those who had been allegedly tortured, disappeared and perhaps even buried within its menacing walls. For unknown to Josefina, except through an unspecific occasional rumour, the post-dictatorship research website Memoria Viva had listed Loyola as one of many hundreds of former torture, detention and disappearance sites throughout the country.[6]

---

4   Vikas Vij, 'Barrick Gold Corp helps underprivileged Chilean families own new homes', Justmeans, 28 January 2013; 'Renacer program: Housing in Chile's Atacama Region', YouTube, 16 January 2013.
5   'Nadezhada Krupskaya was a Russian revolutionary, writer, educator and Secretary of the Bolshevik Faction of the Social Democratic Party. Wife and advisor to V.I. Lenin', 'Nadezhda K. Krupskaya: 1869–1939', Lenin Internet Archive.
6   Memoria Viva lists the site as formerly the property of the CNI, who presumably acquired it from the Air Force after 1984.

Investigating the sites that are the themes of this book, in 2006 the authors visited Loyola, where immediately upon alighting, a passer-by remarked, 'This is where they used to drag the truth out of the young people'. The outer wall was white plastered brick, 4 metres high, topped with barbed wire, covered in graffiti. One read, 'Hasta Siempre Victor Jara' ('Ever onwards Victor Jara'). An elevated guard post stood beside the iron gates marking the entrance and exit to the depot.

Paulo came across the road to introduce himself as a neighbour. As a boy in the 1980s he used to climb the trees close to the wall and call out to the guards. Sometimes they even used to let him in. Paulo had heard screams, hinting at dark secrets and rumours of what had happened inside. From his mother's house just across the road he had heard trucks coming and going all night. Mysterious steps, he remembered, led downwards into passages – could they have been the entrances to cells? On the CNI's departure in about 2002, he had somehow acquired a key to the main gate and installed himself in the guard house. As self-appointed commandant of the abandoned site, he proceeded to offer a guided tour to be undertaken by himself. He would permit the use of a video camera but, doubtless for good reasons, insisted on never appearing in shot.

The tour, 2006

Paulo had arranged himself comfortably in his well-protected domain. He could watch for potential intruders from his lookout tower. In the former guard house he had placed an armchair and, on the wall behind, a girlie calendar. Behind him was the marked-up keyboard where the depot keys had hung: 'main gate', 'light truck', 'kitchen'. Beside that stood a 2-metre iron safe. Just outside he had built himself a little barbecue. His two dogs basked in the sun.

His journey began into what had once been the headquarters of the genuine depot commander and his senior officers, but the real tour began outside. Amidst the rubbish and knee-high grass everywhere lay a cement area the size of two tennis courts, intersected by a number of short channels, 1 metre wide, 3 metres long. In each case their descending steps were interrupted by piles of building rubbish. Were they the truck inspection pits that they logically seemed to be – or did they conceal a secondary and sinister purpose? Was there room for a military helicopter to land on the cement space? At the far end stood the remains of a machinery shed: more inspection pits, more mysterious hooks, steel cables, electrical fittings. At the far left were the remains of classrooms, some still with child-size toilets, others fitted out in barracks style. On the outside wall of the classrooms was a very fair rendition, in chalk, of a helicopter. At the end of the long corridor, the official emblem of the Chilean Air Force. A large pile of rusty railway lines seemed to be the only large objects left behind by the CNI. In truth, anybody entering without suspicion of anything occurring here beside heavy vehicle maintenance would have nothing to suspect. Yet Paulo continued to hint at unspecified menace. No evening candlelight vigils had ever been held outside its walls, but a priest in the 1990s had led processions round the perimeter, singing hymns encouraging Christian valour, and was later found mysteriously dead in a nearby swimming pool! The circumstantial evidence seemed as slight as the physical. And yet Memoria Viva had named Loyola in its enormous master list of 'Centres of Detention Chile 1973–1990'.

***

The first Renacer president, Julieta Varas, had a colourful and radical history in the Quinta Normal district well calculated to rouse the antipathy of Josefina Rodriguez. Her father, Juan Manuel Varas Silva, a MIR militant, was executed by the CNI in 1984.[7] In 2007 she took a prominent part in the *funa*, the public denunciation that denounced 'mad Dimter', the presumed assassin of Victor Jara.[8] Between 2004 and 2013 she was arrested 13 times for robbery, fighting, affray and assaulting police.[9]

---

7 'Juan Manuel Varas Silva', Memoria Viva; 'Varas Silva, Juan Manuel', Archivo Chile.
8 See above, 'Funa al asesino de Victor Jara "Edwin Dimter Bianchi" buena', YouTube; 'La Funa de Victor Jara 1', YouTube.
9 For instance, on 12 July 2012, Varas was arrested for participating in an illegal march organised by radical political movement the Frente Rodriguista, Francisco Águila, 'Detectan participación de rodriguistas en desórdenes ocurridos ayer en el Paseo Ahumada' [Participation of Rodriguistas detected in disorders occurring yesterday in Paseo Ahumada], Emol, 12 July 2012; see also Fernando Duarte M., 'Informe de inteligencia dice que movimientos antisistémicos están infiltrando a estudiantes' [Intelligence report says subversive movements infiltrating students], *La Segunda* online, 21 June 2013.

8. A MEMORIAL DESTROYED

Pinochet had justified his initial persecution of the left by the need to combat 'the intrusion of dogmatic and intolerant ideology inspired by the alien principles of Marxism-Leninism'. While the MIRistas had, in 1973, claimed to be the 'Marxist-Leninist vanguard of the working-class and the oppressed and exploited masses of Chile', by 1989 the party had virtually ceased to exist.[10] Yet that was not the end of leftist violence, for Julieta Varas's political convictions derived from an ideology as overtly combative as the MIR's but in reality much more bellicose. She was a militant of the Frente Patriótico Manuel Rodriguez (the Manuel Rodriguez Patriotic Front), the international urban terrorist cell also known as El Frente and its members Frentistas. While the MIR was decimated, the Frentistas, however, survived. Indeed, as dissatisfied and impatient members of the Chilean Communist Party, they had founded El Frente by breaking from the parent party after it seemed too quiescent in 1983. Despite intense persecution, the members of El Frente organised themselves with tight military discipline under six regional commanders.[11] Frentistas carried out a number of terrorist acts during and after the dictatorship, including arms smuggling, the assassination of the conservative professor of constitutional law, Jaime Guzmán, an attack on a helicopter base, blowing up McDonald's and Kentucky Fried Chicken restaurants, kidnappings and finally a failed assassination attempt, in 1986, on Pinochet himself.[12] On each occasion, enough of its members survived the dictatorship's savage retaliation to continue their violent campaigns. Like the MIR's adherence to the teachings of Che Guevara, a Frentista in 2012 quoted the words of Mao Tse Dong:

> A Communist should have largeness of mind and he should be staunch and active, looking upon the interests of the revolution as his very life and subordinating his personal interests to those of the revolution …[13]

---

10 'Manuel Rodriguez Patriotic Front', Wikipedia; 'Movimiento de Izquierda Revolucionaria [MIR]', 26 June 2009.
11 Cristián Pérez, '"Operación Príncipe": Irrumpe el FPMR-A' [Operation Prince: The FPMR-A erupts]. Its commander was a member of an exiled family, radicalised in Cuba, calling himself Jose Miguel.
12 Rolando Alvarez Vallejos, 'Los "Hermanos Rodriguistas". La división del Frente Patriótico Manuel Rodríguez y el nacimiento de una nueva cultura política en la izquierda chilena. 1975–1987' [The 'brothers Rodriguista'. The division of the Manuel Rodriguez Patriotic Front and the birth of a new political culture in the Chilean left. 1975–1987], *Revista Izquierda* 2(3), 2009.
13 Andrés Figueroa Cornejo, 'Chile. Hablan ex combatientes: La causa del Frente Patriótico Manuel Rodríguez' [The combatants speak: The cause of the Manuel Rodrígeuz Patriotic Front], Dazibao Rojo: Blog marxista-leninista maoísta, 19 September 2010.

If the Frentistas remained ideologically unreconstructed, they were not lacking in courage or conviction. To Varas, and all Frentistas, the ideological base of revolutionary action remained the same, in Chile, Santiago, Quinta Normal, even the humble Renacer in Loyola: to head a grand social movement in the struggle to transform the society that needed it urgently.[14]

Inside and outside the meetings of the management committee, Josefina Rodriguez objected strongly to the direction that the Loyola Renacer was taking under the leadership of Julieta Varas the Frentista. Not by accident did she find herself ejected from it by Varas in the early months of 2007. Shortly afterwards, she found herself also excluded from the list of several hundred people invited to enter Loyola, for the first time in their lives, for the grand opening of the site of their new homes. Had it not been for the well-known political views of their president, they might have been puzzled by the provocative title of the invitation sheet, a 'Grand Fiesta of Popular Justice'.[15] As had occurred just before the opening of Londres 38 and Villa Grimaldi, the invited state officials had caught wind of their likely denunciation during the event and boycotted the opening.

Varas was not about to let slip the opportunity for furthering the cause of the Frentistas. The public notice of the event:

> This feeling [of loss] pierces the people of the *poblaciones*. For this reason they have decided to build on this site a memorial which remembers the victims of the dictatorship of the Quinta Normal. Not that alone. They are preparing a homage for them – this 14th of September to which President [Bachelet] herself will be invited. Memory must be rescued. If we do not tell the story of this place, the cloak of oblivion remains, to never know what occurred here, Julieta [Varas] asserts.[16]

Installing herself on the day as Master of Ceremonies, she explained that recognising Loyola's role as a site of torture and death was essential to its opening. She pointed to the presence of a survivor, Francisco Videla, whose testimony was inscribed on a placard propped against

---

14   Miguel Paz, 'El Frente en la encrujicada. Adiós a las armas?' [The Frente at the crossroads. Farewell to Arms?], Archivo Chile, 2002.
15   Marivic Wyndham and Peter Read, 'Those who have no memorial', *Encounters 5: Memories and Violence, Problems and Debates in a Global Perspective*, Fall 2012, 169–82.
16   'Renacer: La Villa de los Rieles' [Renacer: Villa of Railway Lines], *La Nación*, 31 August 2007.

the wall of the classrooms. One of the very few survivors of Loyola, he had been allegedly detained for 15 days, 'tortured almost to death', and finally had been liberated through error. A painting of a blood-red rose carried the description:

> The Rose of Blood poster painted by the painter Jose Balmes who donated the work to the Renacer cultural area.[17]

Varas asserted that Loyola during the dictatorship was used to detain, torture, rape, and cause people to disappear. Here was a place of death now converted into a place of life for people in their own homes and apartments. Today, she continued, one could still hear the shouts of horror of Chileans suffering directly because of the cowardly actions of state officials. Here the people of the *poblaciones* of North Santiago had been detained. It was not easy to bring together the members of Renacer 'given the despair imposed by the neoliberal model ... Despite this, serious, participative, and transparent work by neighbours broke the ice and generated confidence and the necessary organization to win our rights'. The ponderous Marxist-Leninist phraseology doubtless perplexed, if not instantly alienated, some of her audience as she reminded them: 'The achievement was no gift of the state but a triumph of social organisation, of our intelligence, [of] the audacity of our organisation, and dedication to win.' She concluded that there was much to do – to put out a call to all the organisations of the settlements to construct a grand, popular settlement movement, and to face the task of accommodating more than 300 families who could not find space within Renacer Loyola.

The most solemn moment of the afternoon came as the well-known opponent of the Pinochet regime, Father José Aldunate, blessed the site and unveiled a memorial stone leaning against a classroom wall. Sixty centimetres high, in shape not unlike the way that the Ten Commandments are customarily represented, it was carved in two sections. On them were painted 16 names in black, with the dates of death, and five names in red without dates. Although unspecific as to the rationale for their inclusion, above the names was the inscription:

> Nothing is Forgotten
> Nobody is Forgiven

---

17 Ibid. The report stated that Videla had been held for seven days, and at the time of his release he had seen other detainees, but that he did not wish to discuss the subject further.

and below the names:

Justice and Punishment

The names in black were (for 1973) Simón Cirineo Allende Fuenzalido, Alamiro Segundo Gonzalez Saavedra, Manuel José Gonzalez Allende, Eduardo Cerda Angel, Madrid Galvez, Vasquez Escobar, Jorge Enrique; (1981) Arcadia Flores Perez; (1983) Fabián Onofre Cortes Pino, Gallego Saball, Norbeto Ratier Noguera, Salgado Troquian, Juan Elias Espinoza Parra; (1985) Marisol Varas Linares; (1989) Erick Rodriguez Hinojosa, Ivan Palacios Guarda.[18] They were followed by five names written boldly in red, without dates: Alejandro Pinochet Arenas, José Maltes, Gonzalo Ivan Fuenzalida Navarrete, Manuel Jesús Sepúlveda Sánchez and Julio Orlando Muñoz Otárola.

At a stroke Loyola had jumped from an unsourced entry among a list of many hundred detention sites throughout the nation, to a seemingly official House of Memory and Memorial to the 21 victims of Pinochet; each of whom, apparently, had a close and fatal association with the site in which their memorial stone now was propped unceremoniously against a classroom wall. How to accommodate that recognition would soon become a thorny problem for the management committee of Renacer, as well as the state architects of the 72 new houses soon to be crammed onto the site.

***

Soon after the grand opening, rumours increased that the interests of Julieta Varas in the site went beyond rehousing the 72 families within it. First it concerned the relationship between Julieta Varas, El Frente and the radical leftist Venezuelan President Hugo Chávez.[19] From the somewhat obscure five hectares of Loyola Renacer, it was alleged that Varas was intent on providing a refuge for a sudden evacuation of 'Chavistas' from Venezuela, should it become urgently necessary, that is, Julieta's Frentistas would offer a safe haven for them in the cells

---

18 'Eduardo Elias Cerda Angel', Memoria Viva; Arcadia Patricia Flores Perez', Memoria Viva; 'Fabián Onofre Cortes Pino', Memoria Viva.
19 Brian A. Nelson, 'Hugo Chávez: The Chávez presidency', Encyclopaedia Britannica. Since 2002, when a coup against Chávez had been narrowly and violently defeated, his position seemed always a little insecure. He had won a six-year term in 2006 by a decreased margin, but a package of reform, including a proposal to allow his indefinite re-election, was narrowly defeated in December 2007. It was his first defeat.

still rumoured to lie somewhere below Loyola. Josefina learned that the management committee had been asked to sign an affirmation that such sanctuary would be offered; if it wasn't needed, then the Renacer would become the clandestine Santiago headquarters of the Frentistas!

Events moved swiftly. Suffice it to note here that neither Venezuelan refuge nor political asylum became necessary, Josefina Rodriguez led a community revolt against the plot, and Varas and her *compañera* Rebeca Videla were officially ejected from the committee, and from their recently occupied homes, for having used the Renacer for improper purposes.[20] Varas departed leaving the Renacer with a debt, in Josefina's calculation, of 2 million Chilean pesos. In 2009 Josefina became president of Renacer Loyola.

Such upheavals, and the 2011 earthquake, could only delay the project; but Josefina determined that the rumours of torture, executions, underground cells and burials must be settled. Her committee called in forensic experts, archaeologists, 'people in white coats'. Nothing whatever was found. The underground 'cells' were revealed to be just filled-in vehicle inspection pits no more than a couple of metres deep.

The Renacer began to take shape in the outline of streets, gardens and house foundations. Each year more piles of defence forces rubbish disappeared. The commandant's house went, then Paulo's guard house, even the flagpole. Only a few reminders of its dictatorship past remained: the guard houses perched on top of the wall, the painted emblem of the Air Force maintenance unit curiously allowed to stay, though now adorned by a hammer and sickle.

Why then did the rumours of torture and murder persist? Were the 22 named victims *actually* associated with Loyola, or, indeed, with the Quinta Normal? Were Varas's assertions justified, or, as Josefina Rodriguez suspected, had she hijacked the occasion – as the Family and Friends of the 119 were to do at the opening of Londres 38 in 2010 – solely to advance the cause of the Frentistas? Who were these 'never-to-be-forgotten' victims? Was it true that neighbours knew that behind these walls were no ordinary trucks undergoing routine

---

20 'Atemorizadas las familias con la directiva "que contaba con la personalidad juridical"', Causa no. 1435/2011 (Proteccion). Resolución no. 255716, de Corte de Apelaciones de Santiago, de 5 de Octubre de 2011.

maintenance?[21] Why did Father Aldunate need to consecrate the site? Why did the ex-detainee Francisco Videla, only released in error, refuse to speak about his experiences? Why were the last five of the names on the memorial written so dramatically in red? Indeed, why did Memoria Viva list Loyola as a site of significance at all? Surely there must be records of the alleged victims in the extensive state and private archives of the repression.

Let us test Varas's claims, using the best known online research into the personal histories of Pinochet victims, Memoria Viva, specialising in research into and preservation of records of the detained-disappeared and politically executed, and the more left-orientated Archivo Chile.[22]

The first three victims, Alamiro Saavedra, Gonzalez Allende and Allende Fuenzalida, were gathered in the same house in Quinta Normal 10 days after the coup when drunken members of the security forces burst in at 8.45 pm and killed them. (The DINA was not yet formed.) All three bodies were thrown into the Mapocho River to become, perhaps, among those hauled out by Don Roberto Muñoz.[23] Gonzalez Allende was only 16.[24] Saavedra was a businessman, aged 41.[25] Cerda was a child of eight when, hearing shots outside his house on 12 October 1973 at 11.30 pm, he opened the front door, presumably to see what was happening, and received a bullet in the throat.[26] The solitary victim listed for the year 1981 was that of Arcadia Perez. A long web entry lists her as an active (military) member of MIR, a journalism student at the University of Chile, founder of the Group for the Families of the Detained Disappeared, editor of the journal *The Militiaman*. A leader of 'actions of armed propaganda', she insisted on the formation of a woman-only warrior group standing in the front line of any pitched battle. She was killed in a firefight in her house in Quinta Normal.[27]

---

21 'Renacer: La Villa de los Rieles', *La Nación*, 31 August 2007.
22 Memoria Viva, 'Quienes Somos' [Who We Are], (memoriaviva.com) whose records in relation to the present study are drawn primarily from the Rettig Report; Archivo Chile's subtitle is 'Documentation of the social and political history and the contemporary popular movement in Chile and Latin America' (archivochile.com).
23 'Simón Cireneo Allende Fuenzalida', Memoria Viva; see also 'Archivos de las etiquetas'.
24 'Manuel José González Allende', Memoria Viva.
25 'Alamiro Segundo Gonzalez Saavedra', Memoria Viva.
26 'Eduardo Elias Cerda Angel', Memoria Viva; see also 'Eduardo Elias Cerda Angel', Fotolog.
27 'Arcadia Patricia Flores Perez', Memoria Viva; 'Flores Perez, Arcadia Patricia', Archivo Chile.

8. A MEMORIAL DESTROYED

Much contextual information exists on those whose names are recorded on the plaque as having perished during 1983 at a time of violent upheavals against the Pinochet regime. The global economic downturn in 1981 affected Chile badly. Unemployment rose, the GDP fell, the national debt doubled. In May 1983, united unionists and copper-mine workers demanded a national strike. Some previous Pinochet supporters began to lose faith in the military government's ability to guarantee economic and social stability. A second huge protest was staged in June, and a third in August. The government responded with new legislation proscribing unauthorised demonstrations and newly defined criminal acts, such as spreading false information about terrorist activities. The police and the military adopted the new tactic of indiscriminate shooting into crowds. Brutal repression followed, including 29 deaths.[28] One of the 21 listed by Varas was Cortes Pino, a businessman who defied the curfew to help a wounded child and was shot by indiscriminate fire.[29] Gallego Saball, of Quinta Normal, was shot by one of the 18,000 soldiers rushed to the capital to repress the demonstrations.[30] The MIRista Noguera was killed in a firefight following the assassination of the Governor of Santiago, General Carol Urzúa.[31] Troquian was killed at the same time. Juan Espinoza Parra, another MIRista, having clandestinely returned from Germany in 1981, was taken prisoner by the CNI in December 1983, and executed in the street.[32] The solitary death listed in 1985 was that of Linares, shot by the security forces.[33] The last two names written in black were those of Hinojosa and Palacios, recently joined junior members of a radical group allied to the Frentistas, called Comando Resistencia. Eighteen at the time of their deaths, babies at the time of the coup, Archivo Chile claims they were betrayed by the informer who had recruited them before handing their names to the CNI.[34]

---

28   Rettig Report, pp. 116–17; Orlando Sepúlveda, 'Chile in the time of the Dictator', *International Socialist Review* 53, May–June 2007, 3–5.
29   'Fabían Onofre Cortes Pino', Memoria Viva.
30   'Benedicto Antonio Gallegos Saball', Memoria Viva.
31   'Hugo Norbeto Ratier Norguera', Memoria Viva.
32   'Juan Elías Espinosa Parra', Memoria Viva.
33   'Fabían Onofre Cortes Pino', Memoria Viva; 'Benedicto Antonio Gallegos Saball', Memoria Viva.
34   'Acciones armadas de extrema izquierda' [Armed actions of the extreme left], Wikipedia; 'Iván Gustavo Palacios Guarda', Memoria Viva; 'Erick Enrique Rodriguez Hinojosa', Memoria Viva.

Not one, therefore, of the 16 victims written in black by Varas had a physical connection with Loyola, but each was either a resident of Quinta Normal or a member of an organisation related to her own radical armed political group. That is, none had any known connection to the site at which the memorial to them had just been unveiled.

Research soon revealed that the names of the last five victims were painted in red because, like Varas, they were Frentistas. Alejandro Pinochet, José Peña Maltes, Gonzalo Fuenzalida, Manuel Sepúlveda and Julio Muñoz were members of an organisation that believed in, sponsored, or had taken part in acts of terrorism, and which, even after the demise of Pinochet, continued to propagate the notion of armed rebellion by the masses.[35]

The most notorious of the Frente Rodriguistas' acts was the attempted assassination in 1986 of Pinochet himself, some two hours drive from Loyola, in the year that the Rodriguistas had designated 'The Year of the Popular Rebellion of the Masses'. The daring and minutely planned raid, called by the Frentistas 'Operation Twentieth Century', occurred on a winding road passing through a precipitous valley in Cajón de Maipo. Pinochet frequently used the pass, two hours from Santiago, as he travelled in armed escort to his weekend mountain retreat. More than 20 urban guerillas, many trained in Cuba or Nicaragua, armed with automatic weapons and rocket launchers recently smuggled from Cuba, concealed themselves above the narrow pass. In the violent pitched battle lasting 15 minutes, several vehicles of the presidential motorcade were destroyed and five members of his party were killed. Pinochet's driver, with great skill, reversed the car out of danger after the vehicle was hit by automatic weapon fire. Although all the attackers escaped, Pinochet survived. Shaken but unbowed, he appeared on television to demand a brutal reprisal.[36]

The failed assassination attempt was greeted by the Chilean masses not with popular acclaim or a general uprising but with a hostility unanticipated by the Frentistas. By 1986, the country generally was unsympathetic to terrorist outrages. Real wages and employment prospects had steadily improved since 1982. Inflation seemed at last

---

35 'Iván Gustavo Palacios Guarda', Memoria Viva.
36 For a detailed account of the attack and its aftermath, see Cristóbal Peña, *Los Fusileros*, Debate, Santiago, 2007.

8. A MEMORIAL DESTROYED

to be declining. From 1985, some left and right moderate political parties had been involved in negotiations with the government in working towards a National Agreement for Full Democracy. Talk of a transitional government was in the air. Political parties were to be legalised, and free elections would eventually be held.[37] A demonstration, most unusually in favour of Pinochet, followed the Frentista attempt on his life. Local citizens erected a memorial to the five members of Pinochet's party who had been killed during the attack.[38] In reprisal, the Pinochetistas launched Operation Albania, a dragnet for known armed radicals, which yielded 12 Frentistas in the first month. Public reaction and the Frentistas' own awareness of their recent failures caused the leadership to reappraise its role as the revolutionary vanguard.[39]

Yet one of the six cells into which the Frentistas were organised, refusing to accept the directive, continued to plan a further public gesture. It was this action, a kidnapping, that would cost the five Frentista victims listed at Loyola their lives.

The renegade group, calling themselves FMPR-A (instead of FMPR) determined to kidnap a military officer, Colonel Carreño, particularly associated with the repression. On 1 September 1987 the kidnapping succeeded and Carreño was hidden in an underground cell in north Santiago. After three months, the Frentistas released Carreño in Sao Paulo, Brazil.

Immediately after the kidnapping the government, far from acceding to the ransom demands, launched another sweep of the capital. Carrying out Pinochet's threat of five citizens taken for every one officer kidnapped, troops seized, ostensibly as hostages, the five Loyola Frentistas within a fortnight of Carreño's capture. Gonzalo Fuenzalida Navarrete was last seen at a restaurant at Central Station on 7 September. Next, on the 9th, was José Maltes, 36, who had sought exile in France, returning secretly when the prohibition against

---

37 Rodrigo A. Cerda, 'Labor demand: Chile 1986–2001', *Cuadernos de Economía* 40(121), 2003, 478–84; Sepúlveda, 'Chile in the time of the Dictator'.
38 The freshly painted inscription read, in 2011, 'The community of Cajón de Maipo to the fallen in the fulfillment of their duty. 6 September 1986'.
39 Whelan, *Out of the Ashes*, p. 914, claims that the failures were that the Frentista disruption of the Pope's visit cost the organisation US$700,000, the failed attempt to rescue four Frentistas held in connection with the attack on Pinochet, and the decrease in the ransom demand for Carreño from US$2 million to US$50,000.

him was listed in 1985. Julio Muñoz Otárola, 27, was arrested on 8 September. Manuel Jesús Sepúlveda Sánchez was grabbed and thrown into a utility on 9 September. Alejandro Pinochet Arenas was pulled from a bus next day.[40]

***

It is generally held today that until November 1987 the five Frentista hostages were still being held alive, to be possibly exchanged in return for Carreño and that the decision to kill them was taken only then.[41] Memoria Viva surmises that to release these hideously tortured detainees into the community – and the press – would have reflected badly on the CNI, as well as on Pinochet's regime, with only a year to go before the plebiscite.[42]

What exactly happened to them following Carreño's release has emerged only after many years of investigation, inference and confession. It surely was no coincidence that Julieta Varas had arranged the grand opening of Loyola to match as nearly as possible the exact day of their disappearance 20 years before.

We have seen how the problem of how to dispose of the bodies of people murdered by the regime had emerged less than a day after the coup. Patio 29 served only for a couple of months. The commandants of Londres 38, the National Stadium, José Domingo Cañas, and Villa Grimaldi each had to find his own solution. By 1975 it was plain that neither cemeteries nor burial in remote regions were adequate, while a decade later the government's problems compounded through international investigations. Disposal at sea of the weighted body seemed the most secure method.

It is only at this point, after the execution of the five Frentistas, that Loyola was implicated in their disappearance. It appears that during the 1980s the CNI had requisitioned the site of the Air Force's maintenance depot at Loyola to maintain its own vehicles. Its high walls offered security from enquiry as to what the trucks were

---

40 'Alejandro Alberto Pinochet Arenas', Memoria Viva.
41 Cristián Pérez, '"Operación Príncipe": Irrumpe el FPMR-A' [Operation Prince: The FPMR-A erupts]; see also 'La verdadera história detrás del secuestro de Carreño' [The true history behind the kidnapping of Carreño], *La Nación*, 26 August 2007.
42 'Gonzalo Iván Fuenzalida Navarrete', Memoria Viva.

8. A MEMORIAL DESTROYED

carrying. Since the depot had served heavy construction needs as well as light maintenance, long sections of railway lines were stored there, perfectly obvious as they lay in heaps during the authors' first, unofficial tour of Loyola in 2006. Sections of railway lines were ideal as weights. So in November 1987, all that remained was to arrange for the sections of rail to be cut up and brought from the nearest CNI depot to the place where the Frentistas were to be killed. In 2006 the national newspaper, *La Nación,* reported:

> One of the confessions that confirmed this fact was that of an agent – whose identity *La Nación* withholds – who went, following a phone call to Cuartel Loyola, situated in Pudahuel, and spoke with the Despatch Officer, ordering lengths of iron which were to be used for constructing new rooms. The Despatcher refused to hand them over, but the agent returned next day and took them without authorisation. They were used to weigh down the bodies and it was these that were thrown into the sea, according to the source.[43]

Not for nothing is Loyola referred to on a website as 'The villa of the railway lines'.

No evidence has as yet been unearthed that Loyola actually functioned either as a detention centre or torture centre, but we can perhaps understand Varas's desire to have her comrades-in-arms be remembered somewhere. And in truth, there is a strong case that the Pinochet victims who lived or worked somewhere in Quinta Normal be remembered at a memorial in the regional centre. Surely they deserve it: fearless women fighting on the front line, a returning exile bent on continuing the armed struggle, a curious child accidentally shot dead, a man rescuing a child from danger after curfew, a man simply standing outside his house, two naïve and hot-headed young men jumping heedlessly into a new pocket of the almost defunct MIR, perhaps without thinking more about it than that it stood for rebellious adventure, and certainly unaware of the dangers of informers. None deserved to die, none

---

43 'Una de las confesiones que confirma este hecho es la de un agente – cuya identidad La Nación se reserva – quien llegó hasta el llamado cuartel Loyola, ubicado en Pudahuel y habló con el oficial a cargo, pidiéndole pesados fierros, que eran empleados para estructurar nuevas dependencias. El encargado se negó a entregarlos, pero el agente llegó al día siguiente y se los llevó sin su autorización. Fueron usados para amarrar los cuerpos y que éstos se hundieran en el mar, dijo la fuente'; Jorge Molina Sanhueza, 'Agentes de La Dina vinculados con la desaparación de cinco Frentistas en 1987' [DINA agents linked to the disappearance of five Frentistas in 1987], *La Nación*, 3 February 2006; see also the paragraph 'Rieles de la muerte' [Rails of death] in 'Gonzalo Iván Fuenzalida Navarrete', Memoria Viva.

deserved torture. The five Frentista urban guerillas, too, perhaps deserve recognition, for they understood perfectly well that only a terrible death would await them if captured. It may be argued that even they deserve a memorial; but not in Quinta Normal, and not in Loyola. Josefina Rodriguez remains unimpressed. She states firmly that none of the names on Varas's memorial had or have any connection with the locality.

The 16 residents of Quinta Normal listed in black are buried and honoured in the tombs of their families. The tomb of the five Frentistas is marked only by a few pieces of rusty and dissolving iron rails somewhere at the bottom of the bay of St Antonio.

For a few months Varas's memorial stone continued in position leaning against its classroom wall. On her abrupt departure it was shifted casually to an abandoned flower garden, upside down, the paint peeling off, its original two sections at right angles to each other. Today it is nowhere to be seen. 'That list of names? Oh, we just threw it away.'

8. A MEMORIAL DESTROYED

Little is left of the once-guarded exterior wall (right) of the Loyola CNI Depot.
Source: Photograph by Peter Read, editing Con Boekel.

Part II

9

The memorials today and the advance of the state

The Stadium of Chile

Following a pattern developed in Argentina, Chileans have developed a strategy for punishing Pinochetistas whom the state refuses to name, still less punish, but whose identity is well known. This public spectacle of formal denunciation is known as a *funa*.

In preparation for each denunciation, the 'Funa Commission of Chile' posts on the web the chosen gathering point, though the exact destination or target is not divulged. The crowd, ranging from 50 to several hundred, assembles with placards, flags, a loudspeaker, video cameras and perhaps something for the *funista* to stand on when the moment comes. The leader shouts:

Si no hay justicia (If there is no justice)

The crowd roars in response:

Hay funa (There is the *funa*)!

The procession arrives at the house or workplace of the one to be denounced, whom Chileans call the *funado*, or *condenado*, the condemned, where after a few minutes, or as much as a week of camping outside the residence, the leader formally reads the itemised charges and declares him condemned. The participants then disperse.[1]

Very different was the *funa* of the torturer of Victor Jara.

It was not until 2006 that 'el Príncipe', the Prince, was identified as he who had first recognised Jara in the Stadium of Chile and marked him out for special attention. 'Mad Dimter', Edwin Dimter Bianchi, was a public servant working in white shirt and tie, a senior bureaucrat in downtown Santiago. Such was the fury and grief of the crowd that even today the documentary of his *funa* can still bring an audience to shocked silence.[2]

The video begins with the discussions about who, among the thousands expected to join the *funa*, should enter his office building. Camera following, some 20 people push their way through, to form a crush so tight that the *funista* himself, designated to read the formal denunciation, cannot squeeze in and has to mount his portable podium in the passage outside. Inside the office the protesters push and scream at Bianchi. Perhaps in the commotion the camera loses focus, for the next shot shows el Príncipe lying on his back on his desk, legs flailing, while a woman brandishes a huge photograph of Jara centimetres from his face. Someone pushes open a window, perhaps to let the assembled crowd below hear the tumult. It is impossible to hear a word spoken, not even those of the *funista* calmly proceeding, though inaudibly, outside the door.[3]

In 2009 President Bachelet authorised the exhumation of Jara's remains from his niche burial place, close to Patio 29, where Joan Jara and two communist friends had perilously shoved them in the darkest hours of the night of 18 September 1973. For four days they lay in state while mourners, including the President herself, filed past. An enormous procession followed the cortège to a new and dignified

---

1   For example, see Peter Read, 'Following the Funa: Punishing the state in Chile', *Arena Journal* 32, 2009, 45–51; see also Ernesto Carmona, 'Detención ilegal de documentalistas en Chile' [Illegal detention of documentary makers in Chile], 23 August 2007.
2   Nèlida D. Ruz de los Paños, *La Funa de Víctor Jara*, documentary, 2007; for excerpts see 'Funa al Asesino de Victor Jara, "Edwin Dimter Bianchi"', YouTube.
3   Read, 'Reconciliation without history', pp. 284–85.

tomb. 'Finally,' Bachelet announced, 'after 36 years, Victor can rest in peace.'[4] But Bianchi has not been formally arraigned, although the officer alleged to have pulled the trigger of the gun that killed him, Pedro Núñez, was ordered extradited from Florida to Chile in 2012.[5]

Jara, perhaps, rests in peace, but not the building in which he died. The Stadium of Chile, renamed the Victor Jara Stadium, continued to decline in appearance and status.

The tour, 2014

Juan, different from the guide of 2009, is another stadium caretaker equally committed to sharing oral history with the few who visit the stadium seeking information. Brought through that right-hand corridor, the UTE people sat – Juan points to the far corner – in that green seating area. Beside them, in that yellow area, were forced to sit the factory workers rounded up in those *poblaciones* marked for destruction in the first week of the coup. Above them in that corner, and in each corner, was mounted a 4.5mm machine gun. It was just there – he points – that someone killed himself by jumping off the third storey seating onto the floor. And another one over there. They were the deaths Jara referred to in his last song:

> The other four wanted to end their terror
> One throwing himself into space, others beating their heads against the wall...

And just here was where an eight-year-old, somehow detained with the others, was shot while he was running about.

Now come this way. This left-hand corridor was taken over by the security forces. Not even the ordinary soldiers were allowed in. Totally out of bounds. Each of these little side rooms was taken over too – even the changing rooms. Only last year someone turned up from Britain who identified the holes in the floor as bolt holes to fasten down the *parillas* – two in this big changing room.

---

4   'Chile reburies coup victim and singer Jara', BBC News.
5   Patrice J. McSherry, 'The Víctor Jara case: Justice in 2013?', *Social Justice* Debates, 12 February 2013.

> Since then we've found such holes in every one of the changing room floors. They tied each detainee down naked and attached electrodes all over their bodies. And they could throw water from the basins onto the metal frame to conduct the current better. We had never even noticed those holes before.

He opens another door on the right, the floor and walls covered in tumbling mats.

> This is where children do their martial arts lessons today. But they did the executions in here because it's a long way from the street. Before they covered them up you could see more than 40 bullet marks in the back wall.

The downstairs changing room, centre point of the previous impromptu tour, and site of Jara's torture and execution, is locked.

No more signage is to be seen than what was first fixed in 2003, and there seems no probability of further. Apart from the foyer, no plaque marks the association of detained-disappeared from the UTE or the *poblaciones*. Successive Ministers for Sport control the further erection of historic markers throughout the site and have clearly resisted efforts to further memorialise the precinct.

To this day, the Victor Jara Stadium remains one of the least marked sites of the major torture, extermination and disappearance centres in all Chile. No international band has performed in the Victor Jara Stadium since 2009.

No leftist party except Jara's Communist Party showed much interest in the stadium even at the time, 2003, when the government was prepared to allow a restrained signage. Since then the human rights movement also has shown little interest, in part, of course, because its focus is persons rather than place. Several hundred homeless Chileans continued to shelter on the stadium floor against Santiago's bitingly cold winter nights. For many years the trump card seemed held by the state. It owned the building and in the absence of any current interest group demanding conservation or interpretation, it chose to do nothing. Ageing and somewhat decrepit, it seemed that the stadium had nothing to anticipate but a deteriorating and unmemorialised future.[6] The Minister's control was not, however, absolute. It is rumoured that the Piñera government in 2015 tried to sell the site for a shopping mall, but was forestalled at the last moment by the declaration of the stadium as a Protected Historic Monument. Yet how many resources future governments would deploy towards its preservation remained uncertain.

Patio 29

In 2005 President Bachelet's centre-left government designated Patio 29 as another Protected Historical Monument. In 2010 President Sebastián Piñera's centre-right government constructed a memorial platform at the patio, some 40 metres long and 1 metre high, 3,032 pieces of precast concrete blocks.[7] At irregular intervals marble plaques replaced the concrete. One read:

> Patio 29 represents the horror of mourning that never ends.
> It represents the tireless struggle to know the truth, obtain justice and remember.

The plaque jointly memorialised the detained-disappeared in Patio 29, the Association for the Families of Detained-Disappeared, the politically executed and the rural town of Paine and victims of the bombed seat of government, La Moneda.

Another read:

> Patio 29. Recovery of a public place, where we invite you to reflect on the profound respect that we owe to LIFE, and the NEVER AGAIN that everyone yearns for.

---

6 For conversations, interviews and information on events at the State University of Technology and Estadio Chile, thanks to José Uribe.
7 'Patio 29 Memorial', Architizer; Pascale Bonnefoy M., 'El silencio del cementerio' [The silence of the cemetery], ArchivosChile, 10 September 2013.

And a third:

> They wanted to kill you
> And they killed you
> They wanted to burn your body
> and they burned it.
> They wanted to tear you from the struggle
> And this they could not do
>
> They could not tear you from the struggle!

***

Yet despite the passing of so many decades and so much investigation, nobody today can be certain of how many bodies were taken to the Patio in the first four months of the coup and buried, or later exhumed, or went straight to the crematorium. In 2013 ChileArchive attempted a full-scale determination, both case by case and by comparing the records of the Medical-Legal Institute, where many of the bodies were sent first, and those of the General Cemetery. The Medical-Legal Institute holds records of 1,130 bodies taken to the cemetery, 700 showing signs of bullet wounds. The cemetery records differ markedly both in comparison with the institute's, and internally. Unhelpfully, its administrator allows only 'consultation' (viewing) of the Site Register, but no copying or reproduction. Unlike many other of the mysteries raised in this book about which we can be sure that somebody, somewhere, knows the truth, such were the ad hoc improvisations, daily changes and makeshift solutions at Patio 29 that no final record was kept, or if it was, it would be almost certainly wrong. After months of investigation, ChileArchive concluded rather forlornly:

> Were they cremated in total secrecy, as has been rumoured for years? Were they taken to another place and disappeared? Were they buried as NN [No Name] without any records? Or were they buried in niches or tombs without being recorded in the Cemetery Records?[8]

---

8   Bonnefoy, 'El silencio del cementerio'.

ChileArchive's appraisal, like those of all other leftist research organisations, stresses the need for respect of human life codified as human rights. Introducing the need to reassess the numbers of victims who may have been buried in Patio 29, even temporarily, the Archive stated that on:

> 14th of September, when the bullet-ridden bodies began to arrive, 71 persons were buried, among them the first eight victims of human rights violations, that of an adolescent of 16 years, Tabitha García Gutiérrez.[9]

Notice the fundamental shift away from the 1970s invocation of an unfinished program of left political action, or even of an elected democracy overturned. By 2010 the violation of human rights had become first principle of the signage at all our memorials. From this point Chileans could denounce the contravention of the International Charter of Human Rights as Pinochet's first and fundamental violation. While powerful lobbies were emerging in the United States, Canada, Venezuela and Mexico, it was western and northern Europe with their long traditions of human rights discourse, sympathetic parliaments and existing organisations that were especially fertile soil. In Europe, Chilean exiles played no small part in persuading the International Human Rights Commission to adopt the abuses in their own nation as one of its first specifically directed investigations in the mid-1970s.[10] For some it needed not much more than a close look at a 'people's democracy' to realise its shortcomings. The communist Antonio Leal reflected:

> The earliest Chilean exiles in western Europe began to reassess their failed experiment, while the principle was reinforced by even some who had chosen exile in eastern bloc countries. The vision of socialism, with freedom, with respect for human rights, is an absolute necessity. I have come to believe that the socialist bloc ideologies were unviable ... Dead for me is the orthodox notion of Marxist-Leninism as

---

9   Bonnefoy, 'El silencio del cementerio': 'Ese 14 de septiembre, cuando comenzaron a llegar los primeros muertos por herida de bala al cementerio, fueron sepultadas 71 personas, entre ellas las primeras ocho víctimas de violaciones a los derechos humanos: una era la adolescente de 16 años, Tabitha García Gutiérrez. Los ocho fueron enterrados en nichos comprados por sus familias o en sepulturas familiares, según consta en el Libro de Ubicaciones del Cementerio General.'
10 Patrick Kelly, 'The 1973 Chilean coup and the origins of the transnational human rights activism', *Journal of Global History* 8(1), 2013, 165–86.

something that is really viable. It was expressed in the concentration of power in the hands of one party. The vision of socialism, with freedom, with respect for human rights, is an absolute necessity.[11]

The political scientist Patrick Kelly describes the huge growth of the human rights movement in the 1970s and 1980s as a kind of universal solidarity movement working as a means to galvanise the world against state repression and terrorism. Kelly traces the Chilean origin of the human rights movement to José Zalaquett's seminal work *The Human Rights Movement*, published in 1981, the thinking for which had begun in the United States after his expulsion from Chile in 1976. Thinking and political action snowballed together. Advocates persuaded Amnesty International to ally itself against human rights abuses, past and present. Through the combined effect of both, torture began to supplant exile as the first focus of violations. Strange alliances formed: the leader of the MIR, Miguel Enriquez, in August 1974 wrote to Archbishop Raúl Silva Henriquez, that divided as they were, 'certainly at least we are united in the defence of human rights'.[12] In the two following decades, the presentation of Pinochet's atrocities as violations of International Law or human rights, rather than merely the persecution of the left, remained the dominant voice of Chilean post-Pinochet protest. We have already seen how Viviana Diaz, whose father was disappeared in 1976, stated during a 2005 lecture at Villa Grimaldi that '[t]ime has passed, but the violations of human rights are still an inexcusable aberration; the truth of the deeds has always been here'.[13] Patio 29 – secluded rendezvous first of clandestine meetings in the 1970s, endpoint of mass human rights marches from La Moneda after 1989, key element in Bachelet's 'symbolic reparation' program – was among the first of the Sites of Conscience to forefront the violations of human rights as its *raison d'etre*.

---

11 Antonio Leal, in Katherine Hite, *When the Romance Ended: Leaders of the Chilean Left, 1968–1998*, Columbia University Press, New York, 2000, pp. 137–45.
12 Kelly, 'The 1973 Chilean coup and the origins of the transnational human rights activism'.
13 Diaz, 'Chilean society of today in the light of violations of human rights in the past'.

9. THE MEMORIALS TODAY AND THE ADVANCE OF THE STATE

The tour, 2014

Nena González, 77 years of age, still works as the custodian of Patio 29, sitting down more frequently, consulted often, promised much, receiving little. She saw the first burials, read the surreptitious notes of the disguised priest to his parents, made secret visits and drew maps for the Vicariate of Solidarity, witnessed the clandestine exhumations of corpses, the presidential ceremonies, the memorialisations, the demonstrations, the construction of the memorial platform. She is angry that she has been promised so much, but received nothing even from the Vicariate. Film crews consult her and promise to reward her when filming begins: nothing. She has no idea who will succeed her as caretaker of the precinct. Nobody in her family wants to, yet that is the sole tradition by which the cemetery caretakers have functioned for more than a century. She holds so much knowledge, so many memories, so much torment in what she has seen, heard and absorbed; but it seems of no value to anyone outside the instant gratification of their curiosity. The deep-seated prejudices of the Chilean class system seem to ensure that few, even those leading the human rights movement, will ever take seriously a 77-year-old woman of bent back and hardly any teeth, in an ancient blue dustcoat, born within a stone's throw of this place of enormous symbolic significance, sweeping the paths and keeping alive the memories of those who lay within her domain, with no more equipment than a worn-out broom.

Patio 29 remains, of course, part of the city's General Cemetery, and like the Victor Jara Stadium is the property of the state. None of the collectives, so strong in other Sites of Conscience, has taken the role of *primus inter pares* to demand a certain course of action, for this is shared public space. Nor has any leftist party demanded a dominating voice, not least because the number, identity and political allegiance of bodies buried in the precinct is unknown. The state holds absolute authority, and nobody has challenged it.

The National Stadium

Santiago was host to the 2014 South American Games, most of which took place at the National Stadium. Now that the government had declared itself politically committed to finishing the memorialisation of the National Stadium, it was much more convenient to show itself enthusiastic rather than resistant. It was no accident that the first part of the Kunstmann plan to be completed was the precinct outside the swimming pool adjacent to the main entrance to the whole stadium complex.

As March 2014 approached, forthright as ever, Wally Kunstmann was not going to miss an opportunity for international publicity. Three days before the opening she denounced the Concertación Government for years of passivity, and especially, the 'lack of transparency' in the armed forces. Again she stressed the centrality of women detainees at the expense of the attention thrown on male detainees memorialised (or supposed to be memorialised) within the stadium itself. If the authorities had elevated the status of anybody, it was that of the detained-disappeared and politically executed. The political detainees who had survived had remained forgotten since the transition to democracy. The circumstances of the men were well known, but those of the women, hardly at all.[14]

On 4 March Kunstmann, Sports Minister Ruiz-Tagle and sculptor Guillermo Nuñez presided over the opening of the 'Greece Memorial'.[15]

The tour, 2014

Visitors were left in no doubt as to whom the principal memorial was dedicated.

The self-guided Circuit of Memory designed by Wally Kunstmann's team begins, as was always intended, at the 'Greece Street' entrance near the swimming pool.[16] First stop is the entrance precinct where Don Roberto Sanchez may well be seen working, and it is here that the main work of memorialising currently takes place. An imposing metal plate mounted on an eye-level plinth reads:

---

14   Claudio Metrano, 'Este martes se inaugura el Memorial a prisioneros políticos en Estadio Nacional' [Opening of the Memorial to the Political Prisoners in National Stadium on Tuesday], DiarioUchile, 3 March 2014.
15   'Memorial for political prisoners at Estadio Nacional after forty years', *Santiago Times*, 5 March 2014. The names derive from the 'Greece Entrance', the main entry to the Stadium from 'Avenida Grecia' [Greece Avenue].
16   The tour is described in Spanish, in *Cambio 21* (Santiago), 27 April 2012, www.cambio21.cl/cambio21/site/artic/20120113/pags/20120113131301.html.

9. THE MEMORIALS TODAY AND THE ADVANCE OF THE STATE

Here in this former swimming pool changing room was the place where hundreds of women suffered the brutal repression of the military coup.

It was here in this sombre place where the dream of thousands of Chileans and those from overseas was interrupted by political detention, the horror of torture and death.

Through these walls, curling up round each other against the sneers, hundreds of women, house-wives, students, workers and professional women paid in pain and blood for their decision to be part of the construction of a more just and decent new nation for all.

Here inside, through these walls and beneath the claws of the gaolers, daughters, sisters and mothers were the first women in Chile who had to endure the beginning of a long and dark night of cowardice.

Yet it was also here that the pain wove the unbreakable net of fraternity which gave the prisoners mutual protection against terror, and cared with their lives for their pregnant comrades, for outside these walls tomorrow, it is certain that life will continue and fulfil their hopes.[17]

In memory of all those who suffered within its walls and those who hoped, in the darkness, to see the light of justice and liberty.

Regional Metropolitan Association for Men and Women Prisoners and Political Prisoners

***

The much-reproduced icon of the Metropolitan Association shows clearly a woman, not a man, bound blindfolded in a chair. Everywhere the language is heightened, the passions intense. In the small permanent exhibition installed in front of the changing room, detainees are regularly described as 'prisoners of war'. The former detainee Roland Carrasco writes:

The Stadium, barracks and prison, where artillery points at the entrances of the sporting complex. The (military) patrols tramp on the pavement of the interior paths allowing the echo of orders, greased metal sounds, shouts and discharge of rifles and heavy machine guns.

---

17   También fue aquí donde el dolor tejío la red irrompible de la fraternidad, que hizo a las prisoneras protegerse mutuamente del terror, cuidar con sus vidas a sus compañeras embarazadas porque mañana, fuera de estas paredes, es cierto que continua la vida y se realizan sus esperanzas.

The gunpowder stinging in the nostrils paralyses the prisoners' hearts in the cells like Gate 8. The three long-haired teens were taken away with their heads covered under a blanket and they never returned to be healed at the gate. Neither did the two workers in Dressing-room 4 taken off to interrogation in the frightful Velodrome. Many years later, we understood that their relatives found their mortal remains.[18]

Teresa Anativia López writes:

> We kept guard over a piece of soap for our comrades who had been raped, offering care and caresses, especially when they woke up at night screaming with nausea and vomit.

In November 2014 a temporary exhibition featured stories of individual women, their photographs and stories suspended on the peeling, stained and ugly wall. Inside, in every corner, downstairs and in the farthest recesses, stood the remains of candles burned in collective and personal vigils enacted on the night that President Bachelet presided over the ceremonial opening of the changing room. Each one of the washbasins, deep in brown dust, carried the remains of two or three waxy stumps. A list of the names of some 50 female political detainees also carried the pungent comment that they were copied from the registers of the DINA Commander General Contreras: 'hence the decision of President Lagos to withhold the information collected by the Valech Commission of Enquiry is preventing further investigation'. The demand to release this information, as we shall see, is echoed by the National Institute for Human Rights established in Londres 38 Memory Space.

Outside the detention centre, an imposing sculpture completes the first signed-off memorial in the stadium complex. It is a shallow pool in which stand two large (4 metres by 2) modernist artworks mounted on a concrete frame, the work of the Chilean artist Guillermo Nuñez. The first depicts large black shapes under the title 'A Dark Time', and the other, 'Una Agonía Como Huella', an agony like a deep wound. Beside it stands a stone wall in the same colour as the rendering on the changing-room detention centre. Its shape echoes a prison wall. Towards the top is carved the ridgeline of the Andes skyline as seen from the stadium, towards the bottom is etched the phrase 'estuviste aquí' – you were here.

---

18 Tr. Paula González Dolan.

9. THE MEMORIALS TODAY AND THE ADVANCE OF THE STATE

In a pool of remembrance stands a huge drawing of black, formless shapes personifying the dark time.

A red cement path sweeps purposefully from the swimming pool towards the stadium, but the visitor does not pass the historical signage projected by the Kunstmann plan. It is not built, nor planned in the near future. Entrance way no. 8 into the stadium containing the detainee inscriptions is closed following damage by vandals in August 2014.[19] Nor does the tour take in a building identical to the women's detention centre on the other side of the new swimming pool, but out of sight and unremarked. Don Roberto Sanchez, foreman of the pool precinct, may be the only one who still recounts the rumours that have circulated since the dictatorship, that this building may have been used to hold international detainees. Was, perhaps, Charles Horman held here? Somebody knows, but nobody is telling.

The Via Crucis, the pathway between the Coliseum and the velodrome along which every detainee was frog-marched, is the same as ever. Heading towards the velodrome and the *caracol* torture chamber, the visitor passes another *caracol* on the left, also identical but also unremarked: this was the women's torture chamber, used as a store-shed from the 1990s. Don Roberto, blindfolded and waiting to be tortured, calculated from hearing their screams and his knowledge of the stadium terrain, that it was here that the women were being tortured. Like the changing room out of sight behind the swimming pool, its presence is now a source of unremarked embarrassment and quietly forgotten.

At the velodrome, the passionate narratives last seen at the other end of the stadium begin afresh.

> It was this place that the *caracol*, by chance constructed in the shape of a snail, was chosen by the Armed Forces to commit the most shameful atrocities ...
>
> For a few seconds, imagine raucous military marches filling the air in a vain attempt to disguise the sharp bark of rifles and the deadly thudding of the machineguns and the terrified cries of the victims ...

---

19   'Dolor por la violencia' [Grief at the violence], *Cambio 21*, 28 August 2014.

> The truth of these facts disclosed here must prevail and with that truth the recovery of the dignity of the victims. Night will pass into a day in which the new generations, mindful of the recent history, will never repeat such terrible deeds.

The velodrome, still without signage, is open for cycling events while the *caracol* remains locked. Clearly the next stage of construction, now that military intervention can be discounted, will depend on the determination of the government to pay for it. Nobody has had to set aside Don Roberto Sanchez's preference for a sunny fountain of frolicking cherubs and beneficent angels. He has not told anybody, nobody has asked him.

The last and single most significant element in the Kunstmann plan was the construction of a memorial museum. That, of course, will not now happen since Bachelet, in the last year of her previous term (2006–10), constructed the massive Museum of Memory and Human Rights elsewhere in the city.[20]

After the Victor Jara Stadium and Patio 29, the National Stadium is the third of the three state-owned atrocity sites. It is the only one of the three in which specific interest groups have demanded a voice, even then not the parties, collectives or brigades of the left, but the Association for Families of the Detained-Disappeared, and later the Association for Ex-Political Prisoners. Perhaps they found it a more attractive venue because the issues of the National Stadium were international, the Victor Jara Stadium only party-parochial, and Patio 29 inaccessible. Whatever the interest groups, though, the state commissioned the Kunstmann plan, delayed it, altered it, oversaw it and will determine its final disposition.

Yet within the girdle of control came freedoms manifest in the memorials themselves. Notice how women survivors here are identified not by party affiliation but by occupation:

> Through these walls, curling up round each other against the sneers, hundreds of women, house-wives, students, workers and professional women paid in pain and blood for their decision to be part of the construction of a more just and decent new nation for all.

---

20 Museo de la Memoria y los Derechos Humanos [Museum of Memory and Human Rights].

9. THE MEMORIALS TODAY AND THE ADVANCE OF THE STATE

The writer uses the Spanish reflexive verb *acurrucarse* (literally 'snuggle up') to describe the solidarity of the women detainees at the National Stadium, meaning here in English something like 'nestling round against each other for mutual protection', against the *garras* (claws, talons) and the *vejámenes* (satire, shafts, insults, taunts, sneers) of the gaolers. Both the verb and nouns are evocative words not used in other memorials. They are not those in everyday use in the *poblaciones*, but literary and in this context, poetic. Women survivors make the biting, unequivocal moral judgement of *una noche cobarde, larga y oscura*, a long and dark night of cowardice. The phrase carries a linguistic force different to 'the most ferocious violations of human dignity' that 'demand justice and punishment' but one equally potent in its contempt for a false and corrupt *machismo*. The 2014 text makes no explicit demand for justice, only an implied blazing indictment of the captors' claim to call themselves men. In focus are no longer the dictatorship atrocities, but the human experience of the detainees and their strategies of survival. The decade-long refocus away from the detained-disappeared and politically executed towards the lives of the survivors continues. It is this most recent signage at the National Stadium that leads the direction. We can compare the ascendancy of this educated class of memorialisers with the liberal-left West German establishment's rise to dominance in interpreting the Nazi past.[21] Though from the same social/educational stock, it is the Chilean once-radical left that has seized the public interpretation of the dictatorship. They underline agency not victimhood, resistance, not suffering, not what *they* did to us, but what *we* did to survive. Share our experiences if you can.

What may be the government's final word on the nation's memorials was a new plaque erected in 2015. It read:

National stadium
National monument

The plaque's definitive brevity implied finally that it was here, of all Chile's Sites of Conscience, that the human rights violations of Pinochet were to be finally focused and encapsulated.

---

21   Knischewski and Spittler, 'Competing pasts', p. 167.

Londres 38

A 2014 pamphlet for English speakers greeted visitors entering Londres 38 by informing them that:

> This space now serves to help understand the reality of state terror, enter into the memories of the protagonists of this story, and take an active part in discussions and debates over present day struggles.

The emphasis on the present day, and the absence of historical comment on either the MIR or the 119, indicates the huge discrepancy between the present purposes of 'Londres 38 Espacio De Memoria' (London 38 Memory Space) and the desires and intentions brought by the collectives a decade earlier.[22]

Some time in 2012, the state-dominated consortium managing the use and interpretation of Londres 38 issued a report entitled 'A Memory Space Under Construction: Londres 38 House of Memory'. It began challengingly:

> The working group has developed a memory project which seeks to go beyond the traditional concepts of museum or commemorative space, in line with new currents in critical museology, which privilege relations with the community, that is to say, the world of the subjects and not only objects (monuments and buildings) and their display. (s. II)

At the genuinely community-controlled corporation at Villa Grimaldi, such a statement would signify that the corporation had recognised the need not to shut itself off in its own memories but to engage young Chileans.[23] In the light of the feuding collectives' failed struggle to retain control over the space at Londres 38, the statement could well be construed as a decisive moment of state intervention.

Nor did the following paragraph dealing with the planned role of the collectives give them any encouragement:

---

22   'Former Center of Repression and Extermination', Londres 38 House of Memory, pamphlet (in English), 2014.
23   'Proyecto: Un Espacio de Memoria en Construcción' [Project: A Memory Space under Construction], Londres 38 House of Memory, pdf, n.d. c. 2011.

Unity and Plurality. The three collectives constitute a new organisation for all the objectives relating to the management and organisation of Londres 38, maintaining their autonomy to carry out their original aims, *provided that this autonomy creates neither difficulty nor implementation of the adopted agreement*. (emphasis added)[24]

The site itself, the proposal continued, would provide a space to meet, engage in dialogue and exchange information with those who visited the building; information about the building could be provided in forms like brochures and wall exhibitions.[25]

The first objective of the management committee was 'to make a contribution towards Londres 38 in the construction of a society and a state that guarantees and promotes respect for human rights'.[26] And indeed the proposal looked to have some teeth. A pamphlet of November 2014 stated boldly:

> Forty years after the coup and two decades of civil government
> There are still SECRET ARCHIVES.
>
> We demand their release.[27]

It continued:

> [Keeping state secrets] ... is antidemocratic and holds back the process of truth and justice, perpetuating the impunity of those responsible. For this reason, in cases of grave violations of human rights, the state is obliged to make public all the available information, and can't protect itself by denying the existence of requested documents or restrict access based on the individual privacy or national security, which are the usual reasons for denying access.

---

24 'Unidad y pluralidad. Los tres colectivos se constituyen como una nueva organización para todos los fines relacionados con la gestión y administración de Londres 38; manteniendo su autonomía para actuar en torno a los fines que les han dado origen, siempre y cuando dicha autonomía no contravenga ni dificulte la implementación de los acuerdos adoptados.
III.5.3 Espacio de encuentro, diálogo y acogida
Se habilitará una sala que tenga por fin albergar un espacio de encuentro, diálogo y acogida para quienes visiten la casa. En este espacio, habrá personal a cargo (que puede ser la misma persona que esté a cargo de la visita), y se contará con información en algún formato a definir (por ejemplo, folletos, trípticos, etc) sobre la historia de la casa y temas relacionados. Además, servirá para dar cabida a quienes quieran entregar información o un testimonio. Se ha acordado usar la sala del primer piso que hoy usan los guardias para este fin.' (p. 21).
25 Such a wall exhibition of 2014 was 'Secretos' (Secrets).
26 Section III.2, p. 11.
27 'Proyecto: Un Espacio de Memoria en Construcción' [Project: A Memory Space under Construction], p. 11.

The pamphlet, presumably approved by the Londres 38 Memory Space executive committee, demanded the opening of three discrete state archives. First were the secret parts of the Rettig Report (particularly the names of those implicated in the fate of the politically executed and detained-disappeared) and the Valech Report (particularly the names of those implicated in illegal detention and torture). To the cynical, the assertive tone might have indicated, perhaps, not much more than the government either disassociated itself or did not consider itself bound by publications emanating from Londres 38. It was ironic that the state's proposal seven years earlier, in 2007, to establish exactly such an Institute for Human Rights in Londres 38 was exactly what had united the warring collectives in vociferous and passionate opposition to it.

The pamphlet's third demand was for the further release of documents discovered in Colonia Dignidad.

Colonia Dignidad was a peculiar German quasi-colony, a state within a state in the south of Chile, tolerated uneasily by several post–World War Two governments, then encouraged and protected by Pinochet.[28] There his administration amassed a huge DINA archive. During the transition to democracy more documents were sent for storage and also, probably, to hide them.[29] In 2005 more than 40,000 files, held in larger biographical archives, were discovered to reveal the activities of DINA officers, including some involved in disappearances. Family members, legal investigators and historians also could locate many references to detainees: five, for example, to Victor Jara and two to Muriel Dockendorff, one of which confirmed her brief imprisonment, previously only suspected, in Londres 38.

For Londres 38 to gain the status of clearing-house of such a sensational collection of digitised documents was a major coup. Indeed, it was unclear why the government had allowed such an important archive to be funnelled through the comparatively obscure website of Londres 38. Much more logical would have been its own national Museum of Memory and Human Rights, or the National Archives of Chile itself. It may be that it had concluded that the conduit would

---

28   'Archivo de la Colonia Dignidad', Londres 38 Espacio de Memorias; Bruce Falconer, 'The torture colony', *The American Scholar*, 1 September 2008.
29   'Archivo de la Colonia Dignidad', Londres 38 Espacio de Memorias.

provide a useful justification for its control of Londres 38, while also distracting criticism that its interpretative control, its archaeological investigation and the basic maintenance of the building itself were all drifting aimlessly. The MIR remained nowhere; indeed, it was unsurprising that the democratic state remained unenthusiastic about allowing sympathisers of a party dedicated to armed revolution to install itself in an iconic building, which, in any case, had been the headquarters of the Socialists. Londres 38 had become the Institute for Human Rights that the government had first proposed in 2007 despite enormous opposition. Now its victory seemed complete.

Meanwhile, as the digital archive flourished, the building continued to deteriorate.

The tour, 2014

The first messages to be professionally inscribed on the grimy interior walls seven years earlier,

> This is a past which follows the present

and

> Memory making not inscribed in the present is the same as remembering nothing

seemed ironic in the absence of any signage specific to the building. The rough exploratory holes remained, one even piercing the next room. The staircase ceiling was peeling and part of it missing, and a piece of moulding had clearly fallen away rather than being removed. The signage reassured visitors that the holes in the walls (some made five years previously) were part of the restoration of the building, preliminary to a full archaeological and forensic examination 'that could bring new proofs to the judicial processes into the crimes committed in this building'. The elaborate but now deteriorating signage for the 2013 exhibition on the 119 was stacked, exposed to the weather, in the rear courtyard. On the blackboard inviting comment under the question 'Why are we constructing a memorial?' a single person had answered, 'To teach not to have confidence in mankind'. Beside it another message, 'While there exists no truth or justice there will be vengeance'. The only sign that appeared to be permanent, displayed in government red, aggressively reminded visitors that the interrogators, torturers, vigilantes and executors, employed by the state, still received a pension. Some have been 'condemned ... Others remain on active service'.[30]

The state defeated and ejected the party-driven political left from the building to install its own brand of the modern Chilean human rights movement through an institute that is no more than tolerated by the collectives. 'Human rights' to the Londres management appears to mean not much more than the release of certain archives. To the collectives it means, as it always has, the identification of burial sites, the whereabouts of the detained-disappeared and the identities of the perpetrators. Truth and Justice first and last. The parallel, if not discordant, objectives are unlikely to meet soon.

The MIR has failed to obtain its own commemorative building. Or has it? Roberto D'Orival Briceño's collective, Colectivo 119, may have its eyes on another House of Memory: José Domingo Cañas.

House of Memory José Domingo Cañas

Laura Moya's passing in 2013 initiated changes at first subtle, later more pronounced. The site's 2012 official history listed among its achievements its guided tours, weekly vigils, maintenance of the library, workshops, performances and the general advancement of human rights emanating from its own community of Ñuñoa. A diagram showed four divisions of authority, volunteers and honorary members at the bottom, upwards through the executive director, through the directorate until, at the top of the hierarchy, the unnamed Laura Moya, 'Fundadora':

> The restoration of this place was the result of the tenacity of family, survivors, human rights activists, young people's collectives working together. It was a joint effort, but there is no doubt that Laura Moya was the motor of this struggle. Her tenacity and leadership permitted the achievements which we share today.

---

30 María José Pérez and Karen Glavic, 'La experiencia de la visita y la visita como experiencia: memorias críticas y constructivas', Londres 38 Espacio de Memorias.

The equivalent version of 2014, after her death, omitted 'Fundadora', placing the executive director at the apex of the management structure.[31]

With much more frankness than shown by the other Santiago site custodians, the corporation admitted to its current failings and challenges. First, it had failed to attract young people sufficiently to carry on the work as the generation of the survivors faded:

> We proposed to ... carry out the construction of a society in which justice and respect for human rights comes first thus linked to the new generations of young people in Chile.

The second problem were the internal divisions:

> Different organisations formed during this period, the difficulties of the struggle and the frustration in the destruction of the building broke us up emotionally and sometimes we were not able to maintain unity. Despite having no resources, we discussed different proposals about what to do with the site.

Two particular challenges were to review the agreement among members of the directorate, and, in the only use of capitals in the entire website:

> Train and educate people in memory and NOT IN HORROR[32]

Followed by the affirmation of the significance of the physical site:

> Manuals and recipes of how to shape a place where crimes against humanity were committed don't transfer automatically from one to the other. Despite the differences between the centres, DINA is in the middle of the same history of the country, the contexts of each place are different.[33]

The tour, 2012

In 2012, the money that Laura and the government had invested was splendidly evident. The original walls and passageways were signposted, like 'Prisoners' entrance' or 'Torture room', leaving the visitor to reflect upon how small a space was needed for such

---

31 'Organigrama' [Organisation chart], Fundación 1367 Casa Memoria José Domingo Cañas.
32 'Capacitarse y trabajar la pedagogía de la memoria y NO DEL HORROR'.
33 'Casa Memoria José Domingo Cañas', Sitios de Memoria, 2012.

diabolical deeds to be enacted. Dozens of freshly varnished wooden poles supported billowing sails. Cement seats offered contemplation. A *parrilla* excavated from the ruins stood in its own space. The small swimming pool had been excavated and exposed. At the rear on the right stood a brand-new building capable of holding 80 conference guests, on the left Laura's donated political library. Through the rear door a cement pool of memory where on its plinth were gathered artefacts found among the ruins that the demolishers had left: nails, bolts, unidentified iron pieces. Etched photographs traced the history of the site. Fifty-four polished pebbles each bore the name of detained-disappeared, 10 more discovered since the initial list of names had been inscribed on the street memorial plinth. Lumi's presence was everywhere. A prominent poster read 'Lumi Rebel Light'.

Yet a few tiny details might have portended a deteriorating future: the memorial pool and fountain at the rear of the precinct had yet to be filled because of plumbing difficulties. At the extreme bottom of the memorial outside, the last three names of the detained-disappeared had themselves disappeared because of weather damage.

The tour, 2014

In 2014, a year after the death of Laura Moya, the welcome notice announcing the opening hours was missing. The once arresting murals continued to fade in the blistering Chilean sun. One of two had been crudely retouched, including that of the naked, suspended detainees, but a bench obscured the nudity of the women. The furious demand for punishment and justice painted on the boundary wall

> Here were committed the
> Most ferocious violations
> Of human dignity
> For this reason we demand
>
> JUSTICE AND PUNISHMENT

was now disfigured by an electricity meter stuck on the wall on the left-hand side, half hiding the words. The pool of memory remained dry. One of Laura Moya's last preoccupations, to verify the rumour that detainees had also entered the building through a door in the upper floor of the house next door, was now revealed, though uncaptioned; but peeling paint and huge gaps in the unseasoned wooden poles demonstrated that the government's contribution to the construction had been done as cheaply as possible. The iron frame lying in the 'Torture chamber', re-identified not as a *parrilla* but merely a large iron bedframe, was just a wiry tangle propped against a wall. Pieces of roofing tile, windows and an iron gate leaned uncaptioned against the conference centre, while a poster for gay rights indicated the desire of the remaining volunteer staff member, Bernardo de Castro, to ally the Memory House to other minority causes. Some of the informative text etched in metal had faded to become almost illegible; the sails had blown away or hung in tatters; the wooden pathways were subsiding and hard to negotiate, while a hoarding of all the detained-disappeared in A4-sized photographs fixed outside the conference room was gone altogether. Inside, the photographs of Laura Moya were kept secure by the ever-faithful Bernardo de Castro, while a poster of Lumi Videla Moya bravely greeted visitors entering the building.

Lumi Videla Moya
Justice and Memory
NOW

***

A number of individuals, alienated or driven from the Casa de Memoria's team of volunteers by Laura's strong personality, were beginning to reconsolidate, concerned that the governing body seemed content to allow the whole precinct to fall to bits. Money was desperately short. Account-keeping for donations or sales of posters and Laura's books was not much more sophisticated than a shoebox. Vandals broke into the building twice. Disaster: in the same year the corporation learned that all the timber, including that in the conference centre itself, had been infested by borers and would have to be replaced. Who was to pay for that?

Laura Moya had driven José Domingo Cañas forward through her authority, determination, learning, passion, bureaucratic expertise and finance. Her absence now demonstrated the strengths and weaknesses of a single vision when once that engine failed. She had achieved so much. But for how long would her vision endure?

Villa Grimaldi

The early tensions over what form the memorial should take had by 2015 given way to a more urgent discussion as to what should happen within the grounds. By then the replica tower, erected after much angst on the presumption that it would dominate the entire precinct, had been overshadowed by the dome over the performance space. The corporation, again after much deliberation and contrary opinion, decided that it was more important to attract new visitors than maintain the original conception of quiet serenity. Outreach programs invited school visits and provided student learning materials. Theatre, pop concerts, recitals of poetry and music, album launches, even a wedding ceremony of a son of a detained-disappeared followed.[34]

The changes, though, were internal, not forced upon the corporation, and made possible through its ability to keep government interference at bay. Unlike most other Sites of Conscience in Santiago, Villa Grimaldi still manages its own displays and has the finance to service them.

With the passing of years, corporation members and guides notice that more and more children arrive knowing little even of the dictatorship itself. The historian Katherine Hite, visiting the site at the end of 2009, told a reporter that she saw an impulse in the new team of professionals to educate the young that did not exist previously.[35] In an article written in English, she and her associate Cath Collins found that the site still felt somewhat insular, intended more for human rights activists than others.[36]

Nor was rethinking confined to the corporation members alone, for the program of interviewing 164 survivors of Villa Grimaldi brought some serious reflections to the young scholars well versed in the manifold controversies attending oral history and memory. As was proper, their commentary on the archive that they had compiled was cautious and restrained, but their awareness of what was *not* being said troubled them. In a companion commentary on the transcribed recordings, the interviewer Dr Mario Hercés reflected that historical interviews in

---

34   Villa Grimaldi Corporación por la Paz.
35   'Experta norteamericana Katherine Hite visitó Villa Grimaldi'.
36   Hite and Collins, 'Memorial fragments, monumental silences and reawakenings in 21st century Chile', pp. 387–88.

9. THE MEMORIALS TODAY AND THE ADVANCE OF THE STATE

Latin America, with their prevailing themes of militancy, resistance, torture and resilience, carried an explicitly political dimension reaching beyond the purposes of simple recall but touching the restitution of justice.[37] Evelyn Hevia Jordan conceded that in the interests of neutrality and objectivity, the investigator had to confront what seemed an already predetermined position. How did one deal with cases of denunciation, collaboration and betrayal, themes barely touched upon in the interviews? Bravely, but circumspectly, she surmised that the principal hypothesis of the oral historians was that the political militants had influenced the form in which the survivors relived their experience as detainees. 'This implies that within Villa Grimaldi there grew a certain type of relationship among the prisoners which many times appeared in terms of solidarity, mistrust, isolation and others.'[38] Wisely, in her concluding paragraph to the transcriptions, she let her uneasiness with what she hinted might be a self-imposed hegemony of testimony be articulated by a survivor himself:

> [O]ur history has been constructed on the basis of the myth of heroism, eh? And all of us were heroes (laughs) and they call themselves survivors now, but I don't much like that term, it gives a heroic shade to the thing which (leaning forward) – you're not just a survivor of Grimaldi, you're a survivor of something much more global (silence).[39]

Such an admission is worrying for all oral historians who believe that the medium should have the capacity to reproduce emotions that the speakers felt at the time, not what they felt, or thought they should have felt, later. A more plain-speaking critique of what we might call the politicisation of emotions amongst trauma victims may be found in the tensions between those who fled to Miami after Castro's victory in 1959–61, and those who arrived via a perilous raft journey in the mid-1990s. The oral historian Elizabeth Campisi found immense pressure placed upon Cubans arriving at Miami in homemade rafts to conform to the prevailing narrative that presented the Cuban revolution as

---

37 Diana Taylor, 'Trauma as durational performance', *Open Journal Systems* 1(1), 2009.
38 Evelyn Hevia Jordan, 'Notas para una aproximación al estado de las memorias subterráneas en el Chile actual' [Notes towards an approach to the state of hidden memories en Chile today].
39 'Testimoniante, Archivo Oral Villa Grimaldi', n.p.

invalid, unpleasant or beset with negatives. Experienced interviewers told each other 'you have to get to them before they learn what to say'.⁴⁰

And indeed, behind the transcribed rhetoric, and unlike most of those who never were physically harmed, the Chilean tortured seem to hold little grudge against the well-known and much vilified female 'betrayers' like 'La Flaca Alejandra' (Marcia Alejandra Merino). They seem to understand them as others do not or can not. Some Chilean torture survivors maintain that probably *everyone* revealed something under electrical torture; in fact it is said that MIRista rank and file members were directed that if (and when) they had to betray anyone, they should do so down the hierarchy of leadership, not up it. Such advice is nowhere to be found in the archive. Meanwhile, some other survivors of Villa Grimaldi feel totally alienated from it, or having been once, never return.⁴¹ Clearly their views are not in the transcription archives either. They did not wish to be interviewed, and were not.

How then to interpret Villa Grimaldi faithfully or accurately? Do the terms mutually exclude each other? The struggle for a deeper meaning of the experience of repression by the dictatorship endures, though its manifestations are not always sympathetically received. Michele Drouilly was quite unimpressed with Roberto Merino's guided tours, arguing that she and others had worked so hard to get words like 'detained-disappeared' and 'torture' in the everyday vocabulary of Villa Grimaldi and the nation. 'Suddenly we have this man talking about punishment and actors.'⁴² Yet Merino had made a brave attempt at a Foucauldian interpretation of his humiliation and torture. It may be that he suffered from several of the accepted manifestations of post-traumatic stress disorder like emotional numbing, depersonalisation and dissociative amnesia.⁴³ Would such a mental state affect a guide's interpretation of his or her interpretation? Clearly, yes. Are changes to be expected over time? Clearly, yes. Should such survivors be allowed to act as guides and, if so, who should monitor their interpretation?

---

40   Elizabeth Campisi, 'Talking cure. Trauma, narrative and the Cuban rafter crisis', in Cave and Sloan, *Listening on the Edge*, Oxford University Press, London, 2014, p. 89.
41   Diana Duhalde, discussion, December 2014.
42   Michele Drouilly, interview, 4 April 2015.
43   Peters, in Cave and Sloan, *Listening on the Edge*, pp. 232–33.

9. THE MEMORIALS TODAY AND THE ADVANCE OF THE STATE

That is a matter for the corporation. Describing her tour by Pedro Matta, the performance scholar Diana Taylor pondered the difference between trauma victim and guide:

> Like other survivors, I believe, Matta is both a traumatized victim and a witness to trauma … For Matta, the experience does not last two hours – it has lasted years, since he was disappeared by the armed forces. His reiterated acts of walking, of showing, of telling, of leading people down the paths characterize trauma and the trauma-driven actions to channel and alleviate it. For him, as for the Mothers of the Plaza de Mayo, the ritualized tour offers both personal consolation and revenge. Memory is a tool and a political project – an honoring of those who are gone, and a reminder to those who will listen that the victimizers have gotten away with murder. His tour, like the Mothers' march, bears witness to a society in ruins in which judicial systems cannot bring perpetrators to justice. Yet the walk-through, like the march, also makes visible the memory paths that maintain another topography of place and practice, not of terror but of resistance – the will not only to live but also to keep memory alive.[44]

Six years later, 40 years after the experience, few survivors are prepared to act any longer as guides. The day-to-day interpretation of the site is the province of the younger generation. The strong themes of a decade earlier – blow-by-blow brutality at every corner, the serenity of the rose garden, quiet contemplation of the Wall of Names, the Foucauldian theoretical construct, the loving solidarity among detainees expressed more strongly by women than men, the touching humanising of Michele Drouilly's artefacts in her House of Memory – what remains of these in the modern tour?

The tour, 2014

The modern tour is a self-guided audio tour, invoking, in English or Spanish, 'the painful history' carried out by the 'highest authorities of the Chilean state'. Unlike Matta's tour, which climaxed in the Wall of Names, the visitor follows an anticlockwise circle beginning at the now blocked original detainees' entrance, through which 'no one will ever walk over these paving stones again'. The grove of birch trees symbolises something 'solitary and fragile'. The audio guide acknowledges the death of 'Mauro', the guard executed at the ombú

---

44 Taylor, 'Trauma as durational performance'.

tree, but provides no details of the manner of his excruciating death. The rose garden was said to be revived after 'the corporation decided to re-create it initially as homage' to the women who had died at Villa Grimaldi. The 'House of Memory' was developed to show the disappeared 'beyond their mere names' and 'developed jointly with their relatives'. Michele Drouilly is uncredited for these initiatives. Past the tower – which visitors are still encouraged to enter despite children sometimes fooling about in it – come the memorials to the left political parties. All look much more cared for than a decade ago: the MAPU party, 'dreaming and fighting for justice and solidarity', the rather homespun Socialists' – a little pebble lying on a stone block, reminiscent of Laura Moya's memorial at José Domingo Cañas. The Communist memorial 'fighting in the antifascist struggle to restore democracy' has an excerpt from the Communist Party member Pablo Neruda's 'The Dead of the Plaza':

> And I don't come to weep over where they fell
> I come to us
> I appeal to the living, to you and me within your beaten breast
> Others fell in the past. Do you remember? Yes, you
> Remember
> Others fell who were of the same family, the same name.[45]

The MIRistas, ever the internationalists, have inscribed in bronze the names of 580 fallen comrades, including those killed in Nicaragua, El Salvador and Argentina.[46]

The optional audio subsection 'Daily life in the cells' speaks of the agency of the women, who would sing so as not to hear the screams of the tortured. The guide describes how an individual was deputed to wash everyone's clothes, while others chipped away at the coloured glass to replace it with identically coloured paper that could be removed as a spyhole.[47] The men's testimony to their own solidarity is not mentioned. Any hint of a Foucauldian interpretation has vanished.

---

45 Los Muertos de La Plaza (1948)
    Yo no vengo a llorar aquí donde cayeron
    Vengo a nosotros, acudo a los que viven
    Acudo a tí y a mí en tu pecho golpeado.
    Cayeron otros antes. Recuerdas? Si,
    Recuerdas.
    Otros que el mismo nombre y apellido tuvieron.
46 'Memorial del MIR en la Villa Grimaldi', *Punto Final*, 14–27 May 2010.
47 Tour conducted 8 December 2014.

The passionate intensity of the Ex-Political Prisoners memorial unveiled at the National Stadium in March 2014 is entirely absent; overall the impression is restrained, factual, informative, bland.

Michele Drouilly has very little to do with Villa Grimaldi now. The ideological and museological issues, she says, have been mostly resolved. What depresses her is the endless fights for positions of control and celebrity status amongst the leadership. Her energies are spent, she did what she could. Today the determination that she brought to Villa Grimaldi to reify the memorial of Jacqueline, she has brought to her own site of conscience at home. She holds her sister not in Villa Grimaldi but in her heart.

Loyola, Quinta Normal

Julieta Varas, ever the fighter, did not take kindly to her ejection in 2009 from the governing body of the Loyola Renacer, and from her home within the precinct. She appealed to the Court under Article 20 of the Constitution against her 'arbitrary and unjustified expulsion'. The judgement conceded that she, Rebeca Videla and others had indeed founded the Renacer to develop a housing estate with a 'social project' and a 'memory project concerning the violation of human rights'. However, other 'organisations and persons' had joined 'to produce tensions and difficulties'. Her plea was rejected, the Court ruling that the Renacer committee had acted wholly within its constitution in replacing members of the committee when necessary, and to expel certain members from their homes and from the Loyola precinct.[48] Varas departed and is seldom seen in the area.

Renacer Loyola itself is complete, a gated community within a mixed municipality of small businesses, unemployment and upward mobility. Sections of the original wall remain, but most of the houses are fronted either by an iron grid fence, or a 2-metre cement wall, as ugly as the original, topped with barbed wire. The dwellings are structurally identical even to the uniform colour of a light-brown cement rendering, personalised only with perhaps a satellite dish, gardens and, at Christmas, decorations and lights. The 5-hectare space is jam-packed, the passages narrow, the rooms small, but everything

---

48 Santiago Court of Appeal, 2nd hearing, 5 October 2011.

is modern, everything works. The only public spaces are the still-standing classrooms, where children's outdoor toys, and a garden cared for by Josefina, mark the spot of the last ignominious resting place of Varas's memorial plaque before the committee threw it away.

Josefina is deeply thankful to have a modern home within a secure community that she cannot be evicted from, which she can leave to her daughter, privileges that by no means all Chileans enjoy. But her ethic of hard work and self-sufficiency has come at a cost. One of the well-known sights was Josefina pedalling round the neighbourhood on a three-wheeled bicycle, the front converted to hold an enormous box of utensils and ingredients for on-the-spot *tortillas*. The repetitive strain injury to her wrists that developed over many years has greatly reduced her capacity to earn an independent living. Often, instead, she'll help out at her sister's liquor store three streets away. She is disappointed that the Renacer residents have divided themselves into those who consider themselves – these are her words – the aristocracy and the rest, the proletariat. The former keep to themselves and their children away from the others, don't use the communal space or come to the community meetings, and socialise elsewhere. She would love to secure a second dwelling for her son, but competition is intense. Her community ideals of open community values, like the mandarin tree in a free zone that everyone would share, have been disappointed.

Such a division is, to be sure, likely to occur amongst any group of human beings living together, but in profoundly class-conscious Chile, a small, self-contained, crowded community bounded very distinctly within a high wall would surely be expected to divide sooner rather than later. Such, of course, was never the idea of the Renacer. How then did it happen? Josefina's resentment is directed not at the Julietas of this world – individuals come and go – no, she resents the Chilean state that favours the very poor and the very rich but leave the great majority in the middle subject to corruption and bribery at every level. 'People at both extremes will get the system to work for them, but not those in the middle.' She wonders how the people who should never have never been admitted to Loyola gained their homes.

There is no tour, of course, to be undertaken at Loyola. No memorial plaque attaches to any interior or exterior wall of Renacer and is unlikely ever to do so.

9. THE MEMORIALS TODAY AND THE ADVANCE OF THE STATE

***

Those who wished in 2015 to commemorate the recent past confronted a Chile almost unrecognisable to those who once followed Victor Jara's invitation to gather round where the potatoes were burning. It was true that the class divisions based on family, wealth, position and education seemed as strong as ever, and the Communist and Socialist parties remained viable. But the polarities had softened. The founder of the far-right Fatherland and Liberty political grouping, Roberto Thieme, now believed that Pinochet was a traitor, and at the time of the coup he himself had lacked political sense.[49] Allende's Popular Unity Party had long ago fragmented to other parties. The Frente Rodriguista had committed no outrages for a decade. Laura Moya, lamenting that the next generation was taking only a shallow and passing interest in rebuilding their society, insisted that truth and justice were more urgent imperatives than human rights. Curators at Villa Grimaldi and José Domingo Cañas found themselves confronted by the ignorance and, at times, the flippant uninterest of their young visitors. While in disagreement over other issues, the centre and all manner of leftist opinion were united in the need for educating the young. It seemed that young people sometimes wondered what the struggle was about, since Allende and Pinochet could both seem to represent aberrations in their nation's otherwise stable democracy. Their elders, who had given so much to memorialise their party, friends or family, debated as to who would carry the burden of education. The gap between the looked-for paradise of the 'Socialist Republic of Chile' (as Lumi Videla's 15-year-old friend had put it so long ago) seemed at an unbridgeable distance from the demands of today's student movement for universal free education. Those whose parents had joined revolutionary-action parties like MIR embraced neither an agreed political direction nor what had once seemed to be an inevitable historical program to fulfil. Who would maintain the rage?

The MIR itself never recovered either from its savage persecution or claims that some of its leaders had collaborated with the security forces. By 2015 it existed more as a nostalgic might-have-been among its ageing supporters. Gladys Díaz, one of its few militants known to have revealed nothing under prolonged torture during the dictatorship,

---

49 Roberto Thieme, interview with Tomás Maciatti, YouTube, 17 September 2013.

remained defiant as she reflected, in 2010, on the achievements of her party. 'Were we heroic, altruistic, idealistic or naïve? Historians and sociologists, she surmised, even later MIRista generations, might ask: were we really an elite who gave our best without a moment's thought for ego? Yes, we might have been more aware, more tolerant, reflective, experimental, intelligent, older or wiser'; but Díaz concluded with the triumphant peroration that MIRistas had been enchanted by ideals and ideologies that they were prepared to give their lives for. No one could take away their immense pride in having been the revolutionaries of their time, forgers of the future, their unfulfilled dreams ready to be taken up by new generations.[50] Young people were indeed forming their own judgements, and not always favourably. In 2010 the filmmaker Macarena Aguiló, a child of MIRista parents who left her in Cuba while they returned to continue the armed struggle in Chile, subjected her mother, especially, to an excoriating though implicit interrogation of why she had done so.[51]

As ever, public memorialisation reflects the changing preoccupations of the society that creates them. Chileans do not, any longer, discuss the violence of the dictatorship – neither do their memorials. The confronting emotionalism of Pedro Matta's Villa Grimaldi tour has given way to a flat and unemotional audio tour to mark the endpoint of 25 years of 'polémicas intensas' as to how the history of suffering should be presented there. José Domingo Cañas first displayed what its curators thought, wrongly, to be a *parrilla*; now its Board of Governors prefers its House of Memory to advance 'education and memory and NOT HORROR'. The guide at Londres 38 defended the absence of the instruments of torture such as the *parrilla* in the building as 'contrary to its aesthetic'.[52]

The language of the memorials themselves turns its face from violence too. It is difficult to imagine how this furious invocation, painted in about 1999 on the boundary wall of House of Memory José Domingo Cañas, could be written in 2015:

---

50 Días, Gladys, 'Acto por Memorial del MIR en Villa Grimaldi, 8 de mayo de 2010' [Act of Commemoration at the opening of the MIR memorial, Villa Grimaldi, 8 May 2010], Correo de los Trabajadores.
51 Macarena Aguiló, prod. and dir., *El edificio de los chilenos* [The Chileans' House], DVD, 2010.
52 Leopoldo Montenegro Montenegro, interview, 5 December 2011.

9. THE MEMORIALS TODAY AND THE ADVANCE OF THE STATE

Here were committed the
Most ferocious violations
Of human dignity

For this reason we demand

JUSTICE AND PUNISHMENT

The potent words 'ferocious' and 'demand' would look out of place on any contemporary monument, and for several reasons. The desperate voice that demanded justice and punishment is clearly of the working-class *poblaciones* 'La Legua' and 'La Victoria'. The authors painted them in anguished rage on the wall of José Domingo Cañas at a time when the government was refusing to release the names of the perpetrators identified in its own reports (as it still does). In the following decades their public fury has become private, dulled to a deep resentment or forced acceptance that most of the perpetrators who have not yet been apprehended probably will never be punished. Though it is possible that another hitherto unknown site of execution like Cuartel Simon Bolívar may yet emerge, justice for the politically executed and the detained-disappeared seemed as far away as ever. It is the voices of the *poblaciones* that are absent on the most recent Santiago memorials.

Equally, the interpretative spotlight has moved away from the detained-disappeared and the politically executed. While each of the 2005 plaques outside Londres 38 named the identity and political party of the victim, 10 years later the families of the dead still await the crucial archives to be released by the state. Perhaps all but a few have given up hope that the missing will return. The memorials are already erected – or never will be. Short of the state releasing the secret information in the Rettig and Valech Reports, there is little left to discover, nothing that can further assuage the deepest feeling of mourning, loss and rage. The collectives who form a minority among the board members of the House of Memory Londres 38 have made the best of the state's dominance of the site to lever the further release of state documents.

In 2014 Wally Kunstmann maintained that it was the survivors of detention, especially the women, who remained forgotten, and her priorities were apparent in the very language of the plaques at the National Stadium. The contemporary public interpretation of the dictatorship is in the hands of the survivors.

One explanation for their success may be that, if full democracy may still not have completely returned to Chile, then administrative bureaucracy certainly has. The administration and the educated middle class, who can manipulate it, dominate today's memorialisation. The well-educated survivors, knowledgeable in lobbying, experienced in making the system work for them, strong in friendships in the right places, have seized the microphones and the inscribing tools. The House of Memory José Domingo Cañas is the only substantial memorial specific to the suffering of the *poblaciones* in the entire city; but without the initial lobbying and personal finance of Professor of Psychiatry Laura Moya, that would not exist either. Indeed, only two of the seven site memorials examined in this book have been actually created by the members of the working classes: the Communist Party's Victor Jara Stadium, which despite its heritage listing is in some long-term danger; and Julieta Varas's memorial plaque, which is already smashed and gone. Meanwhile, as the cruellest nightmares passed, highly articulate survivors have begun to speak about their experiences in interviews and documentaries. They write autobiographies and books of poetry. They engage more robustly in what is a process, to many, of self-therapy.[53] They meet their accusers: Gladys Díaz gained much comfort by confronting one of her torturers in court. She found him demystified: short, ugly, poorly educated, so powerless that he was forced to use the respectful second person singular pronoun *usted* rather than *tu* when addressing her.[54] Publicly discussing and composing the passionate but poetic reflections displayed in the women's detention centre and the *caracol* at the National Stadium surely acts as psychological release. Accustomed to rhetoric, the evocative, literary plaques at the National Stadium no doubt fell easier from the pens of middle-class survivors than those of the *poblaciones*. Less preoccupied with daily issues of food and shelter, they are able to focus their energies on memorialisation.

---

53 For example, Jorge Montealegre, *Frazadas del Estadio Nacional* [Blankets of the National Stadium], LOM ediciones, Santiago, 2003; Hernán Valdéz, *Tejas Verdes*, LOM ediciones, Santiago, 1996; Mario Artigas, *Valle de Lágrimas* [Vale of Tears], Pentagrama, Santiago, 2005.

54 Gladys Díaz, in Carmen Castillo, *La Flaca Alejandra*, DVD, 1993. Miguel Krassnoff Martchenko received, in 2011, 144 years imprisonment for over 20 crimes against humanity, Ramona Wadi, 'Dictatorship relics in Chile: Paying homage to Miguel Krassnoff Martchenko', Upside Down World, 14 November 2011.

9. THE MEMORIALS TODAY AND THE ADVANCE OF THE STATE

The survivors understand that both the public impulse to critically memorialise the atrocities of the Pinochet regime and the state's interest in doing so have almost run their course. What they write now is their last chance to interpret their own history, and they know it. Following generations cannot follow them with the same legitimacy or passionate intensity. No one will be able to shout, in Roberto D'Orival Briceño's account of the fiery meeting at Londres 38 on the day that the doors were opened: 'You have no right to speak. You weren't here!'

Yet it cannot yet be claimed that critical memorialisation of the dictatorship is quite complete. Knowledge of secret extermination centres like Cuartel Simon Bolívar only emerged in 2007; others may be revealed. Just as significant, perhaps, was a demand of June 2015 that army conscripts be considered as a victimised group in being compelled to carry out actions against their compatriots. Their suit claimed that they could not be held responsible for their actions.[55] It is not impossible that they too will demand a memorial. A speaker at a meeting of human rights activists at the National Stadium in December 2014 pressed for sites of resistance, such as the Vicaria de la Solidaridad, to be the next sites of commemoration rather than further sites of pain and suffering.[56] The feeling is growing that sites of resistance should be memorialised, not just of 'dead freedom fighters and resistance martyrs', but survivors like 'lawyers, teachers, journalists, archivists and parish priests'.[57] It is possible that State Terrorism is tentatively replacing the naming of the horror as human rights violations.[58]

***

The memorials that stand today, from José Domingo Cañas to the National Stadium, are still points of two shifting decades. While other hopes and expectations have been buried in the collective history of their time, the memorials crystallise the emotions of those that made

---

55 Melissa Gutierrez, 'La eterna batalla legal de los conscriptos de la dictadura' [The conscripts' eternal legal battle against the dictatorship'], *The Clinic* online, 17 June 2015, see also 'Confessions of a Torturer', *Santiago Times*, 25 November 2004.
56 Notes taken at meeting, 11 December 2014.
57 Sebastian Brett, Louis Bickford, Liz Ševcenko and Marcela Rios, 'Memorialization and Democracy: State Policy and Civic Action', p. 10.
58 Aguilera and Caceres, 'Signs of state terrorism…', p. 13.

them. They have survived internal strife, state interference, budgetary crises and vandals. They endure as texts to both their creators and their moment of creation and will continue to do so.

Provided, that is, that the state supports them equally. It is clear that the National Stadium memorials, whether or not the Kunstmann plan will ever be completed, are physically the most secure. Next, in our estimation, is Villa Grimaldi, though it is possible its management by 2030 will be subsidised, if not dominated, by the state. It is likely that Londres 38, at last repaired but under total government control, will endure as a human rights institute situated in a historic building. José Domingo Cañas will only be saved if the state Ministry of Public Works funds a manager/guide/caretaker similar to Londres 38. Beyond this generation, the Victor Jara Stadium as it stands will be secure while it continues to serve useful social purposes such as indoor sport and night-time shelter for the homeless, and while its safe conservation does not cost too much. Nothing more will be, or can be, done at Patio 29, for nothing remains to be discovered. Memorialisation at Loyola has already been swept aside. In the end only the state itself can and will maintain the sites after the passing of the generation that endured the suffering and created the memorials.

***

In 1974 Jacqueline Drouilly, MIRista, third-year social work student, 24 years of age, possibly pregnant, was arrested and bundled away blindfolded. Tortured and beaten, she spent months in Tres Alamos and José Domingo Cañas, recognised by a fellow detainee for the last time in March 1975 at Cuatro Alamos before being transported to Grimaldi, tortured again and disappeared. Throughout the 1970s Norma Yurich and her family never slackened their sleepless attempts through the courts and Red Cross to locate her.[59] But in all probability, Jacqueline died of the effects of torture or was deliberately murdered some time in 1975. Her drugged or dead body may have been transported to a helicopter to be tipped out over Quintero Bay. There her bones lay on the sandy bottom until they too dissolved. Now nothing remains. All that her family, and every family, can do is imagine. All over Chile,

---

59 The legal endeavours are tracked in Sonia M. Martin and Carolina Moroder, *Londres 38 Londres 2000*, CESOC, Santiago, n.d., c. 2005, pp. 159–87. The chapter also contains interviews with Jacqueline's sister, Nicole.

9. THE MEMORIALS TODAY AND THE ADVANCE OF THE STATE

many thousands of relatives are too grief stricken or too old to debate any longer how to memorialise their missing and tortured child, partner or parent. Some are dead, having mourned their murdered child or partner till the end of their days, barely able to conceive his or her agony on the *parrilla*, the terror of lying in the cells awaiting the next summons, every imagined moment fixed in a lifetime of abiding grief.

Michele Drouilly wrote this poem to her detained-disappeared sister.

> **Like a game of chess**
> It was on a beautiful November day that they told us
> It's so long ago now, Jacqueline
> And the years have slipped through our fingers
> And I refuse to accept that of you only are left
> A few faded photographs
> A far-away memory
> An unforgotten echo
> Unfinished knitting
> A few embroidery threads
> That telegram you sent me, do you remember?
> And a name, but what am I saying?
> For … It's not that which only remains, rather, It's that which also remains.[60]

***

Let us bring the survivors, the politically executed and the detained-disappeared together in a symbolic salute to the dead and missing and to their families, at a time when the brief sunlight of the world, as Dickens put it, is blazing full upon them. Here is Norma Yurich,

---

60 Como un juego de ajedrez
    Era un lindo día de noviembre cuando nos avisaron
    hace ya tanto tiempo Jacqueline.
    Y los años se nos han resbalado entre los dedos
    Y me niego a aceptar, que de tí sólo quedaron
    Unas fotografías borrosas,
    Un recuerdo lejano,
    Un eco inolvidado
    Un tejido inacabado
    Unos hilos de bordar
    El telegrama ese que me enviaste, te recuerdas?
    Y un nombre, pero qué estoy diciendo!
    So no es que solo quede eso, sino que ademas queda eso.
    Michele Drouilly, in Martin and Moroder, *Londres 38 Londres 2000*, p. 160.

the mother of Jacqueline Drouilly, writing in 1961 to her 10-year-old daughter about to enter boarding school. Anxiety, excitement, anticipation and motherly love for a lifetime of promise.

List of Things Not to Do

1. Don't hide your neck under a scarf instead of washing it. 2. Don't talk to your teacher like one garbage man to another. 3. Don't get into fights with anyone. 4. Don't talk non-stop so that no-one can interrupt you. 5. Don't throw your expensive coat down under the bed. 6. Don't get about with your hair in a tangled mop like Brigid Bardot with the glooms. 7. Don't store your shoes inside your books. 8. Don't draw thousands of girls with beehive hairstyles because they look big-headed instead of doing your jobs.

... You know that I love you very much and for this reason I want you to study so that you'll be something more than a housewife, because this work can be done by someone who can't read and write. Well, my dear daughter, I'm keeping on writing to you until you know that I'm a bothersome mother. Because the sleepers here don't know that I'm writing to you. It's two in the morning here. Receive my many kisses and from your daddy too, and love from Nicole as well. Clorinda sends her memories. We're all waiting on tenterhooks on Saturday coming to wait for you, because the little girls and I love to see trains. Closing this edition, I've remembered some money that I want to send you, but be patient, I'll put in your hands. DON'T SQUANDER IT. It's better that you send it back to me. Love to those whom I know. Special love to those whom you know I love best. BEHAVE YOURSELF BEHAVE YOURSELF BEHAVE YOURSELF.

Bye my sweet,

YOUR MUMMY AND DADDY[61]

---

61   Norma Yurich to Jacqueline Drouilly, 20 November 1961, reproduced with permission.

References

'A Memory Space under Construction', Londres 38 Espacio de Memorias, pamphlet, 2014.

'Acciones armadas de extrema izquierda' [Armed actions of the extreme left], Wikipedia, es.wikipedia.org/wiki/Acciones_armadas_de_extrema_izquierda_en_Chile.

Águila, Francisco, 'Detectan participación de Rodriguistas en desórdenes occurido ayer en el Paseo Ahumada' [Participation of Rodriguistas detected in disorders occurring yesterday in Paseo Ahumada], Emol, 12 July 2012, www.emol.com/noticias/nacional/2012/07/12/550315/detectan-participacion-de-rodriguistas-en-desordenes-ocurridos-ayer-en-paseo-ahumada.html.

Aguilar, Mario, 'The ethnography of the Villa Grimaldi in Pinochet's Chile: From public landscape to secret detention centre, 1973–1980', paper presented at the Latin American Studies Association conference, Dallas, Texas, 27–29 March 1973.

Aguilar, Mario I., 'El Muro de Los Nombres de Villa Grimaldi, (Chile): Exploraciones sobre la memoria, el silencio y la voz de la historia', *European Review of Latin American and Caribbean Studies / Revista Europea de Estudios Latinoamericanos y del Caribe*, no. 69, October 2000, 81–88.

Aguilera, Carolina and Gonzalo Caceres, 'Signs of state terrorism in post-authoritarian Santiago: Memories and memorialization in Chile', *Dissidences, Hispanic Journal of Theory and Criticism* 4(8), article 7 of digitalcommons.bowdin.edu/dissidences, accessed 3 February 2016.

Aguiló, Macarena, prod. and dir., *El edificio de los Chilenos* [The Chileans' house], DVD, 2010.

Ahumada, Enrique, 'Dr Patricia Hernández: La Ardua Tarea de Identificar los Cuerpos de Detenidos Desaparecidos', *Caso Pinochet*, www.terra.cl/especial/pinochet-in/enrtrevista.cfm?num=9, accessed 15 October 2007.

'Alamiro Segundo Gonzalez Saavedra', Memoria Viva, www.memoriaviva.com/Ejecutados/Ejecutados_G/gonzalez_saavedra_alamiro_segund.htm, accessed 3 February 2016.

'Alberto Bachelet', Wikipedia, en.wikipedia.org/wiki/Alberto_Bachelet, accessed 1 March 2012.

'Alberto Rodriguez Gallardo: La verdad, yo no conozco la palabra justicia, menos voy a conocer la palabra perdón', El Irreverente, memoriaspreniadastestimonios-web.blogspot.co.nz/2014/04/alberto-rodriguez-gallardo-la-verdad-yo.html.

'Alejandro Alberto Pinochet Arenas', Memoria Viva, www.memoriaviva.com/English/victims/alejandro_alberto_pinochet_arena.htm.

'Alfonso Chanfreu', Wikipedia, es.wikipedia.org/wiki/Alfonso Chanfreau, accessed 24 August 2014.

Amorós, Mario, *Neruda: El Príncipe de los Poetas*, Ediciones B, Santiago, 2015.

Anon [Michele Drouilly], 'Testimonio Rieles' [Testimony of the railway lines], Corporación Parque de la Paz Villa Grimaldi, pamphlet, n.d., c. 2008.

Aránguiz, Tamara Vidaurrázaga, *Mujeres en Rojo y Negro*, Ediciones Escapararte, Santiago, 2006, pp. 302–314.

'Arcadia Patricia Flores Perez', Memoria Viva, www.memoriaviva.com/Ejecutados/Ejecutados_F/FLORES_PEREZ.htm.

Arce, Luz, *The Inferno: A Story of Survival and Terror in Chile*, tr. Stacey Alba Skar, University of Wisconsin Press, London, 1984, books.google.com.au/books?id=e6hVSdlsq7AC&pg=PA164&lpg=

PA164&dq=lumi+videla+moya&source=bl&ots=1KdE48l3Y3&sig=tzbFZgfhGNatOENKuYLa456Kcks&hl=en&sa=X&ei=0N16U46QIIXVkQWS-.

'Archivo de la Colonia Dignidad', Londres 38 Espacio de Memorias, www.londres38.cl/1934/w3-article-96548.html, accessed 3 February 2016.

'Archivos de las etiquetas', mqh02.wordpress.com/tag/simon-allende-fuenzalida/.

Artegabeitía, Rodrigo, 'Corporación Parque por la Paz Villa Grimaldi: una deuda con nosotros mismos', Ministerio de la Vivienda, Santiago, 1997.

'Atemorizadas las familias con la directiva "que contaba con la personalidad juridical"', Causa no. 1435/2011 (Proteccion). Resolución no. 255716, de Corte de Apelaciones de Santiago, de 5 de Octubre de 2011, cortes-apelacion.vlex.cl/vid/-326869995.

Artigas, Mario, *Valle de Lágrimas* [Vale of Tears], Pentagrama, Santiago, 2005.

Aylwin, Azócar Patricio, 'El desafio de mirar al futuro' [The challenge to foresee the future], in Larraín, Hernán and Richard Nuñez, eds, *Las Voces de la Reconciliation,* Instituto de la Sociedad, Santiago, 2013, 35–39.

Baxter, Victoria, 'Civil society promotion of truth, justice and reconciliation: Villa Grimaldi', *Peace and Change* 30(1), 2005.

'Benedicto Antonio Gallegos Saball', Memoria Viva, www.memoriaviva.com/Ejecutados/Ejecutados_G/gallegos_saball_benedicto_antoni.htm.

Bonnefoy Pascale M., 'El silencio del cementerio' [The silence of the cemetery], ArchivosChile, [comentario], 10 September 2013, archivoschile.org/2013/09/el-silencio-del-cementerio/, accessed 10 February 2015.

Brett, Sebastian, Louis Bickford, Liz Ševcenko and Marcela Rios, 'Memorialization and Democracy: State Policy and Civic Action', 2007, www.ictj.org/sites/default/files/ICTJ-Global-Memorialization-Democracy-2007-English_0.pdf.

Bustamante, Javier and Stephen Ruderer, *Patio 29. Tras La Cruz de Hierro*, Ocholibros, Santiago, 2008.

Caiozzi, Silvio Caiozzi, *Fernando Ha Vuelto*, Andrea Films Production, documentary, DVD, 1998.

Campisi, Elizabeth, 'Talking cure: Trauma, narrative and the Cuban rafter crisis', in Cave, Mark and Stephen M. Sloan, eds, *Listening on the Edge*, Oxford University Press, New York, 2014, pp. 74–90.

'Carlos Alberto Carrasco Matus', Memoria Viva, www.memoriaviva.com/Desaparecidos/D-C/car-mat.htm.

'Casa Memoria José Domingo Cañas', Sitios de Memoria, 2012, sitiosdememoria.cl/descargas/encuentro2012/Casa_Memoria_Jose_Domingo_Canas.pptx.

Carmona, Ernesto, 'Detención ilegal de documentalistas en Chile' [Illegal detention of documentary makers in Chile], 23 August 2007, argentina.indymedia.org/news/2007/08/541960.php, accessed 2 February 2010.

'Caso de los 119, operación Colombo', Exilio Chileno, chile.exilio.free.fr/chap06b.htm, accessed 7 April 2014.

Castillo, Luz Carmen, *La Flaca Alejandra*, DVD, 1993.

Castro, Roberto, 'Luciernaga Curiosa', in Castro, Roberto, *Puerto Futuro*, Edición Luciernaga, Santiago, 2007.

Causa no. 1435/2011 (Proteccion). Resolución no. 255716, de Corte de Apelaciones de Santiago, de 5 de Octubre de 2011, cortes-apelacion.vlex.cl/vid/-326869995.

Cave, Mark, 'What remains: Reflections on crisis oral history', in Cave, Mark and Stephen M. Sloan, eds, *Listening on the Edge*, Oxford University Press, New York, 2014, pp. 1–14.

Cave, Mark and Stephen M. Sloan, eds, *Listening on the Edge*, Oxford University Press, New York, 2014.

Caviedes, Raúl, 'Memoria Historica. Detenidos Desaparecidos. Los Familiares', elpaskin3.lacoctelera.net/post/2010/08/10/memoria-hist-rica-detenidos-desaparecidos-familiares, accessed 24 July 2014.

Cerda, Rodrigo A., 'Labor demand: Chile 1986–2001', *Cuadernos de Economía* 40(121), 2003, 478–484, doi: 10.4067/S0717-68212003012100014, www.scielo.cl/scielo.php?pid=S0717-68212 003012100014&script=sci_arttext.

Chacón, Alejandra, 'Patio 29: El dolor de verlos desaparacer dos veces' [Patio 29: The grief at seeing them disappear twice], *La Nación*, 22 April 2002, www.archivochile.com/Portada/8_ddhh/18_port_ddhh.pdf, accessed 24 November 2006.

'Chile: Fallece Laura Moya, ejemplar luchadora de los DDHH', Kaos en la Red, 26 October 2013, 2014.kaosenlared.net/kaos-tv/72165-chile-fallece-laura-moya-ejemplar-luchadora-de-los-ddhh, accessed 27 October 2013.

'Chile reburies coup victim and singer Jara', BBC News, 5 December 2009, news.bbc.co.uk/2/hi/8397042.stm, accessed 14 March and 25 May 2015.

'Chile's Villa Grimaldi remembers horror of Pinochet years' (interview with Lelia Pérez), *Santiago Times*, 7 July 2013, www.amnesty.org/en/latest/news/2013/09/life-under-pinochet-they-were-taking-turns-electrocute-us-one-after-other/.

Cifuentes, Luis S., 'Kirberg. Testigo y Actor del Siglo XX', [Kirberg: Witness and actor of the twentieth century], 2nd edition, August 1999, pviribar.files.wordpress.com/2010/05/kirbergtestigoyactor.pdf, accessed 11 February 2014.

Cofre Schmeisser, Boris, 'El movimiento de pobladores en el Gran Santiago: Las tomas de sitios y organizaciones en los campamentos. 1970–1973' [The movement of the poor in Greater Santiago 1970–1973], *Revista Tiempo Histórico*, no. 2, September 2011, 133–157, www.academia.edu/3822682/El_movimiento_de_pobladores_en_el_Gran_Santiago_1970_1973, accessed 4 May 2015.

Colectivo Londres 38, 'Londres 38. Un Espacio Para La Memoria', pamphlet, 10 December 2007.

Committee for Cooperation for Peace in Chile, see 'Comité de Cooperación para la paz en Chile', Arzobispado de Santiago, Fundación Documentación y Archivo de la Vicaría de la Solidaridad, www.archivovicaria.cl/historia_01.htm, accessed 24 April 2015.

'Confessions of a Torturer', *Santiago Times*, 25 November 2004, santiagotimes.cl/confessions-of-a-torturer/.

'Chile's Constitution of 1980 with Amendments through 2012', tr. Anna I. Vellvé Torras, Adela Staines and Jefri J. Ruchti, www.constituteproject.org/constitution/Chile_2012.pdf.

Corporación José Domingo Cañas 1367 [Laura Moya], *Una Experiencia Para No Olvidar*, Corporación José Domingo Cañas, Santiago, 2001.

——, *José Domingo Cañas 1367: Más Memoria*, Corporación José Domingo Cañas, Santiago, 2007.

——, *Lumi Videla Moya, Su Vida, Su Lucha, Su Muerte Heróica* [Lumi Videla Moya, Her Life, Her Struggle, Her Heroic Death], Corporación José Domingo Cañas, Santiago, 2013.

Costa-Gavras, director, *Missing,* feature film, 1982.

Cozzi, Adolfo, *Estadio Nacional*, Editorial Sudamericana Chilena, Santiago, 2000.

Cunningham, Valentine, *British Writers of the Thirties*, Oxford University Press, Oxford, 1989.

'Declaran Monumento Nacional al Patio 29', CIREN, *Cronica Digital*, 13 July 2006.

Díaz, Gladys, 'Acto por Memorial del MIR en Villa Grimaldi, 8 de Mayo 2010' [Act of Remembrance of the MIR, Villa Grimaldi, 8 May 2010], Correo de los Trabajadores, cctt.cl/correo/index.php?option=com_content&view=article&id=1378:acto-por-memorial-del-mir-en-villa-grimaldi-8-de-mayo-de-2010&catid=24.

Diaz, Viviana, 'Chilean society of today in the light of human rights violations in the past', in *A Museum in Villa Grimaldi: Space for Memory and Education in Human Rights*, International Seminar, August 2005, Corporación Parque por La Paz Villa Grimaldi, Muncipalidad de Peñalolén, Santiago, n.d., c. 2006.

'Dolor por la violencia' [Grief at the violence], *Cambio 21*, 28 August 2014, www.cambio21.cl/cambio21/site/artic/20140828/pags/20140828152302.html, accessed 15 September 2015.

Donoso, Dante and Coral Pey, eds, *Villa Grimaldi. Un Parque por La Paz*, Asamblea Permanente por los Derechos Humanos, Santiago, 1996.

Doyle, Debbie Ann, 'Historians protest the new Enola Gay exhibit', *Perspectives of History*, December 2003, www.historians.org/publications-and-directories/perspectives-on-history/december-2003/historians-protest-new-enola-gay-exhibit, accessed 19 September 2013.

Durán, Claudio, 'Autobiografía de un ex-jugador de ajedrez', in Salazar, Gabriel, *Villa Grimaldi (Cuartel Terranova)*. *Historia Testimonia, Reflexión*, Villa Grimaldi, Corporación Parque de la Paz, Santiago, 2013, pp. 44–46.

'Eduardo Elias Cerda Angel', Fotolog, www.fotolog.com/severfil/39774673/.

'Eduardo Elias Cerda Angel', Memoria Viva, www.memoriaviva.com/Ejecutados/Ejecutados_C/cerda_angel_eduardo_elias.htm.

Ensalaco, Mark, *Chile Bajo Pinochet, La Recuperación de la Verdad*, Alianza Editorial, Madrid, 2002.

———, *Chile Under Pinochet. Recovering the Truth*, University of Pennsylvania Press, ebook, 2010, books.google.com.au/books?id=bJxQIK4WHMkC&pg=PA87&lpg=PA87&dq=marta+ugarte+chile&source=bl&ots=2nYRj2VGyL&sig=rnGDC_2EuyKVGUd-F5YodX5yZk0&hl=en&sa=X&ei=efQkVY3gDYj_8QXO5YCIBA&ved=0CFYQ6AEwCQ#v=onepage&q=marta%20ugarte%20chile&f=false.

'Erick Enrique Rodriguez Hinojosa', Memoria Viva, www.memoriaviva.com/Ejecutados/Ejecutados_R/rodriguez_hinojosa_erick.htm.

Escalante, Jorge, 'Asesinato de Lumi Videla: El "Guatón" Romo contó que el general Garín le pagó por su silencio' [Murder of Lumi Videla: 'Pot Belly' Romo reveals that General Garin paid him for his silence], *La Nación*, 25 July 2007, piensachile.com/2007/07/asesinato-de-lumi-videla-el-qguatasnq-romo-contas-que-el-general-garasn-le-pagas-por-su-silencio/, accessed 3 June 2014.

Escalante, Jorge and Javier Rebolledo, 'The "Dolphins" that exterminated the Communist Party', *La Nación*, 1 April 2007, www.memoriaviva.com/English/the_workings_of_the_secret_police.htm, accessed 6 February 2016.

Escalante, Jorge, Nancy Guzmán, Javier Rebelledo and Pedro Vega, *Los Crímenes que Estremecieron a Chile* [The Crimes that Shook Chile], Ceibo Ediciones, Santiago, 2013.

Espinoza Carlos, dir. and prod., *Las Lucienagas* [The Glow-worms], DVD, 2006.

'Estadio Nacional Julio Martínez Prádanos: Concerts', Wikipedia, en.wikipedia.org/wiki/Estadio_Nacional_Julio_Mart%C3%ADnez_Pr%C3%A1danos#Concerts, accessed 22 July 2014.

'Estadio Nacional, Santiago', Memoria Viva, www.memoriaviva.com/Centros/00Metropolitana/estadio_nacional.htm, accessed 6 February 2016.

Estefane, Andrés, 'Materiality and politics in Chile's Museum of Memory and Human Rights', *Thresholds* 41, Spring 2013, 158–171, web.mit.edu/ebj/Desktop/ebj/MacData/afs.cron/group/thresholds/www/issue/41/t41_estefane.pdf.

'Estoy orgullosa de ti' [I am proud of you], Memoria Viva, www.memoriaviva.com/Desaparecidos/D-L/1o2.htm.

'Ex soldier confessed to shooting Victor Jara', Freemuse, 8 June 2009, freemuse.org/archives/1448, accessed 27 May 2015.

'Exiles File Civil Suits', Memoria Y Justicia – Human Rights Today – Exiles, www.memoriayjusticia.cl/english/en_rights-civilsuits.htm, accessed 6 February 2016.

'Experta norteamericana Katherine Hite visitó Villa Grimaldi', Villa Grimaldi, villagrimaldi.cl/noticias/experta-norteamericana-katherine-hite-visito-villa-grimaldi/.

'Fabían Onofre Cortes Pino', Memoria Viva, www.memoriaviva.com/Ejecutados/Ejecutados_C/fabian_onofre_cortes_pino.htm.

Falconer, Bruce, 'The torture colony', *The American Scholar*, 1 September 2008, theamericanscholar.org/the-torture-colony/#.VTX-j2aHmX0.

'Family and Friends Collective' [now 'Collective 119 for Human Rights'], trincheradelaimagen.cl/?p=30285.

Fernando, Duarte M., 'Informe de inteligencia dice que movimientos antisistémicos están infiltrando a estudiantes' [Intelligence report says subversive movements infiltrating students], *La Segunda* online, 21 June 2013, www.lasegunda.com/Noticias/Impreso/2013/06/857707/informe-de-inteligencia-dice-que-movimientos-antisistemicos-estan-infiltrando-a-estudiantes.

Figueroa Cornejo, Andrés, 'Chile. Hablan ex combatientes: La causa del Frente Patriótico Manuel Rodríguez', Dazibao Rojo: Blog marxista-leninista maoísta, 19 September 2010, dazibaorojo08.blogspot.com.au/2010/09/chile-hablan-ex-combatientes-la-causa.html, accessed 21 May 2015.

'Flores Perez, Arcadia Patricia', Archivo Chile, www.archivochile.com/Memorial/caidos_mir/F/flores_perez_arcadia.pdf.

'Former Center of Repression and Extermination', Londres 38 House of Memory, pamphlet (English), 2014.

Foucault, Michel, *Discipline and Punish: The Birth of the Prison*, Vintage, New York, 1975/1995.

'Funa al asesino de Victor Jara, "Edwin Dimter Bianchi" buena', YouTube, www.youtube.com/watch?v=UA9lGZMgoQc.

Garcés, Mario, 'Archivo y Memoria. La Experiencia de Archivo Oral de Villa Grimaldi', *Cuadernos de Trabajo Educativos* 3(VI), n.d., c. 2010, n.p.; villagrimaldi.cl/wp-content/uploads/2011/07/Cuaderno_de_Trabajo_VI.pdf.

Gibson, Lisanne and Joanna Besley, *Monumental Queensland: Signposts on a Cultural Landscape*, University of Queensland Press, St Lucia, 2005.

Gómez-Barris, Macarena, *Where Memory Dwells: Culture and State Violence in Chile*, University of California Press, Berkeley and Los Angeles, 2009.

'Gonzalo Iván Fuenzalida Navarrete', Memoria Viva, www.memoria viva.com/Desaparecidos/D-F/fue-nav.htm; www.memoriaviva.com/English/victims/fuenzalida-navarrete.htm.

Grandin, Greg and Thomas Miller Klubock, Editorial Introduction, *Radical History Review* 97, Winter 2007.

Gutierrez, Melissa, 'La eterna batalla legal de los conscriptos de la dictadura' [The eternal legal battle of the dictatorship conscripts], *The Clinic* online, 17 June 2015, www.theclinic.cl/2015/06/17/la-eterna-batalla-legal-de-los-conscriptos-de-la-dictadura/, accessed 17 June 2015.

Hennings, Erika, public address, 10 December 2009, recording.

Hidalgo, Louise, 'Orlando Letelier: Murdered in central Washington DC', BBC News, 21 September 2011, www.bbc.com/news/magazine-14994035.

Hiroshima Peace Memorial Museum website, www.pcf.city.hiroshima.jp/index_e2.html.

'Hiroshima Peace Memorial Park', Wikipedia, en.wikipedia.org/wiki/Hiroshima_Peace_Memorial_Park, accessed 6 February 2016.

'Historia', Arzobispado de Santiago, Fundación Documentación y Archivo de la Vicaría de la Solidaridad, www.archivovicaria.cl/historia01.htm, accessed 18 March 2014.

Hite, Katherine, *When the Romance Ended: Leaders of the Chilean Left, 1968–1998*, Columbia University Press, New York, 2000.

——, 'Chile's National Stadium: As monument, as memorial', *ReVista*, Spring 2004, 58–61.

Hite, Katherine and Cath Collins, 'Memorial fragments, monumental silences and reawakenings in 21st century Chile', *Millenium* 38(2), 2009, 379–400.

Hoppe, Alejandro, photographer, *Memoriales en Chile: Homenajes a las Víctimas de Violaciones a Derechos Humanos*, Ocho Libros Editores, Santiago, 2007.

Horvitz, Maria Eugenia, in Larraín, Estéban, *Patio 29: Historias de Silencio*, Fondo de Desarollo de los Artes y la Cultura, Ministerio de Educación, Chile, Fundación Ford, documentary, 1998.

'Hugo Norbeto Ratier Norguera', Memoria Viva, www.memoriaviva. com/Ejecutados/Ejecutados_R/hugo_norberto_ratier_noguera.htm.

Hutchison, Elizabeth Quay, Thomas Miller Klubock, Nara B. Milanich and Peter Winn, eds, *The Chile Reader*, Duke University Press, Durham and London, 2014.

Instituto Nacional de Derechos Humanos, 'Beneficios establecidos por ley a las victimas y familiares de violaciones ocurridas durante la dictadura', www.indh.cl.

'Iván Gustavo Palacios Guarda', Memoria Viva, www.memoriaviva. com/Ejecutados/Ejecutados_P/palacios_guarda_ivan_.htm.

'Jacqueline Paulette Drouilly Yurich', Las Mujeres de Villa Grimaldi, 19 May 2007, mujeresdevillagrimaldi.blogia.com/temas/jacqueline-paulette-drouilly-yurich/.

'Jacqueline Paulette Drouilly Yurich', Memoria Viva, www.memoria viva.com/English/victims/drouilly.html.

Jara, Joan, *Un Canto Truncado*, Punto de Lectura, Madrid, 1983.

Jara, Victor, 'Manifiesto', tr. Bruce Springsteen, *The Nation*, 2013, www.thenation.com/blog/176155/springsteens-tribute-victor-jara-forty-years-after-he-was-killed-chilean-coup.

——, 'Questions for Puerto Montt (Preguntas por Puerto Montt)', LyricsTranslate, lyricstranslate.com/en/preguntas-por-puerto-montt-questions-puerto-montt.html, accessed 27 February 2015.

Jordan, Evelyn Hevia, 'Notas para una approximación al estado de las memorias subterráneas en el Chile actual', villagrimaldi.cl/noticias/nuevo-numero-de-cuadernos-de-trabajo-educativos/.

'Juan Elías Espinosa Parra', Memoria Viva, www.memoriaviva.com/ Ejecutados/Ejecutados_E/espinoza_parra_juan_elias.htm.

'Juan Manuel Varas Silva', Memoria Viva, www.memoriaviva.com/ Ejecutados/Ejecutados_V/varas_silva_juan_manuel.htm.

Keene, Judith, ed., *Where Are the Bodies? A Transnational Examination of State Violence and Its Consequences*, The Public Historian 32(1), February 2010.

Kelly, Patrick, 'The 1973 Chilean coup and the origins of the transnational human rights activism', *Journal of Global History* 8(1), 2013.

Klep, Katrien, 'Tracing collective memory: Chilean truth commissions and memorial site', *Memory Studies* 5(3), 2012, 259–269.

Knischewski, Gerd and Ulla Spittler, 'Competing pasts: A comparison of National Socialist and German Democratic Remembrance in two Berlin memorial sites', in Purbrick, Louise, Jim Aulick and Graham Dawson, eds, *Contested Spaces: Sites, Representations and Histories of Conflict*, Palgrave Macmillan, Basingstoke, 2007, pp. 168–187.

Kornbluh, Peter and Katherine Hite, 'Chile's turning point', *The Nation*, 17 February 2010.

Kruass, Taylor, 'In the Ghost Forest, Listening to Tutsi Rexcapés', in Cave, Mark and Stephen M. Sloan, eds, *Listening on the Edge*, Oxford University Press, New York, 2014, pp. 91–109.

Kunstmann, Wally, Alejandra Lopez, Sebastian Insunza, Carlos Duran, Aleksandra Buzhynska, Marcel Coloma and Claudio Guerra, *Open Museum. Site of Memory and Homage*, in *Proyecto Estadio Nacional. Memorial Nacional. Comité Estadio Nacional 2002–2007*, photocopy document in possession of the authors.

'La Funa de Victor Jara 1', YouTube, www.youtube.com/watch?v=2EQlXQTfQeU.

'La Legua', Wikipedia, es.wikipedia.org/wiki/La_Legua.

'La verdadera história detrás del secuestro de Carreño' [The true history behind the kidnapping of Carreño], *La Nación*, 26 August 2007, www.lanacion.cl/la-verdadera-historia-detras-del-secuestro-de-carreno/noticias/2007-08-25/222513.html.

Larraín, Estéban, *Patio 29: Historia de Silencio*, Fondo de Desarrolo de las Artes y la Cultura, Ministerio de Educación, Chile, Fundación Ford, documentary, DVD, 1998.

Larraín, Hernán and Richard Nuñez, eds, *Las Voces de la Reconciliation,* Instituto de la Sociedad, Santiago, 2013.

Larsen, Thomas, 'The anatomy of torture – Villa Grimaldi', tr. from Danish by Thomas Kennedy, *European Review of Latin American and Caribbean Studies,* no. 69, October 2000, 81–88.

'Las raices de desabastecimiento y el "mercado negro"', 7 February 2002, www.blest.eu/biblio/palacios/cap7.html, accessed 27 July 2015.

Lazzara, Michael, 'Tres recorridos de Villa Grimaldi', in Jelin, Elizabeth and Victoria Langland, eds, *Monumentos, Memorials y Marcas Territoriales,* Siglo Vientiuno, Madrid, 2003, pp. 127–147.

Lazzara, Michael, ed., *Luz Arce and Pinochet's Chile: Testimony in the Aftermath of State Violence,* Palgrave Macmillan, Basingstoke, 2011.

Lira, Elizabeth and Brian Loveman, 'Truth, justice, reconciliation and impunity as historical themes: Chile 1814–2006', *Radical History Review* 97, 2007, 42–76.

Liñero, Germán, *El Muro de los Nombres* [The Wall of Names], DVD, 1999.

'Little Boxes', Wikipedia, en.wikipedia.org/wiki/Little_Boxes.

'Lo Prado', Wikipedia, es.wikipedia.org/wiki/Lo_Prado.

'Londres 38', Wikipedia, es.wikipedia.org/wiki/Londres_38, accessed 10 July 2014.

López, Roberto, 'Cardenal Silva Henríquez en el Estadio Nacional (1973): "Vengo a ver a mis hermanos en desgracia"', [journalist], *Cambio 21,* 27 September 2007, www.cambio21.cl/cambio21/site/artic/20070927/pags/20070927000000.html, accessed 24 April 2015.

'Los Allende: con ardiente paciencia por un mundo mejor', by Wessell, Günther, cited in 'Revolutionary Left Movement (Chile)', Wikipedia, en.wikipedia.org/wiki/Revolutionary_Left_Movement_%28Chile%29, accessed 10 July 2014.

Lowy, Maxine, 'How Patio 29 was saved from (total) disappearance', *Human Rights Today,* 2006, www.memoriayjusticia.cl.english/en_rights-patio.htm, accessed 2 August 2007.

'Lumi Videla Moya', Memoria Viva, www.memoriaviva.com/Ejecutados/ Ejecutados_V/videla_moya_lumi.htm, accessed 3 June 2014.

'Lumi Videla Moya' [English], Memoria Viva, www.memoriaviva.com/ English/victims/videla_moya_lumi.htm.

'Lumi Videla Moya', *Punto Final*, 19 December 2013, www.puntofinal.cl/795/homenaje.php.

Luz Parot, Carmen, *Estadio Nacional*, DVD, 2002.

'Malvina Reynolds: Song Lyrics and Poems: "Little Boxes"', people.wku.edu/charles.smith/MALVINA/mr094.htm, accessed 25 May 2015.

'Manuel José González Allende', Memoria Viva, www.memoriaviva.com/Ejecutados/Ejecutados_G/gonzalez_allende_manuel_jose.htm.

'Manuel Rodriguez Patriotic Front', Wikipedia, en.wikipedia.org/wiki/Manuel_Rodr%C3%ADguez_Patriotic_Front.

'Maria Cristina Lopez Stewart', Memoria Viva, www.memoriaviva.com/Desaparecidos/D-L/lol.htm.

'Marta Lidia Ugarte Román', Memoria Viva, www.memoriaviva.com/Ejecutados/Ejecutados_U/ugarte_roman_marta_lidia.htm, accessed 10 February 2016.

Martin, Sonia M. and Carolina Moroder, *Londres 38 Londres 2000*, CESOC, Santiago, n.d., c. 2005.

'Marxistas tratan de imponer historia falseada de Chile' [Marxists try to impose a false history of Chile], Movimiento 10 de Septiembre, 12 April 2012, movimiento10deseptiembre.blogspot.com.au/2012/04/marxistas-tratan-de-imponer-historia.html.

Matta, Pedro Alejandro, 'A Walk Through a 20th Century Torture Centre: Villa Grimaldi, Santiago de Chile. A Visitor's Guide', 2000.

McKiernan, Zachary, 'National Stadium, national memory: A personal letter', Public History Commons, publichistorycommons.org/national-stadium-national-memory-a-personal-letter/, accessed 6 February 2016.

McSherry, J. Patrice, 'The Víctor Jara case: Justice in 2013?', *Social Justice* Debates, 12 February 2013, www.socialjusticejournal.org/SJEdits/McSherry_Victor_Jara.html, accessed 10 February 2016.

Memoria Viva, 'Quienes Somos' [Who We Are], memoriaviva.com.

'Memorial del MIR en la Villa Grimaldi', *Punto Final*, 14–27 May 2010, www.puntofinal.cl/709/memorial.php, accessed 14 July 2015.

'Memorial for political prisoners at Estadio Nacional after forty years', *Santiago Times*, 5 March 2014.

'Memorias del Grupo de Antropología Forense y Suporte al Campo de los Derechos Humanos en Chile', V Congreso Chileno de Antropología, 8–12 November 2004.

Merino, Roberto Jorquera, 'Memoria, olvido y silencios de un centro secreto de sequestro', in (unnamed editor) *Memorias en Busca de Historia, Más Allá de Los Usos Políticos de la Memoria*, Universidad Bolivariana, LOM Ediciones, Santiago, 2008, 87–100.

Metrano, Claudio, 'Este martes se inaugura Memorial a prisoneros políticos en Estadio Nacional' [Opening of the Memorial to the Political Prisoners in National Stadium this Tuesday], DiarioUchile, 3 March 2014, radio.uchile.cl/2014/03/03/este-martes-se-inaugura-memorial-a-prisioneros-politicos-en-estadio-nacional.

'Michelle Marguerite Peña Herreros', Memoria Viva, www.memoriaviva.com/Desaparecidos/D-P/pen-her.htm, accessed 13 October 2014.

Montealegre, Jorge, *Frazadas del Estadio Nacional* [Blankets of the National Stadium], LOM Ediciones, Santiago, 2003.

'Movimiento de Izquierda Revolucionaria [MIR]', 26 June 2009, bigflameuk.wordpress.com/2009/06/26/movimiento-de-izquierda-revolucionaria/, accessed 30 July 2014.

Moya, Laura, *Represión en el Barrio José Domingo Cañas Durante la Dictadura (1973–1990): Memoria de los Vecinos*, Fundación 1367 José Domingo Cañas, Santiago, 2013.

Moya, Laura, Ricardo Balladares, Claudia Videla, Akison Bruey, Hervu Lara, Andres Carvajal, Mario Aballay and Marcelo Alvarado, *Tortura en Poblaciones del Gran Santiago (1973–1990): Colectivo de Memoria Histórica*, Colectivo 1367 José Domingo Cañas, Santiago, 2005.

Muñoz, Arturo Alejandro, 'Quién asesinó a Jacqueline Drouilly?' [Who murdered Jacqueline Drouilly?], www.lashistoriasquepodemoscontar.cl/qmato.htm.

Muñoz, Heraldo, *The Dictator's Shadow: Life Under Augusto Pinochet*, Basic Books, Philadelphia, 2008, pp. 217–8, books.google.co.uk/books?id=e_qN1cY-MEwC&pg=PA219&lpg=PA219&dq=aylwin+cueca+sola&source=bl&ots=IuFIWvBULW&sig=t6zVuXqkeCGgffR7Fa7kidNrfws&hl=en&sa=X&ei=mJAyVP-uLsSWaqivgPgH&ved=0CDgQ6AEwAw#v=onepage&q=aylwin%20cueca%20sola&f=false, accessed 15 July 2014.

'Muriel Dockendorff Navarette', Memoria Viva, www.memoriaviva.com/Desaparecidos/D-D/1g.html, accessed 25 August 2014.

Museo de la Memoria y los Derechos Humanos [Museum of Memory and Human Rights], www.museodelamemoria.cl/, accessed 2 June 2015.

'Nadezhda K. Krupskaya: 1869–1939', Lenin Internet Archive, www.marxists.org/archive/krupskaya/Krupskaya.

National Monuments Council, Chile, *Parque por la Paz Villa Grimaldi*, documentary, DVD, n.d., c. 2006.

Navarrete, Berenice Dockendorff, *Homenaje a Muriel*, self-published, Santiago, March 2008.

Nelson, Brian A., 'Hugo Chávez: The Chávez presidency', Encyclopaedia Britannica, www.britannica.com/EBchecked/topic/108140/Hugo-Chavez/285482/The-Chavez-presidency.

Neumann, Klaus, *Shifting Memories: The Nazi Past in the New Germany*, University of Michigan Press, Ann Arbor, 2000.

Norma Yurich to Jacqueline Drouilly, letter, 20 November 1961.

Ojeda Frex, Jorge, 'Las batallas de La Legua' [The battles of La Legua], Alterinfos, 5 June 2008, www.alterinfos.org/spip.php?article2363, accessed 10 August 2014.

Olson, Lynn and Stanley Cloud, *A Question of Honor: The Kościuszko Squadron: Forgotten Heroes of World War II*, Vintage Books, New York, 2007.

Orella, Carlos, in Villegas, Sergio, ed., *El Estadio*, LOM Colección Septiembre, Santiago, 1974/2013.

'Organigrama' [Organisation chart], Fundación 1367 Casa Memoria José Domingo Cañas, josedomingocanas.org/nosotros/fundacion/organigrama/.

Osieja, Helen, *Economic Sanctions as an Instrument of US Foreign Policy: The Case of the Embargo against Cuba*, Universal Publishers, 2006, google.com.au/books?id=ObzimhWiz30C&pg=PA97&lpg=PA97&dq=allende+US+embargo&source=bl&ots=mDqrVrENvT&sig=4wRBo5zfEW2QRqNY4xPmN6LvL-k&hl=en&sa=X&ei=zwrwUo_COIepkgXvkYF4&ved=0CDoQ6AEwAw#v=onepage&q=allende US embargo&f=false, accessed 8 February 2014.

Osorio, Víctor, 'El Escándalo del Patio 29: Los Errores de Identificación', Ercilla, no. 3293, 8–21 May 2006, www.ercilla.cl/web, accessed 25 September 2007.

Padilla Ballesteros, Elias, *La Memoria y el Olvido – Detenidos Desaparecidos en Chile*, www.archivochile.com/Memorial/doc_gen/memo_docgen000002.pdf.

'Patio 29 Memorial', Architizer, architizer.com/projects/patio-29-memorial/, accessed 24 May 2015.

Paz, Miguel, 'El Frente en la encrujicada. Adiós a las armas?' [The Frente at the crossroads. Farewell to Arms?], Archivo Chile, 2002, www.archivochile.com/Izquierda_chilena/fpmr/sobre/ICHfpmrsobre0009.pdf.

Peña, Cristóbal, *Los Fusileros*, Debate, Santiago, 2007.

Pereira, Pamela, in Ortiz, J.J., C. Uruza and H. Cossio, 'Dramática notificación a familiares de DD.DD por error del SML: Anuncian acciones legales', *La Tercera*, 22 April 2006.

Pérez, Cristián, '"Operación Príncipe": Irrumpe el FPMR-A' [Operation Prince: The FPMR-A erupts], www.casosvicaria.cl/temporada-dos/operacion-principe-irrumpe-el-fpmr-a/.

Pérez, María José and Karen Glavic, 'La experiencia de la visita y la visita como experiencia: memorias críticas y constructivas', Londres 38 Espacio de Memorias, 2011, www.londres38.cl/1934/articles-92502_recurso_1.pdf.

Peris Blanes, Jaume, 'Testimonies of Chilean exile: Between public protest and the working through of trauma', in Hogan, Colman and Marta Marín Dòmine, eds, *The Camp: Narratives of Internment and Exclusion*, Cambridge Scholars Publishing, Newcastle, 2009, pp. 298–319; www.academia.edu/1479529/Testimonies_of_chilean_exile_between_public_protest_and_the_working_through_of_trauma, accessed 16 April 2015.

'Perm-36', Wikipedia, en.wikipedia.org/wiki/Perm-36, accessed 6 February 2016.

Peters, David W., 'A spiritual war: Crises of faith in combat chaplains from Iraq and Afghanistan', in Cave, Mark and Stephen M. Sloan, eds, *Listening on the Edge*, Oxford University Press, New York, 2014, pp. 226–240.

Peters-Little, Frances, Ann Curthoys and John Docker, eds, *Passionate Histories*, Aboriginal History Monograph 21, ANU E Press, 2010.

Piñera, Sebastián E., 'Por un Chile reconciliado y en paz' [For a reconciled and peaceful Chile], in Larraín, Hernán and Richard Nuñez, eds, *Las Voces de la Reconciliation*, Instituto de la Sociedad, Santiago, 2013, pp. 27–29.

'Proyecto: Un Espacio de Memoria en Construcción' [Project: A Memory Space under Construction], Londres 38, Casa de la Memoria, pdf, nd, c. 2011; www.londres38.cl/1934/articles-91296_recurso_1.pdf, accessed 21 April 2015.

'Proyecto de memoria y educación en el Estadio Nacional de Chile: "Museo Abierto, Sitio de Memoria y Homenaje"', Archives Audiovisuelles de la Recherche, www.archivesaudiovisuelles.fr/1860/proyecto-abierto.asp, accessed 6 February 2016.

Proyecto Estadio Nacional. Memorial Nacional. Comité Estadio Nacional 2002–2007, photocopy in possession of the authors.

Purbrick, Louise, Jim Aulick and Graham Dawson, eds, *Contested Spaces: Sites, Representations and Histories of Conflict*, Palgrave Macmillan, Basingstoke, 2007.

'Quienes y por que mataron a Lumi Videla y arrojaron su cuerpo en la Embajada Italiana de Santiago?' [Who killed Lumi Videla and threw her body into the Italian Embassy of Santiago, and why?], Villa Grimaldi, villagrimaldi.cl/noticias/quienes-y-por-que-mataron-a-lumi-videla-y-arrojaron-su-cuerpo-en-la-embajada-italiana-de-santiago/, accessed 7 August 2014.

Quique Cruz, *Archaeology of Memory,* 2014.

Read, Peter, 'The truth that will set us all free: An uncertain history of memorials to Indigenous Australians', in Purbrick, Louise, Jim Aulick and Graham Dawson, eds, *Contested Spaces: Sites, Representations and Histories of Conflict*, Palgrave Macmillan, Basingstoke, 2007, pp. 146–65.

——, 'Following the Funa: punishing the state in Chile', *Arena Journal* 32, 2009, 45–51.

——, 'Where are you Uncle John?' *Australian Cultural History* 27(9), 2009, 13–24.

——, 'Reconciliation without history: State crime and state punishment in Chile and Australia', in Peters-Little, Frances, Ann Curthoys and John Docker, eds, *Passionate Histories*, Aboriginal History Monograph 21, ANU E Press, 2010, pp. 281–98.

Read, Peter, and Marivic Wyndham, 'Putting site back into trauma studies: A study of five detention and torture centres in Santiago Chile', *Life Writing* 5(1), 2008, 79–96.

——, 'The day that Londres 38 opened its doors: A moment in Chilean reconciliation', *Universitas Humanistica. Revista antropologia y sociologica*, no. 71, 2011, January–June 2011, 193–212.

Rebolledo, Javier, *El despertar de los cuervos,* CEIBA, Santiago, 2013.

Rebolledo, Javier and Luis Narvaez, 'Patio 29. Muertos sin nombres' [Patio 29. The Nameless Dead], *La Nación*, 29 April 2006, www.lanacion.cl/patio-29-muertos-sin-nombre/noticias/2006-04-29/215727.html, 3–4.

'Recinto DINA – "Londres 38"', Memoria Viva, www.memoriaviva.com/Centros/00Metropolitana/Recinto_DINA_londres_38.htm, accessed 1 June 2014.

'Renacer: La Villa de los Rieles' [Renacer: Villa of Railway Lines], *La Nación*, 31 August 2007, www.lanacion.cl/noticias/vida-y-estilo/renacer-la-villa-de-los-rieles/2007-08-30/210513.html.

'Renacer program: Housing in Chile's Atacama Region', YouTube, 16 January 2013, www.youtube.com/watch?v=xsus_0zTph4, accessed 5 May 2015.

'Report of the National Commission for Truth and Reconciliation' ('Rettig Report'), Santiago, 1991, en.wikipedia.org.wiki/Rettig_Report.

'Report of the National Commission on Political Imprisonment and Torture' ('Valech Report'), 29 November 2004, en.wikipedia.org/wiki/Valech_Report.

Richard, Nelly, 'Sitios de la memoria: Vaciamiento del recuerdo', *Revista de Crítica Cultural* 23, 2001, 11–13.

Rivera Mejía, Hernán, 'Estadio Nacional de Chile: Un museo abierto', Archivo, 5 February 2009, www1.rfi.fr/actues/articles/110/article_10695.asp, accessed 6 February 2016.

'Roberto Francisco Jorquera Merino', in 'Auto de Procesiamiento de 10.12.1998 contra Augusto Pinochet Ugarte' [Indictment against Augusto Pinochet Ugarte], Puro Chile, www.purochile.rrojasdatabank.info/auto14.htm, accessed 16 March 2015.

Rodriguez Gallardo, Alberto, 'The truth is I don't know the word "justice", and even less the word "pardon"', *El Irreverente*, elirreverente.cl/index.php?option=com_content&view=article&id=38:alberto-rodriguez-gallardo-la-verdad-yo-no-

conozco-la-palabra-justicia-menos-voy-a-conocer-la-palabra-perdon&catid=48&Itemid=198&lang=es, accessed 23 August 2014.

Rojas, Carmen, *Recuerdos de una MIRista* [Memories of a MIRista], edición mimeografiada, Jose Miguel Bravo, Santiago, 1995, www.archivochile.com/carril_c/cc2012/cc2012-073.pdf; www.psicosocial.net/grupo-accion-comunitaria/centro-de-documentacion-gac/116-recuerdos-de-una-mirista?path=aprender-de-la-voz-de-los-supervivientes, accessed 16 April 2015.

Rojas, Paz, María Elena Ahumada and Juanita Méndez, *Segundo Informe. Testimonios de tortura en Chile. Septiembre de 1973 a marzo de 1990s*, Archivo CODEPU (Corporación de Promoción y Defensa de los Derechos del Pueblo), Santiago, 2003.

Rojas, Paz, María Inés Muñoz, María Luisa Ortiz, Viviana Uribe, in *Todas Ibamos a Ser Reinas* [All of us were to be queens], Colección Septiembre, Santiago, 2002.

Rozas, Valentin, 'Tres maneras de explicar la presencia de graderias antiguas' [Three ways of explaining the presence of the old seating], Bifurcaciones revista de estudios culturales urbanos, www.bifurcaciones.cl/2013/10/graderias-antiguas-en-un-estadio-remodelado/, accessed 6 February 2016.

Ruiz, Lucía Sepúlveda, *119 de Nosotros*, Colección Septiembre, LOM Ediciones, Santiago, 2005.

'Russian activists rally round embattled museum of Soviet repression', Radio Free Europe, 2 October 2014, www.rferl.org/content/russian-activists-rally-around-embattled-museum-sovietv-repression/25438139.html, accessed 6 February 2016.

Ruz de los Paños, Nèlida D., *La Funa de Víctor Jara*, documentary, 2007.

Salazar, Gabriel, *Villa Grimaldi (Cuartel Terranova). Historia Testimonial, Reflexión*, Villa Grimaldi, Corporación Parque de la Paz, Santiago, 2013.

Sanhueza, Jorge Molina, 'Agentes de La DINA vinculados con la desaparición de cinco Frentistas en 1987' [DINA agents linked to the disappearance of five Frentistas in 1987], *La Nación*, 3 February 2006, www.lanacion.cl/noticias/pais/agentes-de-la-dine-vinculados-con-la-desaparicion-de-cinco-Frentistas-en-1987/2006-02-02/211022.html.

Sepúlveda, Orlando, 'Chile in the time of the Dictator', *International Socialist Review* 53, May–June 2007, 3–5; www.isreview.org/issues/53/chile.shtml.

Serrano, Bruno, *Exhumación del Olvido*, CEIBO, Santiago, 2013.

'Simón Cireneo Allende Fuenzalida', www.memoriaviva.com/Ejecutados/Ejecutados_A/simon_cirineo_allende_fuenzalida.htm.

Sites of Conscience, www.sitesofconscience.org/members/.

Soto Gutiérrez, Carmen Gloria, 'Hoy un parque para la paz ... ayer, un lugar para la muerte. Villa Grimaldi, ex Cuartel Terranova. Chile, 1974–1978: Un espacio para la memoria colectiva', Revista Sans Soleil – Estudios de la Imagen, No. 4, 2012, 224–242, revista-sanssoleil.com/wp-content/uploads/2012/02/art-Carmen-Gloria.pdf, accessed 31 March 2016.

'South Korea admits ferry disaster dead bodies given to wrong families', *The Guardian*, 25 April 2014, www.theguardian.com/world/2014/apr/25/south-korea-ferry-remains-dead-wrong-families.

Stern, Steve, *Remembering Pinochet's Chile: On the Eve of London, 1998*, Memory Box of Pinochet's Chile bk 1, Duke University Press, Durham, 2004.

——, *Battling for Hearts and Minds: Memory Struggles in Pinochet's Chile, 1973–1988*, Duke University Press, Durham, 2006.

——, *Reckoning with Pinochet: The Memory Question in Democratic Chile, 1989–2006*, Memory Box of Pinochet's Chile bk 3, Duke University Press, Durham, 2010.

Taylor, Diana, 'Trauma as durational performance', *Open Journal Systems* 1(1), 2009, www.seer.unirio.br/index.php/opercevejoonline/article/view/499/426.

——, 'Memory, trauma, performance', *Aletria* 1(21), January–April 2011, 67–76.

'Testimoniante, Archivo Oral Villa Grimaldi', n.p.

'Testimonio de Raimundo Belarmino Elgueta Pinto', Memoria Viva, www.memoriaviva.com/testimonios/testimonio_de_raimundo_belarmino_elgueta_pinto.htm, accessed 10 July 2014.

'The secret history of Brazilian torturers who brought terror to the detainees of this country in the National Stadium', 24 April 2014, imagenesparamemoriar.com/, accessed 15 July 2014.

'The soccer match that disgraced Chile', PRI Public Radio International, 11 September 2011, www.pri.org/stories/2013-09-11/soccer-match-disgraced-chile, accessed 6 February 2016.

Thieme, Roberto, interview with Tomás Maciatti, YouTube, 17 September 2013, www.youtube.com/watch?v=b3usy7JAYw4.

Torres, Ozvaldo, in *A Museum in Villa Grimaldi: Space for Memory and Education in Human Rights*, International Seminar, August 200 (sic), Corporación Parque por La Paz Villa Grimaldi, Muncipalidad de Peñalolén, Santiago, n.d., c. 2006.

Torres, Veronica, 'Los Escritos de los presos politicos del Estadio Nacional: El pergamino, la lápida y la canción de Bebo' [The writings of the political prisoners at the National Stadium], *The Clinic* online, 10 November 2010, www.theclinic.cl/2010/11/10/los-escritos-de-los-presos-politicos-del-estadio-nacional-el-pergamino-la-lapida-y-la-cancion-de-bebo/, accessed 2 June 2015.

Traverso, Antonio and Enrique Azúa, 'Villa Grimaldi; a visual essay', *Journal of Medical Practice* 10(2&3), 2009.

Valdes, Cecilia, 'Torture charge pits professor v professor', *New York Times*, 8 September 2001, www.nytimes.com/2001/09/08/arts/torture-charge-pits-professor-vs-professor.html, accessed 15 July 2014.

Valdéz, Hernán, *Tejas Verdes*, LOM ediciones, Santiago, 1996.

Vallejos, Rolando Álvarez, 'Los "hermanos Rodriguistas". La división del Frente Patriótico Manuel Rodríguez y el nacimiento de una nueva cultura política en la izquierda chilena. 1975–1987' [The 'brothers Rodriguistas'. The division of the Manuel Rodriguez Patriotic Front and the birth of a new political culture in the Chilean left. 1975–1987], *Revista Izquierda* 2(3), 2009.

Vann, Bill, 'Chilean court reenacts stadium execution of American journalist' [Charles Hormann], World Socialist Web Site, 17 May 2002, www.wsws.org/en/articles/2002/05/horm-m17.html.

'Varas Silva, Juan Manuel', Archivo Chile, www.archivochile.com/Memorial/caidos_mir/V/varas_silva_juan.pdf.

Vial, Gonzalo, *El Mercurio*, Santiago, 30 April 2006.

'Víctor Jara', Biographías y Vidas, www.biografiasyvidas.com/biografia/j/jara_victor.htm, accessed 25 May 2015.

'Victor Jara biography', Encylopaedia of World Biography, www.notablebiographies.com/sup/Supplement-Fl-Ka/Jara-Victor.html.

Videla, Dago Pérez, 'Los asesinos no pudieron con mi madre' [The murderers couldn't handle my mother], Rebelión, 7 April 2004, www.rebelion.org/hemeroteca/chile/040407dago.htm, p. 3.

'Videla Moya, Lumi', Centro de Estudios Miguel Enriquez, www.archivochile.com/Memorial/caidos_mir/V/videla_moya_lumi.pdf, accessed 3 June 2014.

Vij, Vikas, 'Barrick Gold Corp helps underprivileged Chilean families own new homes', Justmeans, 28 January 2013, www.justmeans.com/blogs/barrick-gold-corp-helps-underprivileged-chilean-families-own-new-homes.

Villa Grimaldi Corporación Parque por la Paz, villagrimaldi.cl/, accessed 19 June 2015.

'Villa Grimaldi, História y Características de las Grandes Mansiones', tourist brochure, n.d., c. 1960.

Villegas, Sergio, *El Estadio,* LOM, Santiago, 2013.

REFERENCES

Wadi, Ramona, 'The right to memory in Chile: An interview with Erika Hennings, President of Londres 38', Upside Down World, 4 May 2002, upsidedownworld.org/main/chile-archives-34/3618-the-right-to-memory-in-chile-an-interview-with-erika-hennings-president-of-londres-38, accessed 25 August 2014.

——, 'Dictatorship relics in Chile: Paying homage to Miguel Krassnoff Martchenko', Upside Down World, 14 November 2011, upsidedownworld.org/main/chile-archives-34/3356-dictatorship-relics-in-chile-paying-homage-to-miguel-krassnoff-martchenko, accessed 19 June 2015.

Waldman, Gilda, 'La "culta de la memoria": Problemas y reflexiones', *Política y Cultura* 26, 2006, 1–12.

Whelan, James R., *Out of the Ashes,* Regnery Gateway, Washington, 1989.

Wills, Denise Kirsten, 'The Vietnam Memorial's history', *Washingtonian*, 1 November 2007, www.washingtonian.com/articles/people/the-vietnam-memorials-history/, accessed 17 September 2013.

Wright, Thomas, *State Terrorism in Latin America: Chile, Argentina, and International Human Rights,* Rowman and Littlefield, Lanham, 2007.

Wyndham, Marivic and Peter Read, '"From state terrorism to state errorism": Post Pinochet Chile's long search for truth and justice', in Keene, Judith, ed., *Where Are the Bodies? A Transnational Examination of State Violence and Its Consequences, The Public Historian* 32(1), February 2010, 31–44.

——, 'Those who have no memorial', *Encounters 5: Memories and Violence, Problems and Debates in a Global Perspective*, Fall 2012, 169–82.

——, 'The disappearing museum', *Rethinking History. The Journal of Theory and Practice* 18(2), April 2014, 165–180, dx.doi.org/10.1080/13642529.2013.858454.

Zangana, Haifa, 'Foreword: Abu Ghraib: Prison as a collective memory', in Purbrick, Louise, Jim Aulick and Graham Dawson, eds, *Contested Spaces: Sites, Representations and Histories of Conflict*, Palgrave Macmillan, Basingstoke, 2007, pp. xi–xvi.

Interviews and guided tours

The authors are deeply grateful to the following for interviews granted to them:

- Aguiló, Macarena
- Diaz, Vivianas
- D'Orival Briceño, Roberto
- Duhalde, Diana
- Drouilly Yurich, Michele
- Espina Espina, Juan
- González, Elena [Nena]
- Graciela Huinau
- Kunstmann, Wally
- Medina, Juan
- Montenegro, Leopoldo
- Rodriguez, Rogelio
- Merino, Roberto Jorquera
- Moya, Laura
- Peña, Victor
- Rodriguez, Josefina
- Sanchez, Roberto
- Silva, Marcelo
- Uribe, José
- Varas, Julieta

www.ingramcontent.com/pod-product-compliance
Lightning Source LLC
Chambersburg PA
CBHW040319170426
43197CB00022B/2964